TEN YEARS IN THE DEATH OF THE LABOUR PARTY

TEN YEARS
in the
DEATH
of the
LABOUR PARTY

———

TOM HARRIS

Biteback Publishing

First published in Great Britain in 2018 by
Biteback Publishing Ltd
Westminster Tower
3 Albert Embankment
London SE1 7SP
Copyright © Tom Harris 2018

ISBN 978-1-78590-223-9

10 9 8 7 6 5 4 3 2 1

A CIP catalogue record for this book is available from the British Library.

Set in Adobe Caslon Pro

Printed and bound in Great Britain by
CPI Group (UK) Ltd, Croydon CR0 4YY

MIX
Paper from
responsible sources
FSC® C020471

CONTENTS

To Carolyn, for her love, support and ceaseless encouragement.

PREFACE

In 1984, the year I joined the Labour Party, I read a book by Austin Mitchell, a serving Labour MP at the time, depicting the civil war that had engulfed his party in the aftermath of its defeat at the 1979 general election and which, even then, showed little sign of waning. It was titled *Four Years in the Death of the Labour Party* and it was one of the first books I read once I decided to bite the bullet and join the party that, only a year earlier, I had felt unable to support in the general election.

Looking back at that tumultuous and dramatic time from the perspective of 2017 is illuminating. After being thrown into opposition, Labour MPs – only they had the power at the time to select party leaders – chose the left-wing Michael Foot to replace defeated premier Jim Callaghan. There then followed an intense battle between the party's right and left wings, the former personified by Labour's deputy leader Denis Healey, the latter by demagogue and former Industry Secretary Tony Benn. The feud between the two men culminated in 1981 when Benn challenged Healey for the deputy leadership, perfectly exposing just how split the Labour movement was, when the incumbent held on with a majority equivalent to less than 1 per cent of the vote.

The newly empowered left saw a chance to throw their weight around and did so by threatening to deselect any Labour MP who didn't sign up to their own exclusive, elitist brand of socialism, which included unilateral nuclear disarmament, taking the UK out of the European Economic Community (EEC) without a referendum and nationalising a large section of British industry. This in turn led to the biggest split the party had endured since 1931, with the creation of the Social Democratic Party (SDP) by the so-called Gang of Four: former Home Secretary and Chancellor, Roy Jenkins, recently returned to these shores after a stint as president of the European Commission; David Owen, Foreign Secretary under Callaghan; Shirley Williams, the former Education Secretary who had lost her seat at the 1979 election; and former Transport Secretary, Bill Rodgers.

Thanks in large part to the nature of Britain's first-past-the-post electoral system, a hangover of the kind of two-party politics that prevailed throughout much of the twentieth century, the SDP failed in its stated aim of 'breaking the mould' of British politics. It succeeded only in splitting the anti-Conservative vote, helping to deliver three-figure majorities for Prime Minister Margaret Thatcher at the 1983 and 1987 general elections.

We now know, thanks to the patience and determination of individuals like Neil Kinnock, John Smith, Tony Blair, Gordon Brown and many others who refused to walk away or give up on the Labour project, that the party eventually recovered and went on to win the 1997 and 2001 general elections with unprecedented landslide majorities, as well as the 2005 election with a handsome, though more modest, majority. So, only a few years ago, a more appropriate 'sequel' to Mitchell's 1983 book might have been titled *Fourteen Years in the Resurrection of the Labour Party*.

Alas, the resurrection was not as successful for Labour as it was for Lazarus, at least in terms of longevity. Whatever the continuing debates over New Labour's achievements and failures, its domination of British politics lasted for a shorter period than anyone would have expected on that bright new dawn in early May 1997. Thirteen years remains the longest unbroken period of government in Labour's history, with Blair becoming the first Labour leader ever to win two, let alone three, consecutive working majorities. But when it all came to an unedifying end in the frantic, dramatic days following the 2010 general election, Labour was already on a downward spiral that exclusion from office only seemed to accelerate.

This book does not aim to present an impeccably fair sequence of events from 2007 to 2017; it can be fairly criticised for overemphasising many of the protagonists' failures and missteps, while ignoring their (occasionally) impressive achievements. Yet the purpose of this book is to identify those events and judgements that were pivotal to the demise of the Labour Party during (and, perhaps, beyond) this period. I make no apology for accentuating the negative while eliminating the positive, for only by doing so can we understand the voters' judgement.

To state that Labour is dying is not to predict categorically that it will, ultimately, kick the political bucket. After the drama of Theresa May's snap election and disastrous campaign in 2017, few would bet their house on Labour's imminent demise. Conceivably, it could yet return to government under its most left-wing leadership in its (or Britain's) history. And, if not, who is to say that the period of 'dying' might not take years, even decades before the process reaches its natural conclusion? It might even be the case that Labour enters a state of living death, the Nosferatu of

British politics, doomed to wander aimlessly through the political twilight, not quite dead, yet not quite attached to the reality of life, condemned to hover in the purgatory between irrelevance and government. A bit like the Liberal Democrats.

Ten Years in the Death of the Labour Party has not been written from an objective point of view. I am decidedly partial in my perspective. The last decade has been one of desperate frustration for me; were I not a Labour member and supporter it would have seemed a lot more entertaining. Yet, having been a member of the party almost all of my adult life, and having spent fourteen years as a Labour MP, recent history has been a genuinely heartbreaking experience. Perhaps I hoped that writing this book would prove a cathartic experience – that remains to be seen.

My deep gratitude goes to the staff at Biteback and particularly to Iain Dale, whose experience in publishing my previous book, *Why I'm Right and Everyone Else is Wrong*, did not discourage him from giving me another opportunity to see my name on the nation's bookshelves. Gratitude is also due to Henry Hill who, despite being a Tory, has offered me genuine friendship and wonderful advice (and proofing expertise) in this project.

Most of all, thank you to my friends and former colleagues in the Parliamentary Labour Party (PLP) whose friendship during my time in the Commons lifted my spirits every day. Nowhere in the country can be found more dedicated or indefatigable public servants. I do not envy them their task, in these troubled times, of trying to guide our party back onto the straight and narrow. But if anyone can do it, they can.

Tom Harris
October 2017

CHAPTER ONE

BUTTERFLY'S WINGS

I t had all been going so well.

On Friday 5 October 2007, the Prime Minister, Gordon Brown, had a decision to make. In some respects it was the simplest one a Prime Minister ever has to make, with a binary yes-or-no answer: should he call a general election and seek a fresh mandate for his premiership from the electorate?

The Iron Chancellor (or 'Irn Broon', as a Scots wag had labelled him) had finally reached his ultimate political goal, the goal that had driven him all his life, from being the youngest ever rector of Edinburgh University to Member of Parliament, to the front bench of the Labour opposition and, more rapidly than virtually anyone had expected, to become heir apparent to John Smith as leader of the Labour Party. When Smith took over the helm of the party after its shattering fourth consecutive general election defeat in 1992, Brown had been appointed shadow Chancellor, a role that seemed perfect for the dour yet charismatic politician. But it was not, to him, the perfect role. For a start, it was in opposition, not government, and Brown craved the power that government would bring, the power to put into practice his ideas of a modern form of old-fashioned, electorally unpopular socialism.

And, in 1992, as Smith put the finishing touches to his first shadow Cabinet and prepared to do battle with the triumphant Prime Minister John Major, the wider party acknowledged that the leadership was in safe hands. That acknowledgement included an understanding that, whenever Smith chose to stand down from the role, the identity of his successor was only too obvious.

This was a view shared by the Dunfermline MP. It was not, however, a view that was shared as widely or as enthusiastically as Brown would have liked among a significant proportion of his parliamentary colleagues. His abilities were never doubted; his grasp of the finer points of economic policy, his ability to distil complicated facts and figures into easy-to-swallow sound bites for the media and their audiences – that was accepted and welcomed as a major contribution to Labour's fightback after yet another defeat. Brown's talents were an indispensable part of Labour's courageous, and ultimately successful, strategy to regain the trust of voters, to be seen as a viable, serious alternative government in a way that eluded Smith's predecessor, Neil Kinnock, for the nine years of his leadership.

Perhaps to other Labour MPs, Brown's ambition was just a little too naked, his estimation of his own abilities just a touch overgenerous. There was a humourless arrogance, shared by his exclusive inner circle, about the inevitability of their man's succession, an assumption that irritated a significant section of the PLP. What's more, Brown, like Smith, was Scottish; would the party and the country be content for two successive leaders to hail from north of the border? The last Labour leader to represent an English seat had been Harold Wilson. Most importantly, one of the things on the short list of reservations about Brown was his personality. He could certainly affect charm when it suited him, but it didn't always suit him, and MPs had doubts that the natural likeability that he possessed might not be easily communicated to a mass audience.

Such considerations were not of immediate concern, to either Brown or to the wider party, until the morning of 12 May 1994, when Smith's untimely death instigated another leadership election, at which point Brown realised, to his dismay, that the man he regarded as his 'junior partner', shadow Home Secretary Tony Blair, enjoyed more support than Brown himself did. If Brown didn't acknowledge this explicitly, it was only because, by not standing himself and by affecting the role of magnanimous party loyalist, he could pretend that the crown could have been his had he wanted it. But the party must come first and a divisive contest between its two leading 'modernisers' would not be in its best interests.

So, smiling for the cameras as much as he was able to, the shadow Chancellor remained in the post originally given to him by Smith and supported his former friend.

On Tuesday 15 June 2004, Brown became the longest continuously serving Chancellor of the Exchequer since the 1820s, beating David Lloyd George's record of seven years and forty-three days. But Chancellor wasn't the role he wanted for its own sake – he saw it as a stepping stone to the highest office, an office he never stopped believing had been unfairly denied him by the perceived (as he saw it) treachery of Blair ten years earlier. The alleged betrayal, recounted and enforced repeatedly by a coterie of friends and allies in Parliament and the media throughout Blair's leadership of the party and the government, defined Brown; arguably it impeded his success as Chancellor, undermined his many achievements and allowed his opponents to emphasise his failures. Rumours of his stormy relationship with Blair inevitably percolated through to the public, forcing both men to admit that yes, there were tensions, but only tensions that added to the creative forces at the centre of government. There had been a deal, Brown's allies insisted, a deal to which Blair had agreed as far back as 1994; a deal that meant Blair would fight two general elections and then retire, bequeathing the leadership to the Chancellor. The terms of any deal, if there ever was one, were always hotly contested by the followers of both sides. Brown fully expected – felt he was led to expect – an announcement by Blair in 2004 that he would resign as Prime Minister, allowing a smooth transition before an expected general election in May of the following year. But in September 2004, Blair announced that he intended to fight a third general election and would serve an entire parliamentary term before stepping aside in time to allow his successor to fight the next general election. A furious Brown told Blair: 'There is nothing that you could ever say to me now that I could ever believe.'

In 2006, more than a year after Blair had led his party to an unprecedented third election victory, achieved despite the growing shadow of Blair's – and Parliament's – controversial decision to join the US-led invasion of Iraq in 2003, the dam burst. Using the pretext of the Prime Minister's reluctance to condemn Israel's insurgence into nearby Lebanon, seventeen MPs, all allies of Brown's, struck, signing a letter to Downing Street, a letter demanding Blair's resignation. Wrongly believing that the signatories represented the wider consensus in the PLP, Blair announced he would be gone within the next year and that the forthcoming party conference in Manchester would be his last as leader. TV cameras caught Brown smiling broadly as he jumped into his ministerial car on leaving a meeting with his embattled leader.

Following the local, Scottish and Welsh elections in May 2007,

Blair duly announced the date of his retirement: following a process within the Labour Party to choose his successor, he would leave Downing Street for the last time as Prime Minister on 27 June.

This time, Brown left nothing to chance. Despite the resentment of a large minority of Labour MPs towards him for perceived disloyalty to his leader over more than a decade, and even deeper resentment at the coup that finally dislodged Labour's greatest election winner of all time, no one was prepared to challenge Brown for the top job. Senior Cabinet members and some junior ministers complained of threats by Brown's allies against anyone who even contemplated standing against him to replace Blair. 'I was told, in no uncertain terms, that if I even supported the principle of an open election, rather than a coronation, I could say goodbye to my ministerial car,' one junior minister said.

As for senior figures, although less susceptible to intimidation, they could see no point in fighting an election they believed Brown would win heavily anyway. John Reid, Blair's pugnacious Home Secretary, regarded as the government's best communicator, received a number of invitations to throw his hat in the ring, but his response – that by standing in the contest he would feel obliged to serve in Brown's Cabinet afterwards, and that he was simply unprepared to do so – echoed the reservations and assumptions of other would-be candidates. John Hutton, Blair's Work and Pensions Secretary, told the BBC as the September 2006 coup was unfolding that a 'serious, Cabinet-level candidate' would emerge to challenge Brown. Yet, by May the following year, he had declared his support for Brown after all. The Environment Secretary, David Miliband, widely seen as the Blairites' next great hope, announced that he, too, would support Brown. Even Charles Clarke, Neil

Kinnock's ex-chief of staff and a former Home Secretary to Blair, known to be an opponent and critic of the Chancellor's within government, who had told the *Sunday Times* in April 2007 that if Miliband declined to stand then he himself would, eventually capitulated to the inevitability of a Brown tenure at No. 10, even going so far as to suggest he would be willing to return to the Cabinet under him (he was not offered any post by Brown).

It was the same old story, the same old excuse, at every turn: Brown was going to win anyway, so why bother? Why mount a challenge guaranteed to fail, whose only reward would be the undying enmity of the new Prime Minister?

Blair duly became one of Brown's nominees in the leadership election, as did 312 other MPs, out of a parliamentary party numbering 356.

In fact, there was one challenger: John McDonnell, the hard-left MP for Hayes and Harlington, was a leading member of the small but voluble Socialist Campaign Group of MPs, made up of those who saw themselves as keepers of the true flame of 'proper' socialism, committed to high taxes, unilateralism and workers' control. He announced he would be a candidate and duly started to seek the nominations from parliamentary colleagues that he would need in order to make it on to the ballot paper. Party rules at the time provided for each nominee to secure the support of 12.5 per cent of the PLP, or forty-five MPs. McDonnell failed to persuade colleagues, most of whom he did not know and with whom he almost never socialised, even to 'lend' him their nomination, a tactic used frequently to allow a no-hope candidate to stand for the sake of 'broadening the debate'. In 2007, however, MPs were very well aware that the heir apparent (Brown had graduated from his 'presumptive' status of 1994) would brook no complications in the shape of another candidate on the ballot paper. And anyway, it was inconceivable that a member of the Socialist Campaign Group could ever be taken seriously as a leader of the Labour Party. Nevertheless, before nominations closed on Thursday 17 May, there was an open hustings event at which McDonnell was invited to participate (though, unfortunately, the media were not asked to attend). The Hayes and Harlington MP's long record of voting against the Labour government encouraged one government whip, the Cardiff MP Kevin Brennan, to consider posing the question: 'If you become leader and Prime Minister, will you start voting with the government?' The question, sadly, was never put.

One argument for there to be only one candidate that was occasionally, though unenthusiastically, proffered was that it would save the party money; there would be no need to issue ballot papers if only a single name was on the ballot paper. Coronations cost little in the Labour Party.

However, this argument quickly fell through when John Prescott, Blair's deputy since 1994, announced that he would step aside at the same time as the Prime Minister. A contest, and an expensive mass mailing of ballot papers to the party membership, was now inevitable, at least for the junior job. Six candidates duly stepped up to fill Prescott's shoes: Harriet Harman (the then Minister of State for Constitutional Affairs), Peter Hain (the Northern Ireland Secretary), Alan Johnson (the former postman and postal workers' union boss, who had risen to the position of Education Secretary under Blair, and who was regarded as the favourite at the outset of the contest), Labour Party chair, Hazel Blears; Hilary Benn (the International Development Secretary, whose father, Tony, had split the party down the middle with his own ill-fated challenge for the same job in 1981, in a very different era, of course), and backbencher Jon Cruddas, who had only entered Parliament in 2001. Six high-profile, capable, articulate and clever candidates for deputy; one talented, ambitious and flawed candidate for leader.

At close of nominations on 17 May, Brown was declared the winning (and only) candidate (by securing more than 308 nominations from fellow MPs he had made it mathematically impossible for any other candidate to secure enough qualifying nominations). But he had to wait until the party's special leadership conference on 24 June for his long-awaited victory to become official. At that conference, Harriet Harman unexpectedly pipped Alan Johnson for the No. 2 spot by a margin of 50.43 per cent to Johnson's 49.56 (Johnson having led the field, albeit narrowly, in all four preceding rounds of voting) and became Brown's deputy.

Prime Minister's Questions on Wednesday 27 June witnessed unprecedented scenes. Clapping is officially not allowed within the chamber of the Commons, but as Blair, standing at the despatch box for the last time, said an emotional goodbye to the place, the ranks of Labour MPs behind him and to the sides roared their appreciation, then stood to applaud. The Speaker Michael Martin looked on, smiling indulgently, unwilling to rebuke members for their defiance of protocol. Then the Leader of the Opposition, David Cameron, stood up and beckoned his own side to join in the applause.

The smooth transition of power dictated by Britain's uncodified and ever-changing constitution operated smoothly, as Blair headed back to Downing Street and then left, his wife, Cherie, accompanying him, to head to Buckingham Palace to offer his resignation to Her Majesty. Ten minutes after Blair's departure from his audience, Brown and his wife, Sarah, arrived at the palace to be appointed the Queen's eleventh premier of her long reign.

Returning from the palace to the iron gates of Downing Street at precisely 2.55 p.m., Brown rather awkwardly recited the words he knew would define the beginning of his leadership: 'If we can fulfil the potential and realise the talents of all our people then I'm absolutely sure that Britain can be the great global success story of this century,' he told reporters standing excitedly across from the famous black door, confined safely behind their metal barricade. Then, quoting his school motto, he said: 'I will try my utmost [inexplicably, he pronounced it *out*-most]. This is my promise to all of the people of Britain. And now let the work of change begin.'

And the work did begin.

The new Prime Minister was finally where he believed he was destined to be, albeit ten years later than he felt was fair. And he could not have asked for a more confident and assured start. His first act was to appoint his Cabinet and junior ministerial ranks, a task unexpectedly interrupted by his (and his new Home Secretary, Jacqui Smith's) first crisis: two car bombs were discovered parked in London's busy West End early on the Friday morning, one directly outside Tiger Tiger night club in Piccadilly Circus. Both vehicles were removed and the explosives and nails they contained safely disposed of. The next day, Saturday, in what investigators later confirmed was a related incident, an Islamist terrorist carried out a violent attack at Glasgow International Airport by driving a car through the plate-glass walls at the front of the main terminal building.

Brown was forced to interrupt his phone calls to expectant would-be ministers in order to deal with the security aspects of the operation. On Monday 2 July, when Smith updated the House of Commons on the previous weekend's events, she and her boss were broadly praised for their deftness in reassuring the nation and dealing with the unexpected attacks.

The next crisis Brown faced was a more typically British one. June had already proved to be one of the wettest on record, with double the average rainfall for the month. But July proved even worse for homeowners and farmers, and few areas of England escaped the threat of flooding. Again, Brown seemed in his element. Chairing regular COBRA (Cabinet Office Briefing Room A, to give its rather more pedestrian, less dramatic full title) emergency meetings, Brown was methodical and analytical, demanding facts and figures from the officials present. In July he decreed that every government minister, whatever their official remit and wherever they were in the country, should make sure they visited at least one site where residents had been badly affected by the floods.

The strategy worked. Brown's personal ratings, already satisfactorily high as a result of the change of faces at the top of government, improved still further. His high-profile work on behalf of the nation helped capitalise on an opinion poll bounce reported during his first weekend at No. 10: an ICM poll for *The Guardian* reported a seven-point increase in Labour support, its best polling score since David Cameron became the Tory leader in December 2005. Brown personally could bask in one particular finding: a 35–23 per cent lead over Cameron on the question of 'Who would make the best Prime Minister?', reversing a Cameron lead of 5 per cent just three months earlier.

The omens were good for the double by-election due on 19 July, prompted by Blair's resignation as MP for Sedgefield in the north-east of England, and by the death of Piara Khabra, the Labour MP for Ealing Southall in London. Despite five visits to the Ealing campaign by Cameron, his party failed to improve on the third place it had achieved at the previous general election; in Sedgefield, the Conservative candidate failed to hold on to second place and was beaten into third by the Liberal Democrats. In both seats, Labour held on comfortably. And, perhaps inevitably, talk began of an early general election.

Brown's closest advisers were split. Spencer Livermore, one of his most senior advisers and confidants at No. 10, was in favour of going to the country in the autumn of 2007, despite the parliament having another three years to run. In this he was supported by Brown's closest friend and supporter in government, the Schools Secretary Ed Balls. Other advisers expressed caution. Why needlessly risk a solid parliamentary majority and, perhaps almost as importantly, Brown's personal political authority?

As rumours grew, it became apparent that the Conservative Party, too, was divided on the issue. As Parliament coasted towards the start of the long summer recess in July 2007, Lord Elder of Kirkcaldy was alerted in an unusual way to the normally well-hidden tensions within the main opposition party. Murray Elder had been a childhood friend of Brown's and had remained one of the new Prime Minister's closest friends and supporters ever since. He spent four years as secretary of the Labour Party in Scotland before becoming chief of staff to John Smith on his election to the leadership. After Smith's death, Elder worked briefly for Smith's successor before heading off to the private sector. He was ennobled in 1999. Other members of the Lords, of whichever party, regarded Elder as a reliable source of information as to what Brown might be thinking on any particular subject. It was in this capacity that he was approached one evening by a Tory peer who asked him: 'Is Gordon going to call an early election?'

Elder replied, 'Not that I'm aware, no.'

'Fuck!' replied the disappointed Lord.

Elder asked him, 'Are you that confident of winning it if he did?'

'No,' came the reply. 'We'd lose, and that means we could get rid of Cameron.'

And the Tory leader, in his various and energetic attempts to 'detoxify' the Tory brand after three calamitous and unprecedented general election defeats, had indeed incurred the ire of many of his party's more traditional elements, elements that were content not to rock the boat until after the current leader had led the party to an expected fourth defeat. The prospect of dispensing with the sled-riding, bicycling, hoodie-hugging metropolitan Witney MP was one that was regarded as a substantial consolation prize in the event of Brown returning to No. 10 after an October poll.

So, the decision facing Brown, in late summer and early autumn 2007, just weeks after becoming Prime Minister, was an excruciating one. If he held an election now, would he return to Downing Street with an increased majority over what his predecessor had won just two years earlier? And if not, what would have been the point? Voters in Britain are widely thought to resent being expected to vote for no good reason.

And yet the attraction of having his own mandate, rather than one inherited from Blair, was one that was difficult to resist. If he fought and won, he would avoid the easy comparison with the last Labour Prime Minister who had gained office in midterm, James Callaghan, who plodded on to defeat at the messy end of a tortuous parliament. But what if he fought and lost? A Tory majority was never on the cards, but what if, as often happens in politics, unexpected events derailed Labour's re-election campaign? What if Brown lost his majority entirely and ended up leading an enfeebled minority government, or having to do a deal with the Lib Dems in the next parliament? After getting used to large, sometimes overwhelming, Commons majorities in the last decade, Brown knew his party would never forgive such a careless, arrogant loss of a majority, which would have been seen as an act of hubris. Losing a 66-seat majority, when there really was no urgency to go to the country at all except to satisfy his own ego, could end his premiership after only a few short weeks.

According to Anthony Seldon's *Brown at Ten*, Brown's inner circle, though divided on the wisdom of an early election, had received explicit instructions on the eve of Labour's annual conference to 'talk up the possibility with journalists in order to destabilise Cameron'.

As delegates to the conference arrived in Bournemouth on Saturday 22 September, the attendant media wanted only to talk of one subject. Across the country, the word went out from regional and local organisers to candidates, MPs and campaign teams: get ready.

Throughout conference week and the week that followed, when the Conservatives' conference was taking place, Labour MPs in marginal seats were told through official channels that an autumn election was on the cards. Gisela Stuart, who had gained her Birmingham Edgbaston seat with an impressive 10 per cent swing from the Conservatives on the night of the 1997 general election, had seen her 5,000 majority shrink in subsequent elections. Two years earlier she had held on with a majority of 2,349. Now, warned of what regional party offices in the West Midlands assumed were Brown's intentions, Stuart and her campaign team rolled up their sleeves. If Labour's majority in the Commons was to be preserved, her seat was exactly the kind that had to be successfully defended.

Some media outlets reported that there was even a possibility that Brown might announce the election during his conference address on the Tuesday. This proved another false hope, though the immediate post-speech polls gave further encouragement to those pushing for an autumn election. Still Brown prevaricated, while across the country local organisers made preparations.

And not only local organisers.

The party's general secretary Peter Watt had been put on a campaign footing before the conference began. In fact, the number of full-time officials in Bournemouth had been drastically reduced, because Watt had sent so many of them back to London to finalise preparations for the general election. 'The assumption all week was that it was going ahead,' said Watt. 'We actually cancelled annual leave for the coming period.'

After the conference and back in London, Watt oversaw lists of potential candidates and seats not yet filled. And introductory leaflets ('pretty generic but with local candidates' details in them') were delivered to the party's headquarters for distribution during the crucial first seventy-two hours after the election was called.

Even if Brown had been more confident of the way forward, shadow Chancellor George Osborne's announcement at the Tories' own conference the following week would have caused him to think again. To great acclaim and good media reviews, Osborne announced that a future Conservative government would raise the threshold on inheritance tax to £1 million. And he would pay for it with a levy on foreign 'non-doms', wealthy foreign residents living in the UK.

Whatever the economic arguments for the move, it was a masterstroke in terms of political tactics, putting Labour on the back foot and making the Tories look optimistic and confident. Brown's unannounced visit to British troops serving in Iraq the same week, on the other hand, dealt a blow to his personal reputation:

a convention of British politics is that rival leaders don't try to upstage their opponents' conferences – a particularly distasteful move when government resources and British troops in a combat zone are used in order to achieve it.

Watt recounts:

> The week before, we [the election team, including Watt, Spencer Livermore and Douglas Alexander] had had a discussion and we asked what we would do if we were the Tories. And that [the inheritance tax announcement] is what we would have done. We needed to have a response, but we didn't have one.

And by the end of that week, the decision had still not been made. If it were made now, an October poll was out of the question; now, the earliest that polling day could be arranged for was November, after the clocks had been turned back an hour at the end of October, heralding darker, decidedly voter-unfriendly evenings.

And then, on Friday 5 October, Brown was briefed on new polling that suggested a modest Tory poll lead in the marginal seats that would decide any election – and he bottled it.

There was spluttering outrage from Ed Balls, who believed his friend and mentor was making a calamitous mistake, particularly so given the briefing that had already taken place specifically to heighten expectations. That such expectations were now to be dashed was bad enough. The manner in which it had been done cast a long shadow over Brown's reputation with the media.

On Saturday 6 October, Brown gave a pre-recorded interview to Andrew Marr for his Sunday morning political show on BBC1. The idea, opposed by some close to the Prime Minister, was to include in the interview the revelation that there would, after all, be no early election either in 2007 or, barring unforeseen events, the following year. It was optimistic, to say the least, to expect such political dynamite not to leak before the programme aired the following morning. In fact, it never had a chance to be leaked. As Brown left Downing Street after the interview finished, Marr briefed journalists standing outside on what Brown had said. The news led all the major news bulletins for the rest of the day.

Whether with regret or relief, candidates across the country stood down their operations. 'We're being told [by the party's regional office] there's going to be a general election,' said Gisela Stuart. 'We're getting ready to have a targeted mailing out – I think 15,000 letters ready, addressed, bundled into rounds, all in crates. We check with regional office: "We're still on, aren't we?" "Yes, we're still on."

'Then [a couple of hours before it hit the news] I get a phone call from Harriet Harman saying there's no election.' Stuart's response was to invite all her core campaign team to share a crate of champagne while they made a bonfire of the 15,000 undelivered, and now useless, direct-mail letters.

The die was cast: the choice made, for good or for ill. It had never been an easy one to make in the first place, but the decision to stand down his troops after so much preparation had gone into 'the election that never was' had been Brown's and Brown's alone. Over the course of barely a week, his government made the transition from master of the British political sphere to its hapless victim. Brown's sin was not in refusing to call an early election, but in authorising his allies to talk up the possibility of one. The sight of the country's new Prime Minister, having marched his troops to the top of the hill only to reluctantly march them back down again without firing a single shot, sat uneasily with voters, who now started to look, however reluctantly and unenthusiastically, to David Cameron and the Conservative Party for leadership.

'People had a sense that something pretty huge had happened,' says Watt. 'You didn't need to see the headlines about "Bottler Brown" to see that. Something devastating had happened.'

Watt, who had been a strong supporter of Blair's, said that, at the time of Brown's arrival, other Blairites employed at party headquarters had had deep misgivings about the new Prime Minister.

But Gordon had had a fantastic summer, had completely exceeded our expectations. He almost had 'Father of the Nation' status. He'd had a pretty good conference; the No. 10 operation seemed to be doing a pretty good job. For a predominantly Blairite head office, we were pretty excited. It still felt like we were working for the number one political party in the country.

That week [of the Conservative Party conference] destroyed that. It felt like we were working for a second-rate political party.

Watt's misgivings were reinforced on the following Monday, during a conversation with Fiona Gordon, Brown's director of political relations.

She told us there was going to be a series of announcements to get the initiative back. But when I said that cancelling the election was a disaster, she denied the election had ever been called, so how could it have been cancelled? They just didn't realise the enormity of what had just happened.

Labour's poll ratings took an immediate dive from the moment the decision was announced. Voters began to suspect that 'Irn Broon' wasn't the steadfast and reliable leader they had been led to believe. A year later, *Guardian* journalists Nicholas Watt and Patrick Wintour concluded: 'On one thing only is there agreement. It marked a watershed in public perceptions of Brown, and represents the biggest unforced political error in the history of New Labour.'

Having reversed the Tories' previous opinion poll lead in the immediate aftermath of Blair's resignation – and often by double digits – Labour was behind again. In the twenty-nine months that were left of the parliamentary term, Labour only rarely – and fleetingly – took a lead in the national polls.

* * *

It had all been going so well. And it could have been so different.

If Brown had been more courageous (some might say 'cavalier') and gone to the country in October 2007 and won, he would have become the fourth Labour leader in history to win a general election in his own right. He would have been given the option of serving up to five more years. Having won his own mandate, he may well have chosen to step aside at a time of his own choosing, unharried by his enemies (an achievement only ever accomplished once by a serving Prime Minister, Harold Wilson, since 1945), once his preferred replacement as leader and Prime Minister had been lined up.

The 2008 financial crisis and MPs' expenses scandal (see Chapter Two) would still have happened, but the consequences for the Conservative Party of losing a fourth consecutive general election may well have rendered them incapable of exploiting such difficulties. Cameron would undoubtedly have been forced from his job as party leader and who would have replaced him? Who was respected enough to be able to renew, reform and modernise the party while maintaining an appeal to the old guard? An unprecedented fourth loss and the resignation of Cameron might well have ended the Conservative Party's ambitions to govern for a generation or more.

The future would have been Labour's to own.

It was a future that didn't materialise. Indirectly, from that one pivotal moment – the decision to confound and frustrate the expectations of candidates and media alike – flowed a succession of consequences that would, within ten years, transform the Labour Party, one of Europe's oldest political parties, the founder of Britain's welfare state and NHS, into an unrecognisable, extreme version of itself.

The supreme irony is that Labour could not point the finger of blame for this calamity at any of its political opponents or the media or big business or any of the range of its traditional enemies. All of its subsequent troubles were therefore self-inflicted; every poor decision and overreaction was the conscious and deliberate choice of Labour's leaders. The party had no one to blame for its predicament but itself.

CHAPTER TWO

HOW TO GIVE A CAR CRASH A BAD NAME

The PLP was badly split, fractious and – at least parts of it – bitter by the time Gordon Brown made his first speech in Downing Street at the end of June 2007. Blairites, many of whom continued as ministers under their new leader (in fact, Brown would have found it almost impossible to fill all the spaces on his front bench without them) had had months, and in some cases years, to prepare for life under the new regime and so were prepared to lick their wounds, keep their heads down and give the new boss some time to prove he was fit to follow in the footsteps of Tony Blair.

But, as with the general electorate, such existing patience quickly evaporated when the shock of the election that never was reverberated around the country. Until that point, MPs known to have been critical of Brown while he was Chancellor were generous in their praise and honest in their surprise that they could have been wrong. Perhaps Brown was, after all, exactly the right face to present to an electorate that had become too cynical and jaded after ten years of Blair's easy charm and wide smile. In the Members' Restaurant (the stately dining room in the House of

Commons, where only serving MPs and Lords who had also once been MPs could dine) talk during the late summer of 2007 was tinged with the smug satisfaction of the Brownites (most of whom never quite got round to saying 'I told you so', but then, they didn't need to) and the more or less equal measures of disappointment and relief felt by the Blairites.

All that changed during the first weekend of October. From that moment onwards, the administration of Gordon Brown became defined by a series of disasters and, more importantly, from a political point of view, by a never-ending series of conspiracies by ministers and others to depose him and replace him with a candidate whom the electorate might consider more appealing. In fact, despite the global financial meltdown that threatened the world's economies in 2008 and the rather more prosaic, though politically colossal, scandal involving MPs' expenses in 2009, Brown's tenure at No. 10 came to be defined by the almost permanent conspiracy (or conspiracies) by his own MPs to oust him as leader and Prime Minister. With hindsight and, arguably, even at the time, this could be seen as unfair to Brown, whose decisive leadership of the G20 may well have averted some of the more destructive consequences for jobs and economies of the bankers' greed and hubris. The frustrating aspect for Brown and his advisers was that, according to the consistent conclusions of various polling organisations, such efforts were barely appreciated or even recognised by the British electorate.

Brown's missteps began almost immediately, on Monday 8 October 2007, the day after the Marr programme was broadcast, with its, by now, not even remotely exclusive nugget about Brown's decision not to hold a general election. This was the day the Prime Minister hosted his monthly press conference at No. 10. Inevitably, he had to field questions about the election that never was. Inexplicably, he denied that his decision not to hold the election had been anything to do with the opinion polls. Had this been true, he would have been the first Prime Minister in living memory who had taken such a decision without reference to them. And no one believed him. Journalists present would remember this occasion when, two years later, Brown was to deny another obvious truth in the aftermath of another crisis (see Chapter Three).

Under the headline 'Crisis for Brown as election ruled out', *The Guardian* reported on Conservative leader David Cameron's largely successful attempt to exploit Brown's difficulties: 'The Prime Minister has shown great weakness and indecision and it is quite clear he has not been focused on running the country these last few months. He has been trying to spin his way into a general election campaign and now has had to make this humiliating retreat.'

Two days later, Cameron took full advantage of Brown's travails when, at the weekly joust between the pair at Prime Minister's Questions, he drew positive headlines (for himself and his party) by attacking Brown as 'phoney'. For Brown and for Labour, this was a dangerous line of attack, given that the party had promoted Brown as 'Not flash, just Gordon' in a series of posters unveiled during Labour's annual conference a fortnight earlier. Brown's dour and apparently humourless demeanour was the very thing Labour strategists felt they could capitalise upon, making a virtue out of what, in the television age, would ordinarily have been seen as a weakness. So Cameron's attempt to challenge this perception, to paint the Prime Minister as a phoney, risked undermining fatally the central value of what the Brown government had to 'offer'.

In a carefully rehearsed sound bite that had his own benches rocking with laughter and, more importantly, which caused many in the press gallery above the Speaker's chair to emit enthusiastic guffaws, Cameron told the House: 'He is the first Prime Minister in history to flunk an election because he thought he could win it!'

Throughout all this, Brown barely hid his anger at each barb thrown in his direction. It was his worst performance, up to that point, at the despatch box, either as Prime Minister or as Chancellor. He was unaccustomed to being the butt of the joke, not in this chamber over which he had held such sway so often in a career that had lasted twenty-four years. Brown was used to praise – much of it deserved – for his easy command of the facts, and in the first fifteen weeks of his premiership he had clearly enjoyed the positive reviews he had received. He was not used to ridicule, and it showed.

If observers were unconvinced about the degree to which the media had changed its perception of Brown and his government, they only had to peruse the coverage of new Chancellor of the Exchequer Alistair Darling's pre-Budget statement to the Commons on the Tuesday of that same week. A month earlier, perhaps Darling's announcements would have been described as politically clever or imaginative, and would have acted as an indication that here was a government that knew what it wanted to achieve and how to make those aims a reality. But in the immediate aftermath of Brown's decision not to hold an early election, after Brown had told them to their faces that the likelihood of winning such an election had played absolutely no part in his calculations, members of the press gallery found themselves with the bit firmly between their teeth. Here was a government that was vulnerable, a government that wasn't about to face the voters any time soon, and so a government that had to be properly scrutinised and taken to task in a way that, arguably, its predecessor (and Blair himself) had not been.

Darling's announcements were widely seen as political measures concocted for a general election. His statement failed to find favour with Labour's left wing, which was unhappy about the doubling to £600,000 of the couples' inheritance tax allowance, the consequent cost to the Exchequer of £1.4 billion a year by 2010 and by the fact that this was clearly a reaction to George Osborne's own inheritance tax announcement to his own party's conference a week earlier.

Darling also announced that, as the BBC reported: 'UK economic growth will slow from 3 per cent this year to 2–2.5 per cent next year, a reduction from the previous forecast of 2.5–3 per cent made in March.' It did not go unremarked upon that the March forecast had been made by Brown in his last Budget statement as Chancellor.

Even commentators who were normally sympathetic to Labour were hardly encouraging. Polly Toynbee wrote in *The Guardian*:

> To give the children of the well-off a £1.4 billion inheritance bonus while the children of the poor only got another 48p a week in tax credits is symbolically far worse than that notorious 75p for pensioners. The halfway mark to abolish child poverty by 2010 will be missed by miles. Holding down public sector pay rises to 2 per cent for three years, only half next year's expected private sector increase, will increase inequality.

Darling's announcement of a cut in capital gains tax was, wrote Toynbee, 'as shameless as it is dysfunctional'.

Morale within the PLP had taken a hit, but at this point few were panicking. There was still a great deal of good will towards Brown and the government from the Labour back benches and, after all, since no election was imminent, there was plenty of time to mount a fightback. The next general election was still at least eighteen months away, possibly two and a half years. As events developed, however, there was precious little time for such a fightback, since events seemed to conspire to knock the government continually onto its back foot.

On 20 November 2007, Labour whips texted MPs to urge them to attend the chamber to support the Chancellor, who would be making an emergency statement. To a hushed House and to genuinely outraged Members on both sides, Darling revealed that two data discs relating to child benefit claimants and containing the personal information of 25 million citizens – nearly half the country's population – had gone missing in the internal mail system of Her Majesty's Revenue & Customs (HMRC). The news brought widespread political and public condemnation, sparking fears of data fraud and dealing a near-fatal blow to Brown's hopes for the introduction of a mandatory national identity database. In no way could Brown or his ministers be blamed for such a catastrophic error. Nevertheless, the incident played into the poisonous narrative, understandably encouraged by the Conservative opposition, that this government's reputation for quiet competency was ill deserved and unravelling fast.

In his last Budget as Chancellor, as well as making a prediction on growth that had to be downgraded by his successor at No. 11, Brown had announced the reduction from 22p to 20p in the standard rate of income tax. In order to pay for this generosity, he also announced that the 10p rate of tax, which had been introduced in 1999 and mainly benefited lower-paid workers, would be abolished.

The announcement at the time, in March 2007, had caused little debate in the country or in the PLP at the time. But at the start of 2008, as the new financial year hoved into view, awareness of the change – and the impact it would have on 5 million low-paid workers who benefited from the lowest tax band – began to filter through to MPs. A particularly – and unexpectedly – hostile meeting of the PLP in January took Brown by surprise as normally supportive MPs expressed their dismay at the impact the abolition of the 10p rate would have, both on individual workers and families, but also on the party. Brown's anger at being challenged on the issue was apparent from his facial contortions, and he left the meeting in a foul mood while news of the exchange leaked to journalists waiting in the corridor outside.

As more and more MPs spoke out against the change, the independently minded former minister Frank Field stepped up to make life even more difficult for Brown by tabling an amendment to the Finance Bill then before the Commons, which demanded compensation for every taxpayer who lost out because of the 10p rate abolition. Enough Labour MPs – forty-five – signed Field's amendment to guarantee a defeat for the government if they all followed through by voting for it when a division was called on the floor of the House. Such a scenario was utterly unthinkable as far as Brown was concerned; he despatched his Chancellor to do the surrendering for him. After lengthy negotiations and one-on-one meetings between Darling and the rebels, during which it was promised that compensation would be provided to those affected by the 10p rate abolition, Field agreed to withdraw his amendment. On 13 May, the retreat was formalised by Darling in a statement to the Commons: personal tax allowances would be increased by £600 at the lower end of the scale (backdated to the start of the tax year), while the higher tax threshold would be reduced by the same amount, to avoid the politically explosive prospect of higher earners gaining a tax cut.

Brown had blinked. Nine months after being marched to the top of the hill and back down again without the anticipated general election, backbenchers were feeling less restrained in their criticism. Much of the unhappiness about the 10p tax rate abolition was clearly redirected anger at Brown himself. The discipline that had prevailed in the PLP during Brown's short-lived honeymoon was beginning to disintegrate.

But another defeat was just around the corner, a defeat that, like the 10p tax debacle, went to the heart of what a Labour government is for. In this case, the issue wasn't redistributive taxation, but civil liberties.

In 2006, true to his conviction that the 9/11 terrorist attacks on the United States had 'shaken the kaleidoscope' for ever, Tony Blair had tried, and failed, to introduce unprecedented detention powers to deal with terrorist suspects. Plans to introduce an upper limit of ninety days before a suspect had to be charged were defeated in the Commons after an intense campaign by civil liberties campaigners and a rebellion by a significant number of Labour MPs (although the maximum time limit for detention without charge was doubled from fourteen to twenty-eight days).

Now, in 2008, after pressure from the security services, Brown tried again. This time the aim was to increase the limit from twenty-eight to forty-two days of detention without charge as part of the Counter-Terrorism Bill. Again, the government found itself up against severe criticism from parts of the media and civil liberties groups. The crucial clause was voted upon in June 2008 and was passed by the Commons despite a rebellion by thirty-six Labour MPs (the votes that came to the government's rescue were cast by the Democratic Unionist Party (DUP) of Northern Ireland). Four months later, the measure was overturned by a vote in the House of Lords. Rather than face another heated and knife-edge debate in the Commons, Brown agreed that the 42-day detention should be consigned to the dustbin. This was another defeat for a man who valued his reputation as a stout defender of the nation against external and internal enemies.

By this point, as pratfall followed misstep and the polls continued to reflect a bleak outlook for Labour, a number of government ministers of various levels of seniority embarked on manoeuvres against Brown. Their thinking was ruthless, if simplistic: since the UK has a parliamentary rather than a presidential system of government, then what would it matter if Brown were deposed and replaced with yet another 'unelected' Prime Minister, provided he (or she) had better prospects of keeping the party in power? Even if the strategy were to fail, and Labour found itself in opposition after the next general election, why would such an outcome be any worse than the certain defeat to which Brown was now leading Labour?

On 1 May 2008, voters across England and Wales cast their ballots in local authority elections (Scots had chosen their own local councillors a year earlier). Labour came a dismal third place, one percentage point behind Nick Clegg's Liberal Democrats and, with just 24 per cent of the vote, a full twenty points behind the Conservatives. Later that month, the Conservatives won the constituency of Crewe and Nantwich in the north-west of England, in a by-election triggered by the death in April of the formidable

Gwyneth Dunwoody MP. With a swing from Labour to the Conservatives of over 17 per cent, the result was enough to give David Cameron a comfortable Commons majority in the (admittedly unlikely) event that a UK-wide general election would deliver the same result nationally. More importantly, the result represented the first gain in a parliamentary by-election the Conservatives had made since losing office in 1997; in fact it was the first since the Mitcham and Morden by-election in 1982.

The next electoral test Brown had to face was staged in his own backyard, in the Scottish seat of Glasgow East. Sitting Labour MP David Marshall had stunned and perplexed colleagues by resigning with immediate effect from his rock-solid safe Labour seat in the east end of Scotland's largest city. Rumours at the time suggested Marshall had resigned in anticipation of criticism he expected to receive when his (and all his parliamentary colleagues') parliamentary expenses were published; unaware that that particular drama was nearly a year away and, in the event, Marshall's own record elicited no criticism whatsoever.

Scottish Labour had always been nervous of by-elections, and with some justification. The days when the Conservatives could win unexpected victories in traditional working-class areas like Pollok were forty years in the past; since John Major had lost every single Conservative MP in Scotland in 1997, so his party had not been considered as a serious threat to Labour's continued monopoly of its political heartlands in west and central Scotland. But as the Tories waned, the Scottish National Party (SNP) waxed. Offering a message that was unashamedly left wing, while slamming Labour over its failure to deliver real improvements for the most impoverished of communities, despite decades of dominance at all levels of government, the nationalist message was seductive and, for Labour, dangerous. It had been twenty years since an SNP candidate had overturned a seemingly impregnable Labour majority, in Govan in 1988. Could they pull it off again in a seat that was, to all intents and purposes, identical to Govan?

Yes, they could. In 2005, when fewer than half of eligible voters had cast their ballots, Marshall had held the seat with more than 60 per cent of the vote, securing a Labour majority of 13,500. On 24 July 2008, the SNP's John Mason was returned to Parliament with a majority of just 365.

The result was particularly humiliating for a Prime Minister who had been the first since Alec Douglas-Home to represent a Scottish seat. The result set the hare running on a number of challenges, some less overt than others, against Brown's leadership. There had been much speculation in the media as to which prominent figures might resign from the government in protest at Brown's continued leadership of the government. The Health Secretary, Alan Johnson, and Foreign Secretary, David Miliband, were regularly identified as possible or likely successors were Brown to fall on his sword. Both were known to be critics of the Prime Minister and both received numerous requests from parliamentary colleagues to provoke a contest in order to oust him. But it was Miliband, the older brother of Ed, the Energy and Climate Change Secretary, on whom the rebels' hopes were pinned as the summer recess progressed. Writing in *The Guardian* on 29 July 2008, just a few days after the Glasgow East defeat, Miliband said that 'the times demand a radical new change'. His own aides had briefed journalists the evening before that the article – which failed to mention Brown – was the starting pistol on a challenge for the leadership of the party. The article was duly reported as such and, fielding questions about it during a press conference he was hosting in London alongside Franco Frattini, the Italian foreign minister, the Foreign Secretary pointedly refused to rule out a challenge to Brown.

Enthusiastically cheering Miliband on from the sidelines were a number of Labour MPs well known for their devotion to their former leader, Blair, and, in equal measure, for opposition to the man they saw as their hero's usurper – among this number was Mitcham and Morden MP Siobhain McDonagh. Two weeks after Miliband's *Guardian* article, McDonagh became the first member of the government (she was an assistant whip at the time) to call for a leadership election. She was promptly sacked.

Resigning at the same time from her party role as 'vice-chairman' was Enfield North MP, Joan Ryan, a close friend of McDonagh's, and Barry Gardiner, MP for Brent North, who walked away from the (unpaid and non-governmental) position of 'Forestry Envoy' (a post few knew he held; even fewer knew what the title meant).

With the BBC's political editor Nick Robinson reporting that as many as another half-dozen ministers were set to follow in the next few days, the press went into a frenzy as it hunted down the next character in the story. It wasn't long before they found their quarry.

David Cairns had worked for McDonagh after her election to the Commons in 1997. In 2001 he had himself been elected as Labour MP for Greenock and Inverclyde, the seat in which he was born and had grown up. He achieved a degree of notoriety following his adoption as candidate when the government was obliged to change the law to allow ordained Roman Catholic priests – in which capacity Cairns had served in his earlier years – and certain other clergy to take their seats in the Commons.

Having proved himself to be a popular and able advocate of

the government, Cairns was appointed as Scotland Office minister following the 2005 general election, and a year later was given additional ministerial responsibilities in the Northern Ireland Office. Acquitting himself well (he was one of a very small number of Labour politicians not intimidated by First Minister Alex Salmond of the SNP and was equal to him in debate), Cairns was nevertheless frustrated by his role at the Scotland Office, as most of its responsibilities had been devolved to the Scottish Executive (or Scottish government from 2007), and hankered after a UK portfolio. Forming his first government in June 2007, Brown, recognising Cairns's sure touch in Scotland, only managed to persuade him to remain in post by offering the Inverclyde MP a promotion to minister of state level (the job had previously been designated at a parliamentary under-secretary of state level, the most junior of ministerial ranks).

A firm supporter and confidant of Tony Blair, Cairns had often warned colleagues that Brown, were he ever to achieve the office to which he aspired, would be a disaster for the country and the Labour Party. Now, in the summer of 2008, his predictions were coming true. And in mid-September, as Labour's annual conference hoved into view, Cairns repeated his views to BBC political correspondent David Thompson, who reported them as unattributable. But the source was described as a 'minister of state', immediately reducing the pool of suspects to a manageable number for No. 10 investigators.

The Secretary of State for Scotland at the time, Des Browne, was a friend and admirer of Cairns; the pair had developed an easy and productive working relationship. Browne did not want to lose his junior colleague, but his name was being openly talked of as the source for the BBC story. The only way to kill the story, Browne told Cairns on 16 September, would be for him to issue a statement of support for Brown's continued leadership of the Labour Party. The alternative would be his resignation. Cairns chose resignation.

Would Cairns's departure represent the bursting of the dam? Or would a semblance of loyalty and discipline descend on the party's parliamentary ranks? The able and respected Blairite himself insisted his actions had been motivated by a devotion to the Labour Party that he simply couldn't reconcile with support for a Prime Minister he was certain could not regain the trust of the British electorate.

Miliband had by this time already disappointed supporters by seeming to pour cold water on his own prospects of challenging Brown. The initial enthusiasm for a challenge, even among Brown's enemies within the party, had waned as the global economic crisis continued to rage. Lehman Brothers, the US-based global financial services company, had declared bankruptcy on 15 September, the day before Cairns's resignation, by which time Miliband was already rowing back from his challenge at the end of August. Nevertheless, as Labour's conference approached and the media and backbench MPs gossiped excitedly about the resignations of McDonagh and Cairns, speculating about who else might volunteer to jump ship in order to pressure Brown to step down, Brown's team found it frustratingly difficult to regain control of the political narrative. There had been no major ministerial reshuffle since Brown's first one after assuming office. Observers had started to speculate that his reluctance to embark on a reshaping of his government was founded on nervousness which, in turn, was seen as a sign of weakness.

Against this background, Labour's 2008 conference kicked off in Manchester. Had it really been just a year since Brown's first conference speech as leader and Prime Minister, when the conference centre was electric with the anticipation of an impending general election victory?

On Monday 22 September, David Miliband took to the stage for his annual set-piece speech, a lacklustre affair that praised Brown but stopped short of endorsing his continued leadership. Two events beyond the conference stage managed to diminish the Foreign Secretary and any challenge he may or may not have been considering mounting. The first was what wags in the media started to label 'Bananagate', when Miliband allowed himself to be photographed on the way into the conference awkwardly brandishing the fruit. Coupled with Miliband's already well-established 'geek chic', the images did nothing for his credibility as a future Prime Minister, certainly not when compared to the grave and dour images of Brown as he prepared his own speech and made the traditional rounds of conference fringes.

The second event was rather more substantial and, for Brown, worrying. Miliband, who was relaxing in the conference bar on the evening of his speech, was overheard – and subsequently reported – by a BBC journalist referring specifically to the question of a leadership challenge. In a clear sign that he had considered being more overtly critical of Brown in his speech, Miliband told a friend that he had eventually chosen to avoid a 'Heseltine moment', a reference to the former Conservative Defence Secretary's decision to challenge Margaret Thatcher for the leadership of their party in 1990. In an atmosphere already bubbling with speculation about the only story the media were interested in, this was valuable intelligence that was duly reported online the following day – the day of Gordon Brown's second conference speech as leader of the Labour Party.

Introduced by his wife Sarah, Brown delivered a speech that was widely seen as uninspiring. As Chancellor, Brown had frequently set delegates' pulses racing; as Prime Minister, he perhaps felt the weight of the office and allowed caution to overrule his instinct for demagoguery. As Theo Bertram, who worked as an adviser to both Blair and Brown, later recounted, some of the backroom dilemmas that shaped Brown's speech nearly sank it. His 2008 speech included a quote from the shadow Chancellor, George Osborne, but was misrepresented to suit Brown's political agenda; the actual quote: 'It isn't pleasant to watch people making loads of money out of the misery of others but that is a function of financial markets', became, in Brown's speech (and, as if to compound his 'error', Brown prefaced the quote with the words 'and I quote…'): 'It's a function of financial markets that people make loads of money out of the misery of others.'

'Gordon wanted to show how reckless and uncaring the Tories would be and so he quoted George Osborne,' said Bertram in 2016. 'But George Osborne had not said that. Definitely not.' Bertram added: 'Conference speeches are difficult things. Someone has to be in charge of it. But it was never clear exactly who was in charge in 2008.'

As if acknowledging the need to sate the appetites of journalists hoping to write more about the *sotto voce* battle for the leadership, Brown, in a reference to Cameron but using language that was easily interpreted to be aimed at his own Foreign Secretary, declared that now 'is no time for a novice'. Miliband was careful to make sure he was captured applauding and smiling at his leader's turn of phrase.

The rivalries among Brown's disciples in No. 10 were to play a major role in the development of the perception that the government was in disarray; it is a matter of some speculation whether such a dysfunctional situation could have been averted had Brown been freshly elected as Prime Minister in 2007 as he originally intended. The most controversial figure, and one of Brown's closest friends and advisers, was Damian McBride.

A former civil servant at the Treasury while Brown was Chancellor, he was later recruited to Brown's own staff as a special adviser and made the transition alongside him to No. 10 in 2007. McBride was hated by the Blairites in the party, an enmity in which it was said he took great pride. From the start of the period when Brown's leadership started to come under threat until McBride's resignation in April 2009 (and, critics suggest, from a much earlier point), he was considered Brown's enforcer, undermining critics within the party by the use of press briefings and the promise of titbits about ministers and others. In this way, ministers became wary of being seen publicly to criticise the Prime Minister, even indirectly.

It was careless, or perhaps rival, briefings that helped end the week of conference on a sour and chaotic note. On the Tuesday night, the BBC's *Newsnight* programme helped cast a shadow over coverage of Brown's speech by speculating on reports that the long-awaited reshuffle was now imminent, and that three Cabinet ministers – Ruth Kelly at Transport, Chief Whip Geoff Hoon and Scotland and Defence Secretary Des Browne – were all to lose their jobs. This was hotly denied by at least one of Brown's aides, but at 3.00 a.m. on Wednesday morning, McBride was seen in the conference bar briefing journalists and confirming that Kelly would indeed be leaving – of her own volition – at the next reshuffle. In the febrile atmosphere of conference, suspicions were raised that the Bolton MP had been pushed for some imagined act of disloyalty to Brown and that McBride was getting his retaliation in early. In fact, Kelly had decided to stand down for personal reasons; she was later to announce her departure from the Commons at the subsequent general election.

It was a messy end to what should have been a confident, successful week. Brown, considering the shape of his new government, needed to pull something out of his hat that would persuade the media and the public that he was in command and that he knew what path the country needed to take.

Peter Mandelson was a former TV producer who had risen to national prominence in charge of the Labour Party's communications under Neil Kinnock in the 1980s. His rebranding of the party, the adoption of the red rose to replace the red flag, his ruthless promotion to the media frontline of telegenic frontbenchers like Blair and Brown, made him a target of adoration and hatred, depending on which wing of the party you occupied. In 1992, he became an MP, representing the north-east seat of Hartlepool, following some manoeuvring by his long-time ally Blair, whose seat was nearby. Following Labour's defeat in 1992, while John Smith was leader, Mandelson found his talents as a spin doctor were no longer required. But, following Smith's sudden death in 1994, Mandelson had little hesitation in throwing his weight behind Blair's leadership bid, much to the consternation of the Brown camp. Brown himself had never forgiven Mandelson his 'treachery', believing that he, not Blair, was more deserving of Mandelson's considerable promotional talents.

The feud continued up to and beyond Mandelson's eventual departure from UK politics, with his appointment in 2004 as Britain's representative on the European Commission. So Brown's announcement on 3 October 2008 that Mandelson was to be given a seat in the House of Lords and appointed to the Cabinet as Business Secretary, achieved exactly what it was intended to achieve: front-page headlines and copious analysis of the theme that he was a man confident enough to appoint one of his (former) foremost critics to a key government post. The Prime Minister and the country needed 'serious people for serious times', said Brown. Mandelson's appointment was in 'the national interest'. Petty personal grievances would not define his government, was Brown's message.

* * *

Governments rarely lose votes on opposition day debates – at least governments with healthy working majorities rarely do. And even when such a thing occurs, the result of a vote on these occasions can have no formal or legal bearing on any particular area of policy. Nevertheless, when, on 29 April 2009, the Commons supported an opposition day motion criticising the government for its refusal to allow former members of the Gurkha regiments of the British Army who had retired before 1997 to obtain residency in the UK, it felt like a major, confidence-sapping defeat.

TV star Joanna Lumley, whose own father had fought with the Gurkhas during the Second World War, led the high-profile campaign to alter the government's policy, and Nick Clegg, the Lib Dem leader, was quick to spot an opportunity to receive some reflected starlight from the former *New Avengers* and *Absolutely Fabulous* star. After a heated debate in the Commons, the Liberal Democrat motion demanding that the government accede to Ms Lumley's demands was carried by a majority of twenty-two, after a large number of Labour MPs either abstained or voted with the opposition. Brown quickly took the view that it was better to retreat and concede. But it was too late to avoid the impression that the government was drifting, buffeted by events, rather than commanding them.

Ministers may at that point have hoped for some form of distraction that might remove the spotlight from defence and immigration policy. One week after the defeat on the Liberal Democratic motion, they were to get their wish.

The history of MPs' expenses is one steeped in opportunism, dishonesty and cynicism. Successive Prime Ministers of either party believed that while Members deserved a substantial salary increase, to grant one would entail potentially catastrophic consequences for whichever government made that decision. So for decades a dishonest game was played whereby allowances – non-taxable and without receipts – could be allocated to MPs to cover a range of costs, from London accommodation to food and furniture. Other allowances – petty cash to cover day-to-day costs of running a constituency office, for example – could also be claimed and the use of such sums left to the discretion of the Member in question. Again, no receipts were required and such sums were free from tax.

It was a system that was Westminster's grubby little secret. While journalists knew that some MPs had made a fortune by buying London accommodation entirely at the taxpayers' expense and then selling it on for huge personal gain, there were precious few official figures for them to pore over and confirm, in print, that what they knew was happening could be proved to be happening.

Until the Labour government passed the Freedom of Information Act 2000.

Ministers had cavilled at explicitly excluding parliamentarians from the Act's remit, accepting officials' vague reassurances that only the broadest sums covering entire annual budgets – travel, London living costs, etc. – rather than the details of individual items, would ever be released to the public.

Ministers' misunderstanding of the legislation they themselves had piloted through Parliament were dramatically exposed when, against objections by House of Commons authorities, the Information Tribunal approved a Freedom of Information (FOI) request for details of MPs' claims. After the High Court concurred with the tribunal's conclusions, the Commons capitulated and the Speaker, Michael Martin, decreed that details of all Members' expenses – the Incidental Expenses Provision (IEP, or office costs) and the Additional Costs Allowance (ACA, or London living allowance) – would be published in due course. However, in order to prevent the release of individuals' private information, such as credit card numbers and private home addresses, much of the detail would be redacted, or obscured by acres of black ink. This was a source of frustration to journalists, who were convinced the withholding of such detail might prevent exploitation of the system – particularly with regard to MPs' arrangements over their constituency and London accommodation – being exposed.

Rumours began to circulate of the existence of a CD that contained not just the details of the four years of expenses that had been collated for publication, but the *unredacted* files. The disc was being offered to various newspapers. It was only a matter of time before an editor with the right news sense took the bait.

Snippets of what was to come had found their way into the media in early 2009. Home Secretary Jacqui Smith faced humiliating reports that her husband had not only paid to watch a pornographic movie, but had somehow managed to claim the cost on his wife's parliamentary expenses. Then, at 10.00 p.m. on Thursday 7 May,

Sky News revealed what almost every sitting MP had dreaded: the disc containing the unedited details of every claim in the last four years was in the possession of the *Daily Telegraph*, which would begin publishing details in the following day's edition.

Parliament entered a state of panic; the media entered a feeding frenzy. The revelations involved MPs of all parties, and many of the more dramatic and egregious claims had been made by Conservative MPs, including the infamous 'duck house' whose cost was claimed by (but not paid out to) Gosport MP Sir Peter Viggers. Nevertheless, it was a Labour government that was left holding the parcel when the music stopped. And it was Gordon Brown to whom the country turned, more in resignation than expectation, for a solution. The Prime Minister himself had been the subject of one of the *Telegraph*'s exposés, raising questions (subsequently answered entirely satisfactorily) about an arrangement Brown had had with his brother over the shared costs of a cleaner. And to this son of the manse, the product of a morally strict Presbyterian upbringing, even the suggestion that he could be dishonest in such a matter – let alone having the details of the allegation splashed across the front page of the nation's biggest-selling broadsheet – cut him to the quick.

Brown had to take charge of the situation; he was planning yet another reshuffle to take place in the aftermath of June's expected crushing defeat in the European Parliament election. The last thing he wanted was to appoint ministers who might then have to resign if an examination of their own expenses revealed an item that might embarrass the government – and him. At the same time Brown needed to be seen to lead efforts to draw a line under the whole messy affair by putting his weight behind a new scheme that would satisfy an angry public while not leaving his MPs in penury.

Brown came to prominence on Labour's front bench, first as shadow Trade and Industry Secretary under Neil Kinnock, then briefly standing in for John Smith while the shadow Chancellor was recovering from his first heart attack in 1988. He had a reputation of being a master of the sound bite as well as the TV interview, displaying an astonishing and impressive grasp of detail while phrasing it in such a way as to be digestible by the average viewer. Yet by 2009, Brown found himself acutely awkward when dealing with some of the new forms of media and campaigning. His agreement to appear in a YouTube video proclaiming confidence in a brand-new system of parliamentary expenses was widely mocked for his stilted and uncomfortable delivery. He seemed unsure when to smile (apparently none of his advisers thought to caution him against smiling at all, given how angry MPs' behaviour had made the entire country) and displayed an inappropriate grimace at what seemed quite random points, a grimace that would fade to a scowl from one moment to the next.

The second problem with the video was the scheme he was promoting, a daily allowance that could be claimed by any MP attending Parliament, for however long the individual in question was present in the Palace of Westminster. Such a scheme (still operating in the House of Lords at time of writing) had already attracted severe media criticism after a number of their Lordships were seen entering the building and leaving minutes after claiming their £300-a-day attendance allowances. Neither Labour MPs nor MPs of any other party had been consulted about the proposed change. It is still unclear why Brown and his advisers thought this would draw any line at all under the devastating scandal that had done so much to undermine people's trust in their representatives.

The third problem was that MPs' expenses was one of those

issues that was generally addressed on a cross-party basis for very obvious reasons: given the unpopularity of paying MPs anything at all from the public purse, successive generations of ministers had managed to hide behind their decisions because they were taken, normally behind closed doors, in agreement with the opposition parties. It quickly emerged, after the Brown video had been uploaded, that neither the Leader of the Opposition, David Cameron, nor the leader of the Liberal Democrats, Nick Clegg, had been consulted about Brown's proposals. Neither turned out to be supportive of the initiative and it was summarily and quietly dropped from consideration.

The expenses scandal had far-reaching consequences, both for the public's relationship with those it elected to represent their interests and for a government unlucky enough to be in power when the dam broke. It's fair to assume that whichever government, whichever leader, happened to be in power at the time would have had to shoulder more of the blame for MPs' bad behaviour than the opposition parties. Nevertheless, it wasn't any other government in power at the time, it was a Labour government, a Labour government headed by an unpopular Prime Minister who, when called upon to lead a way out of the mess that Parliament had itself created over years of opacity and lack of backbone, had fallen at the first hurdle. Brown eventually presided over the creation of a new system of expenses via the passing of the Parliamentary Standards Act in 2009, but only after the dramatic resignation of Speaker Michael Martin and the announcement by a number of MPs, both Labour and Conservative, that they would not seek re-election at the following year's general election. More seriously, four Labour MPs spent time in prison, having been found (or pleaded) guilty of fraud.

And despite an obsession with personally vetting the expense claims of members of his government to ensure that none of his new appointments would be forced to quit prematurely and embarrass the government further, Kitty Ussher, after only eight days in her new job as Exchequer Secretary to the Treasury, resigned her post following revelations that she had avoided paying capital gains tax on her London property.

Aside from the appalling results of the nationwide election to the European Parliament, held on 4 June (see Chapter Three), the expenses scandal had more of a direct electoral impact on Gordon Brown's government, one for which Brown was unable entirely to avoid responsibility. Dr Ian Gibson was a respected medical academic who had spent seven years as a member of the Trotskyite Socialist Workers' Party (SWP) before joining the Labour Party in 1983. Having unsuccessfully stood for election to his Norwich North constituency in 1992, he was successfully elected five years later in the same seat. He subsequently became chair of the All-Party Parliamentary Group on Cancer (he had, when he was the Dean of Biology at the University of East Anglia, been head of a research team investigating cancer), and was awarded a 'Champion' award by Macmillan Cancer Relief for his work in support of people with cancer. But, in May 2009, it was revealed by the *Telegraph* that Gibson had allowed his daughter to stay in his London (taxpayer-funded) flat rent-free and had subsequently sold it to her for half the market value – neither of which was forbidden either in law or by the Commons' expenses rules that applied at the time.

A Labour Party panel, set up on Brown's orders in an attempt to claw back some control of the situation, ruled that Gibson should be prevented from standing for the party at the following general election. Understandably offended by what he saw as a slur on his character, Gibson resigned his seat, causing a by-election that was held on 23 July. The contest was won by the Conservatives, giving them their second by-election gain in a year.

And as if 2009 – and the expenses scandal – could not get any worse for Labour, Brown had one more bullet left to fire directly into his foot.

After a gruelling three months of exposure, public humiliation and high drama, MPs were looking forward to the start of the long summer recess which would begin during the last week of July. Members would be able to spend the entire summer licking their wounds and building bridges with their constituents in the hope that some of the more distasteful memories of the scandal might slip from public consciousness. But that assumption didn't take into account Brown's need to be seen to be *doing something*. Too often his opponent and rival for the keys to No. 10, David Cameron, had received good press for the robust response he had been seen to make to his own MPs' exploitation of the expenses system. In an attempt to win back some of the initiative, Brown had decided he would appoint Sir Thomas Legg, a former senior civil servant, to lead an independent review of all MPs' claims of the Additional Costs Allowance between 2004 and 2008. Sir Thomas would report in October 2009 – the first week when MPs were due back in the Commons.

This meant that MPs, having spent the first few weeks of the recess trying to unwind and recover from the stress of the scandal as it had developed in early summer, would spend the last few weeks of recess girding their loins in anticipation of the inevitable renewal of media interest in the scandal. Legg's inquiry would demand repayments from hundreds of MPs who had received, in its chairman's view, money to which they were not entitled. They had assumed the worst was behind them, but for many, autumn brought with it a second dose of scandal. And it was done at Brown's command.

And the expenses scandal had a further, hidden, consequence for Gordon Brown's government: two years earlier, the world had been officially informed that despite speculation he himself had encouraged, Brown would not hold an early general election, either that year or in 2008. He specifically and deliberately held out the prospect that a poll might yet be held in 2009. Four years was, before the advent of the Fixed Term Parliament Act in 2010, the preferred length of time for a parliament from any premier's perspective. On the two occasions when he was able to choose the date of an election, for example, Tony Blair had opted for the fourth anniversary of his previous triumph. Thatcher did likewise in 1983 and 1987. Unless forced to by circumstances, no Prime Minister wishes to delay beyond that point because it immediately begins to reduce their room for manoeuvre.

Had the expenses scandal never happened, it is unlikely anyway that Brown would have found himself in a position that would allow him to go to the polls with any confidence of re-election. But after the scandal, it was truly out of the question. The un-avoidable confrontation with the voters was now guaranteed to take place in 2010.

CHAPTER THREE

THE BITTER END

In government, Labour had never done well in elections to the European Parliament. Normally, this didn't matter: no one seriously feared that the heavy losses to the Conservatives under William Hague in 1999 or Michael Howard in 2004 presaged a similar result at the following general election.

However, 2009 was different, not because of the scale of the defeat – although no governing party had ever before limped across the finish line in third place with less than 16 per cent of the vote – but because the result was merely a reflection, albeit a somewhat exaggerated one, of Labour's continuing performance in the national opinion polls.

The campaign itself was lacklustre on all sides. The exception was Nigel Farage's UK Independence Party (UKIP), which had avoided entirely any blame for the ongoing expenses scandal and was now campaigning enthusiastically for the only issue it cared about – persuading Britons to vote against continued membership of the EU. In the event, Farage's party won thirteen seats out of a possible seventy-two – the same number as Labour, but with 116,000 more votes. Cameron's Conservatives topped the poll with twenty-six seats, one fewer than the total won five years earlier.

From the beginning of May, for six long weeks, the *Telegraph* continued to publish the uncomfortable details of MPs' expenses gleaned from the CD containing the stolen data. That six-week period included the entire official campaign period for the European elections, undoubtedly the most depressing and disheartening campaign that veterans of all parties had ever fought. Voter anger was undisguised and activists were reluctant to campaign, particularly in constituencies where the local MP's behaviour had been reported in a bad light.

Polling day, on Thursday 4 June, felt as anticlimactic as such days often do, even when voting isn't taking place against such a dramatic and shameful backdrop. At midday, Blairite MPs started to share an intriguing rumour that an unnamed Cabinet member would resign that night at 10.00 p.m., at the precise moment the polls closed, in protest at Brown's leadership. Such suggestions had been made before and always the conspirators were left disappointed when, inevitably, none of the 'big beasts' could muster the courage of their oft-expressed convictions. Would tonight be any different?

At the stroke of ten, the national news networks announced that James Purnell, the Work and Pensions Secretary, a Blairite and known critic of Brown's, had resigned from the government, becoming the first Cabinet minister to call explicitly and publicly for Brown to go. 'I now believe your continued leadership makes a Conservative victory more, not less likely,' he wrote in a letter that had been distributed to the press earlier in the evening and emailed to Downing Street shortly before ten. 'I am therefore calling on you to stand aside to give our party a fighting chance of winning.'

Immediately, the votes cast that day – already lacking in news interest because the results of the European Parliament elections had to be held back until Sunday in order to allow all the EU states to announce them on the same day – became irrelevant; journalists and politicians alike started speculating openly that this, surely, was the final crisis that would end Gordon Brown's premiership. If even one more Cabinet minister followed Purnell's example – indeed, even if one didn't – how could he survive such an assault?

Rumours that David Miliband might announce his own resignation had observers in a state of high excitement. Although a Blairite, Jim Knight, the Education minister, was also a strong supporter of Brown's and was one of the first faces to appear on TV to assure viewers that the Prime Minister would not be resigning and that neither should he. Next was another Blairite, Europe minister Caroline Flint, who gave a similarly supportive interview. But where was Miliband? What of Alan Johnson, the Health Secretary and bookies' favourite to take over in the event of Brown's resignation?

Both were contacted by No. 10 in the early hours of Friday morning; both, either reluctantly or otherwise, made their pledges of loyalty. It seemed that Purnell had, after all, been working alone and not as part of a wider Blairite conspiracy.

Brown's next reshuffle – and, presumably, his last before the general election – had been planned to take place on the following Monday. This would help detract attention from the expected poor results in the European elections that would have been announced the previous day. English local elections had been held on the same day as the European elections and the results were already indicating Labour's worst performance for three decades. Now, following Purnell's bombshell, the decision was made to bring the reshuffle forward to Friday.

No. 10 'sources' had already made it clear that the Prime Minister intended to promote Ed Balls, the Schools Secretary and Brown's closest cabinet ally, to the position Balls had always craved: Chancellor. The briefings against Alistair Darling had intensified during the year, particularly when Darling himself ran into difficulties with his expenses and was forced to repay £600 after it was revealed he had made claims for a second home in London while he was living at No. 11 Downing Street.

Darling, however, made it clear to his boss that he would not go quietly. Brown realised that his position was, following Purnell's resignation and the local election results, precarious to say the least. He simply couldn't afford to have an enemy as powerful and popular as Darling on the back benches. Yet he had made little secret of his desire to replace the Chancellor with Balls. His solution? Just like in 2007, when he denied any plan to hold a snap autumn election, Brown would reject any claims that he intended to replace Darling with Balls.

At a press conference on the Friday, when asked explicitly why he had changed his mind about replacing Darling, Brown said he had never entertained such an idea. The journalists present exchanged quizzical looks, as they knew the opposite to be true.

The number of serving ministers from across the government who voluntarily stepped aside at that reshuffle was indicative of how confident they were of Brown leading the party to victory at the next election. Home Secretary Jacqui Smith, Local Government Secretary Hazel Blears, Defence Secretary John Hutton, Transport Secretary Geoff Hoon, Europe minister Caroline Flint and DEFRA minister Jane Kennedy all departed of their own volition.

With Peter Mandelson now promoted effectively to the position of Deputy Prime Minister (or 'First Secretary of State' as the official title read), Brown had the team he was going to lead into the general election, now almost certainly scheduled to coincide with the local elections on 6 May the following year.

Nevertheless, when the results of the European elections were announced on Sunday 7 June, tensions and rumours of plots were merely encouraged. Labour had polled just 15.7 per cent of the vote, a calamitous result. Following Purnell's resignation, this might have spelled the end for Brown, except for the fact that the Conservatives had managed to poll only 28 per cent – a lead, but far short of what a party hoping to govern with a majority might expect. Nevertheless, the results were poor for Labour; had the results been announced on the same evening that Purnell had resigned, Brown may have found the pressure to go overwhelming. But the three-day delay, in order for all EU states to announce their results on the same day, helped lessen the impact. By the time Parliament reassembled on Monday 8 June, at least some of the heat from Purnell's resignation had subsided. Brown's strategy of conducting an earlier-than-planned reshuffle was also having its intended effect, with MPs hoping for a call from the Prime Minister, rather than from a conspirator.

Brown was due to address the weekly meeting of the PLP, held each Monday in Committee Room 14 while Parliament is sitting. The whips had organised the event well and ensured that when Brown entered the room, after most of the attendees had already arrived, he was greeted with enthusiastic applause and cheers. Tony Lloyd, the Manchester MP who chaired the meetings, and a friend and supporter of Brown's, made sure that the half-dozen Brown critics intending to speak were called early on so that the majority of speakers who supported their leader's continued reign would dominate the latter part of the meeting. Big beasts such as

Kinnock himself (Labour Lords may attend meetings of the PLP) and former Foreign Secretary Margaret Beckett spoke powerfully (although Kinnock strained the patience of many, including the chair, by speaking for far too long).

The rebels were beaten, and the whips were satisfied that they had done their job of protecting the leader. It did not go unremarked upon that members of the Opposition Whips' Office, on learning that Brown had survived, wore their smiles just a little wider. But the rebels hadn't given up quite yet.

MPs and ministers spent Christmas and New Year at the end of 2009 contemplating the year ahead, knowing that the general election could be delayed no longer than the middle of 2010. There was a sense of resoluteness about the PLP as it gathered at Westminster on Tuesday 5 January. But as the debate and voting on the government's Fiscal Responsibility Bill progressed, the former Home Secretary and arch Brown critic, Charles Clarke, was up to mischief. Clarke had served as Neil Kinnock's chief of staff when Kinnock was leader of the party and had subsequently been elected as MP for Norwich South in 1997. Carving out a niche for himself as an arch reformer and Blair supporter, he had gained a reputation as something of a fixer, an articulate and effective minister whose ministerial career came to an end when, in April 2006, it was revealed that more than a thousand foreign prisoners had been released from jail without being subjected to deportation orders. Bowing to public and media pressure for a ministerial sacrifice, Blair sacked Clarke at the reshuffle the following month. By this stage in Blair's premiership, it had become virtually customary for disappointed ministers to throw in their lot with the brooding, ambitious figure of Brown, in the hope of rapid promotion back into the ranks of the government come the day of his coronation. On the back benches, however, Clarke maintained his long-term suspicion and criticism of Brown. Having played a key role in the plotting the previous summer, in January 2010, he gave the dice one last throw.

Holding court in the Members' Lobby, just outside the main doors to the Commons chamber, Clarke told a select few colleagues to be ready for the next day, and to keep an eye on the *Evening Standard* for news of the latest plot to unseat Brown.

There was a degree of nervousness on both sides as MPs filled the chamber for the year's first session of Prime Minister's Questions on the Wednesday. The polls had continued to show a consistent Conservative lead, but Tory MPs were still unsure if it was large enough to deliver an overall working majority come polling day. For Labour, defeat seemed inevitable but its MPs, now that they (or most of them) thought that the leadership rumblings had finally abated, were determined to go down fighting. And who knew? Perhaps there was still some way to fend off defeat, either by beating the Tories fair and square on the subject of the economy or by agreeing a post-polling-day deal with the Liberal Democrats in a hung parliament.

As a particularly heavy snowfall continued outside the Palace of Westminster, inside a pedestrian run around the main economic issues at PMQs ended at precisely 12.31 p.m., at which point the press revealed that two senior former ministers, the former Health Secretary Patricia Hewitt, and former Chief Whip and Defence Secretary Geoff Hoon – both of whom had already indicated their intention to stand down from Parliament at the general election – had written to all Labour colleagues suggesting that the future of Brown's leadership should be decided by a ballot of all MPs. The letter was published in full in that evening's *Standard*.

'As we move towards a General Election it remains the case

that the Parliamentary Labour Party is deeply divided over the question of the leadership,' Hewitt and Hoon wrote. 'Many colleagues have expressed their frustration at the way in which this question is affecting our political performance. We have therefore come to the conclusion that the only way to resolve this issue would be to allow every member to express their view in a secret ballot.' Hewitt and Hoon argued that such a contest would present 'a clear opportunity to finally lay this matter to rest'.

Throughout the rest of the afternoon, with the media now frantically searching for MPs who would either publicly support or oppose this latest challenge, the conspirators received a torrent of emails from colleagues, each one copied in to every other colleague so that the extent of their anger towards the rebels – and support for Brown – might be understood. But whereas support for Brown from backbench colleagues was loud, angry and easily given, some of Brown's senior colleagues who would normally be expected to rally to his aide early on proved suspiciously difficult to trace. Only after a delay of many hours were Harriet Harman, David Miliband and Alan Johnson persuaded to offer their obviously reluctant endorsements of the Prime Minister.

The 'snow coup' was another blow for Labour morale, as it delivered an unexpected New Year double bonus to Cameron: not only was Labour exposed once more as divided over its leadership, but Gordon Brown remained in post.

*   *   *

The choreography had been planned and thought through. When Brown, on Tuesday 6 April 2010, announced he had asked Her Majesty to dissolve Parliament and call a general election for Thursday

6 May, he was not standing, as previous incumbents of No. 10 had stood, alone, on the famous steps. Achingly aware of polls that showed voters' dislike of Brown, Labour communications advisers had recommended that he should present himself as *primus inter pares* indeed – as the leader of a team of young, diverse, enthusiastic and capable ministers, rather than as the dominant figurehead of the campaign. There they were, lined up behind the Prime Minister as he made his first pitch for support in the long campaign ahead.

It didn't work.

Two developments earmark the 2010 campaign as unusual in British politics. The first was the advent of live televised leaders' debates. These have formed the backbone of US presidential elections since 1960 but in the UK, much to the frustration of journalists, they had always been resisted. Now, with the polls still telling him he faced defeat, Brown had nothing to lose in acceding to Cameron's boastful challenges. A slight complication was the involvement of Nick Clegg as leader of the Liberal Democrats.

The debates, broadcast on 15 April (by ITV), 22 April (Sky News) and 29 April (BBC), were so tightly controlled by the rules the parties had themselves insisted upon before participation, so rehearsed and prepared was every answer given by each of the three leaders, that very little news was generated by what was said, other than the historical fact that they had happened at all. As could have been predicted at the start, Clegg gained the most in terms of immediate post-broadcast polling, capitalising on the third party's ability to cast a plague on the houses of both main parties.

But it was Gordon Brown's catastrophic encounter with a voter in Rochdale, Greater Manchester, that sealed his reputation as an accident-prone politician of slapstick proportions. In a conversation, captured on live TV, with Gillian Duffy, a traditionally

Labour-voting local woman who was unhappy about recent immigration into her community from Eastern Europe, Brown did his best not to offend her while defending the government's immigration policies. Back in his car, as he grumpily related to his aides how, in his opinion, the encounter had been 'a disaster', he dismissed Mrs Duffy as 'just a sort of bigoted woman'. Unfortunately, Brown had forgotten that he was still wearing a live microphone attached on his suit lapel by Sky News for an earlier interview. Sky now possessed, and duly broadcast, the incriminating remarks.

Naturally Brown apologised publicly, both to Mrs Duffy in her home later in the day, and on Jeremy Vine's afternoon show on Radio 2. TV clips of the Prime Minister, head in his hands, listening to the surreptitious recording as it was broadcast to the nation, accurately reflected the morale of every Labour candidate in the country at that point.

It was clear from 10.00 p.m. on the evening of Thursday 6 May 2010 – polling day – that Britain was heading towards a hung parliament for the first time since February 1974. Supporters of Brown subsequently argued that denying Cameron the majority he craved was an achievement in itself and that the decision by the PLP not to replace him as leader when it had the chance had been vindicated. Brown's detractors, however, pointed out that winning just 29 per cent of the vote – a single percentage point more than Michael Foot's disastrous election performance in 1983 – can hardly be claimed as any sort of victory. More to the point, given the public's then scepticism of the qualities of the Tory leader, Brown's replacement would have had an excellent chance of defeating him.

It was not to be. Few Labour MPs who rushed to Brown's defence in June 2009, and even fewer in January 2010, believed he could lead the party to victory. But loyalty is an important commodity in the Labour Party, more valuable, in some quarters at least, than ministerial office.

And now Labour was well and truly out of government. Labour won just 258 seats out of 650. The Conservatives, with 306 seats, were twenty seats short of an overall majority. The Lib Dems, despite Clegg's triumph at the TV debates and a consequent 1 per cent increase in the proportion of votes won since 2005, lost five seats, holding fifty-seven seats in the new parliament. A coalition deal between the Conservatives and the Lib Dems looked by far the most obvious outcome from the five days of party bargaining that ensued. Despite a desperate attempt to defy the voters' judgement and cobble together some kind of 'rainbow coalition' with the Liberal Democrats to remain in power – a coalition that would have had to depend on the good will of Ulster Unionist and Scottish Nationalists to survive – Brown could see the writing on the wall earlier than some of his colleagues. On Tuesday 11 May, as Clegg and Cameron neared an agreement, Brown announced he would be going to Buckingham Palace to offer his resignation to Her Majesty. This was despite a last-minute plea from Clegg, who asked for more time to consider his options, hoping to keep the Labour option alive for at least a short while more.

But Brown had had enough. His time at No. 10 had not been a happy one and he understood that while Cameron had not exactly won the election, he, Brown, had certainly lost it.

Flanked by his wife, Sarah, and the couple's two young sons, John and James, Brown said his farewells to the gathered media before leaving Downing Street for the last time. He had occupied the office of Prime Minister for exactly two years, 319 days – the shortest period since Alec Douglas-Home, and the shortest serving Labour Prime Minister in history.

CHAPTER FOUR

'WE'VE GOT OUR PARTY BACK!'

Assumptions have rarely served Labour well. It was assumed, without any serious level of debate, that Gordon Brown would succeed Tony Blair as leader at some point, and so it transpired, with catastrophic electoral consequences. And when Labour MPs were finally summoned to attend a meeting of the Parliamentary Labour Party in Committee Room 14 on Wednesday 12 May, most MPs assumed that the (now former) Foreign Secretary, David Miliband, would be next in line.

The actual event of the meeting, presided over by acting leader Harriet Harman, spoke volumes about the newly acquired role of the Labour Party, post-general election. While few MPs had expected to return to the government benches after polling day, the new political realities were harsher than most had expected: the PLP was meeting the day after the formal invitation by the Queen to David Cameron to form a new government. While newly elected and re-elected Labour members had been exchanging texts and phone calls from their constituencies over the last five days while their leaders sat in exclusive conclave at No. 10, Tory and Lib Dem MPs had been in and around Westminster in order to be regularly consulted about the progress or otherwise of coalition talks. The exclusion of Labour MPs from a symmetrical process either indicated Brown's lack of confidence in his ability to reach an agreement with Nick Clegg, or (more likely) his imperious assumption that whatever deal he might have reached would be rubber-stamped by a compliant and grateful parliamentary party whose actual presence on the parliamentary estate would have been inconvenient and unnecessary.

Whatever the reasons, as the country woke up to a new dawn and the first coalition government since 1945, Labour MPs were acutely aware that they had been the least informed of any major party over the last few hectic and historically important days. Perhaps it had been the broad acceptance that Labour was always going to lose the election that led to the sedate and even good-humoured meeting in Committee Room 14. Brown's absence was noted but not criticised, at least not from the floor. If there were some comrades speculating about the possibility of whether a new deputy leader would be elected at the same time as the new leader, Harman disabused them of such a notion. It is expected common practice that when a Labour leader's career ends in electoral defeat, both he and his deputy depart the scene – a tradition that had been respected by every leadership team in living memory. Even when John Smith died unexpectedly in 1994, Margaret Beckett, Smith's deputy at the time, could easily have insisted that her mandate had some years still to run. Instead she stood down in order to place her candidacy before the party. Perhaps it was that example (Beckett lost the contest to John Prescott) that persuaded Harman to remain in post.

That afternoon, as MPs greeted each other in the tearoom of the Commons before heading back home to their constituencies –

the Commons itself wouldn't meet for another six days – flanked by fifteen of his colleagues and standing outside the St Stephen's entrance to the Commons, David Miliband declared his intention to stand as Labour leader. This was hardly a surprise, not least to MPs, some of whose support was solicited by David's parliamentary supporters as early as the Friday after polling day. Crucially, he was publicly backed by the one person who might have leapfrogged him as the bookies' favourite: Alan Johnson, the former Home Secretary. Miliband, forty-four, had all the right qualifications for the post. He was a gifted speaker, particularly in the Commons where he had a commanding presence, usually equipped with facts and a surprisingly quick sense of humour. By talking of drawing a line under Blair and Brown's era of New Labour ('What I'm interested in is Next Labour'), Miliband hoped to distance himself from his former boss, Blair, and not be painted as merely the continuity candidate.

But on the same day as the former Foreign Secretary stood before the press to tell them what they already knew about his leadership bid, his brother informed him that he would also be a candidate. Ed subsequently claimed that a conversation with former Labour leader Neil Kinnock in February 2010 – three months before the party lost office – had encouraged him to think seriously about challenging his brother after the inevitable defeat at the polls. On formally announcing his bid the following weekend, Ed immediately became the second favourite in the race, although in the early stages of the contest, in the immediate aftermath of the general election defeat, few believed he could beat his older brother.

David and Ed were the products of a wealthy, upper middle-class upbringing, sons of the renowned Marxist intellectual,

Ralph Miliband. Although they spent most of their childhoods in London, they also spent some time living in Leeds as well as in Boston, Massachusetts, where their father secured teaching work. Both attended Corpus Christi College, Oxford, where they studied Philosophy, Politics and Economics (PPE). David graduated with a first-class degree, while Ed achieved a 2:1 after dropping philosophy. While David studied for a master's degree at the Massachusetts Institute of Technology (where he was a Kennedy Scholar), Ed gained his own master's from the London School of Economics (LSE).

Brothers with such academic abilities and privileged backgrounds were always destined to make their mark in the political world. Ed's first job in politics was as an intern in left-wing MP Tony Benn's office, then MP for Chesterfield, while David cut his political teeth as an analyst for the National Council for Voluntary Organisations (NCVO). In 1994, David became head of policy to Tony Blair, the newly elected leader of the Labour Party, and, after the 1997 general election, he became head of the Prime Minister's Policy Unit, a post he held until he was elected as MP for South Shields at the 2001 election.

Ed, having worked for a short time for then shadow Chief Secretary to the Treasury, Harriet Harman, was appointed as a special adviser (spad) to Gordon Brown, the then shadow Chancellor. He continued working for Brown until his own adoption as a Labour candidate in Doncaster North in time for the 2005 general election.

Neither David nor Ed were, on paper, obvious successors to their predecessors as MPs for South Shields and Doncaster North. That they were both selected without much opposition locally raised some eyebrows, and cast an unwelcome spotlight on the leadership's tendency to 'parachute' favoured candidates into safe

political berths – a practice that had become a source of increasing resentment and tension between grassroots members and
the leadership. This was a natural reaction to successive leaders'
determination to promote favoured sons (and they were mostly
sons rather than daughters) over the wishes of local parties who
wanted the freedom to choose whoever they wanted as a candidate. When a sitting MP had been duly selected by his or her local
party to fight the next election but then announced, with just a few
weeks to go until the expected dissolution of Parliament, that he
had changed his mind and wished to stand aside, Labour's NEC,
rather than local party officials, took control of the shortlisting
process. By sidelining the local candidate most likely to win the
nomination and replacing them with an ambitious special adviser,
with or without local connections to the area, leaders could usually
get their way. In such circumstances it was not unusual to see the
conveniently retired members nominated for a place in the House
of Lords in subsequent Honours lists.

The experience of candidates without friends in high places
was very different from that of the favoured sons. Seats had to be
'nursed', often for years, through hard work and by building networks with other local activists. If eventually successful in winning
a nomination and the subsequent election, they then had to be
prepared to put in the hard graft of parliamentary life: service on
interminable standing committees scrutinising government bills,
dutifully asking the right questions at question time, sponsoring
adjournment debates and, if they were lucky and patient enough,
working for a couple of years as an unpaid ministerial aide (parliamentary private secretary, or PPS). Then, and only then, might
an optimistic MP have cause to wait for the call from Downing
Street that might or might not come.

As newly elected MPs, the Miliband brothers had no reason to doubt that their talents would be called upon as soon as the opportunity arose. For David this came a year after the 2001 general election, in the mini-reshuffle that followed Stephen Byers' unexpected resignation as Environment, Transport and Regions Secretary. He was appointed a Schools minister, the first of the 2001 intake to win promotion. A similar period on the back benches awaited his younger brother four years later: after the 2005 general election, Ed, along with another newcomer and Brown protégé, Ed Balls, waited barely a year before receiving the call – Miliband became a minister at the Cabinet Office and Balls a Treasury minister.

Neither was there any doubt that the two Eds would be made Cabinet members as soon as Brown became Prime Minister, whenever that happened and however long each of the Eds had served as MPs by then. For all three of them – the two Milibands and Balls – politics was easy. The pole was considerably less greasy when you knew the right people, particularly when the 'right people' happened to be two Prime Ministers. It was hardly surprising, then, that in 2010, both Ed and David regarded the leadership of their party as something of an entitlement.

As soon as Ed declared for the leadership, the battle lines were drawn along very traditional Labour Party lines: right v left, with David and Ed representing those respective wings. It wasn't an entirely accurate or relevant distinction: the idea that Ed Miliband was, in 2010, the last Cabinet's left-wing conscience was a stretch. Nevertheless, as an opponent, on the grounds of potential environmental damage, of Brown's plan to give the go-ahead to Heathrow's third runway, he had carved out a progressive niche for himself that immediately appealed to those in the party and the trade union movement who had had enough of New Labour, of either the Blair or the Brown variety.

To the media, the normal aspects of a leadership contest – the politics, the chances of winning, the policy platform, the breakdown of support across the movement – all took second billing to the dramatic spectacle of fratricide.

The tendency of the Labour Party to veer leftwards in the immediate aftermath of being thrown out of office is almost a tradition. In the early 1950s, following Margaret Thatcher's victory in 1979 and now, again, in 2010, Labour favoured self-flagellation, almost self-hatred, as it came to terms with being out of office. There had always been a substantial minority of members who viewed government office itself with suspicion, akin (to borrow from the party's working-class and trade unionist traditions) to taking the foreman's job and lording it over the 'proper' workers. The myth of betrayal by Labour ministers of the party's left-wing founding principles traditionally began on the first day after general election success and never really went away. Thus, after the longest uninterrupted period of Labour government in history, there was much for purists to complain about: the landslide majorities were wasted and could have been used for a much greater degree of (usually unspecified) radicalism; budget cuts following the 2008 financial crash should never have been allowed to hit local services; the rich never paid enough tax; there was no attempt to revoke Thatcher's 'anti-trade union' legislation; and, of course, Iraq.

Ed's shorter service in government – he had been a Cabinet member for only three years and a minister for just four (compared to David's eight-year service) – proved an advantage, as did the identity of the brothers' respective former bosses. Despite the absolute absence of any evidence to support it, an impression had been given – and duly encouraged – during the years of government that Brown had been more left wing than Blair. This was a useful fantasy, which Brown used to full effect during his years of brooding grievance while Blair was Prime Minister. And so, in 2010, Ed, by virtue of having worked with Brown before becoming an MP, was deemed more of the left than his older brother, who had worked for Blair. Blair having won three general elections and Brown none impressed few on the party's left.

Meeting on Tuesday 18 May, at the same time that Parliament reassembled for the first time since the general election, Labour's National Executive Committee (NEC) agreed the timetable for the election of Gordon Brown's successor: nomination of candidates by MPs would open on Monday 24 May, and close three days later. The result would be announced on Saturday 25 September, on the first day of Labour's annual conference in Manchester. The timetable raised eyebrows in Parliament and in the media. It was not immediately apparent why the election needed to take eighteen weeks; the previous (deputy) leadership contest in 2007 and the combined leader and deputy contest in 1994, following the death of John Smith, had each taken less than seven weeks. Immediately, David Miliband's campaign team smelled a rat. They knew that a short contest would benefit their man as the existing front-runner; a longer contest, therefore, could only benefit his opponents in general and Ed in particular. This seemed, in fact, to be the motivation of trade union representatives on the NEC – supported by Harman – although one serious consideration that favoured such an elongated timetable was the cost to the cash-strapped party of staging a special conference before September.

Oddly and counter-intuitively, the brothers' personalities played, during the campaign, to Ed's advantage. A supporter standing outside one of his campaign events declared that 'Ed speaks human' – an unambiguous slight on David, whose policy-wonk reputation was well established. Yet friends and colleagues could testify that of the two, David was the more socially relaxed, more apt to share (or even understand) a joke and chat about subjects unrelated to high politics. The charge against David of not speaking human was immediately and sincerely disowned by Ed, who was acutely aware of the potential damage that could be caused to his campaign if he was seen to be making such attacks on his older brother. But it found its mark, at least partly because of David's perceived (and actual) aloofness.

Before the changes to the system for electing Labour leaders in 2014 (see Chapter Six), the party used an electoral college. Introduced at a special conference in 1981, the college was seen at the time as a victory for the Bennite Left, which had mounted a vigorous grassroots campaign to change the system whereby the leader was elected solely by the votes of MPs. After 1981, future leaders would be elected by a college with three different sections: 30 per cent of the vote would be the votes of MPs, another 30 per cent would be active Labour members and 40 per cent would be decided by the leaders of those trade unions affiliated to the party. This particular iteration of the electoral college never elected a future Prime Minister; reforms by John Smith in 1993 introduced a significant level of democracy into the process whereby every individual party member, rather than just those who attended local general committees of constituency parties, would now be given a vote, as would individual trade unionists who paid the political levy through their union dues. The 40/30/30 split among unions, MPs and members was also rebalanced to exactly a third of the college each.

This meant that no candidate could reasonably expect to be successful unless they won a substantial portion of MPs' support.

This part of the college represented David Miliband's greatest strength and his greatest weakness. He could rely on a substantial number of his colleagues supporting him simply because they had seen his strong performances at the despatch box and in the media. But he struggled to overcome charges of elitism – he was, after all, a close friend of former Prime Minister Tony Blair, someone who had worked at the top levels of the party and of government for well over a decade. Too often, that aloofness could become disdain for, or impatience towards, parliamentary colleagues. For example, as Parliament careered towards the long summer recess that started in July 2010, MPs' support was being carefully nurtured by all the candidates. This necessarily included glad-handing around the tables on the House of Commons' Terrace which, on a warm summer evening, becomes the most attractive pub in the world. Yet, while Ed was seen schmoozing and charming his way around tables of MPs with their guests, David was rarely visible. His supporters, on at least one occasion, called him to warn him his brother was on manoeuvres on the Pimm's circuit, but David was nowhere in sight. He was advised to make an appearance, which he duly did, but the reluctance with which he did so was noted, as was the considerably shorter time he spent there in comparison with his younger brother.

One newly elected Labour MP stated that she had expected to support David for the leadership. But after the general election, she had been surprised and hurt that he hadn't called her to ask for her support, so she had decided to support Ed instead. This was not an isolated case.

There were three other candidates: former Schools Secretary

and another Brown protégé, Ed Balls; former Health Secretary Andy Burnham; and Diane Abbott, the candidate of the Socialist Campaign Group of MPs. Abbott was not only the sole female candidate, she was also the only ethnic minority candidate, the only candidate who was not a former spad and the only candidate who needed the support of her opponents to meet the minimum threshold for nominations – her name was accepted as an official entry into the contest after David Miliband 'lent' her his nomination.

Throughout the contest, during the long, wet British summer, there was no doubt in the minds of David Miliband's campaign team that Ed was gaining ground. The larger trade unions were making their preferences known: the executive committees of both the GMB and Unite the Union, two of the party's biggest affiliates, had decided to support Ed on the basis that he had the best chance of defeating David. This allowed them to contribute financially to Ed's campaign as well as to send their own members promotional material on behalf of their preferred candidate. Party rules prohibited ballot papers being sent to members in the same envelope as any promotional material endorsing a candidate, but that didn't stop the unions doing precisely that. Their 'defence', that the ballot paper was in a separate envelope from the promotional material, held little weight since both envelopes were posted in the same, larger envelope.

In polls published throughout the summer, the story was consistent: David was in the lead in all sections of the electoral college, but by a slimmer margin over Ed than he would have liked. The second preferences of voters, particularly the votes of MPs, would be crucial. Because of the weighting in the electoral college, an MP's vote carried nearly 500 times more weight than an ordinary member's vote and 750 times the weight of a member of an affiliated trade union. Neither Miliband could hope to win on the first round of voting and would have to depend on the second, third and fourth preference votes cast by supporters of their opponents.

On the eve of Labour conference, at which the result would be announced, Sky News carried news of a rumour that Ed Miliband would be declared the winner the next day.

The atmosphere in the Central Conference Centre the next day was electric and expectant, at least among Ed's supporters. David's supporters had succumbed to pessimism after the Sky News report and were clinging to the hope that it had been wrong. It hadn't.

David led on the voting in every round, except the fourth and final one. Abbott dropped out first, then Burnham, then Balls. The final votes tally showed that David had secured the support of 54 per cent of ordinary members and 53 per cent of the party's parliamentarians. But in the third section, the affiliated members of trade unions, Ed had triumphed with 60 per cent of the vote in the final round, giving him 50.7 per cent of the final vote.

David put on a brave face when the results were announced, but left the conference soon after his already scheduled speech as shadow Foreign Secretary, in which he urged the party to unite behind his brother. He returned to his home in South Shields from where he announced, in a letter to local members, that he would not be seeking election to the shadow Cabinet in the weeks ahead. 'This is now Ed's party to lead and he needs to be able to do so as free as possible from distraction,' he wrote.

The scale of David Miliband's defeat is worth considering. When local party members' votes were later broken down, it was revealed that David had topped the ballot in 577 constituencies, his brother in just sixty-seven. Had six MPs or MEPs among those who had supported Balls, Burnham or Abbott switched to David instead of Ed, then Labour's recent history might have been very different. But such can be said about almost any close election result, and while such speculation can be entertaining and even informative, the facts do not alter: Ed Miliband was now the leader of the Labour Party.

Immediately following the announcement, the author, in conversation with a friend who worked for the Unite union, was interrupted by a woman who was one of the union's full-time officials. 'Well, we did it!' she said triumphantly. Meanwhile, outside the conference hall, bitter and shell-shocked Blairite MPs shared their own analyses, using colourful language to express their disappointment. The recently elected MP for East Kilbride, Michael McCann, who shared many of his colleagues' enthusiasm for the *Godfather* movies as a reliable political metaphor, told glum colleagues: 'We've just made Fredo the head of the family!'

One of the most delighted people at conference was the same man who had told Ed, even before the 2010 election, that he should consider running. Neil Kinnock had a ringside seat for Miliband's first leader's speech three days after his victory was announced. At the end of it, an equally delighted trade union delegate leaned over to the former Labour leader and said excitedly, 'Neil, we've got our party back!' Kinnock might have asked who 'we' had got the party back from, but did not. He later told journalists: 'I thought that was so accurate as an instantaneous response to the leader's speech.'

CHAPTER FIVE

OMNISHAMBLES

E d Miliband wasted little time in setting out the new direction in which he wished to take his party. Two events in particular, during conference week in those very early days of his leadership, illustrated a different approach both in terms of ideology and in party management.

The new leader had made an initial, short acceptance speech from the platform following the declaration of results. That night he made the obligatory and traditional round of visits to the various receptions being hosted by trade unions and other organisations, receiving a particularly warm welcome from those unions who had nominated him and who saw the result as the start of the fightback against Blairite compromise.

His first formal speech as leader, in the traditional 2.30 p.m. slot on the Tuesday of conference, was warmly received, though perhaps lacking in natural oratorical magic. The point of controversy emerged when he described the 2003 invasion of Iraq as 'an issue that divided our party and our country'. He added:

Many sincerely believed that the world faced a real threat. I criticise nobody faced with making the toughest of decisions and I honour our troops who fought and died there. But I do believe that we were wrong – wrong to take Britain to war and we need to be honest about that.

This drew the prolonged applause intended, including that of Miliband's deputy, Harriet Harman, who had herself voted for military intervention seven years earlier. Sitting next to her, David Miliband ostentatiously refused to join in and instead was seen to turn to Harman, asking: 'You voted for it – why are you clapping?'

'I am clapping for him because, as you know, I am supporting him,' she replied, and continued with her applause.

Ed Milband's election victory had already signalled a desire, at least in certain parts of the party, for a break with Blairism; Miliband had decided he would satisfy that desire on the most iconic issue of Blair's legacy.

A day later, the new leader surprised many in the party by a manoeuvre that few outside the Westminster bubble either noticed or cared about, but which suggested Miliband had hidden reserves of strength he had previously been able to keep under wraps.

Nick Brown had served as Chief Whip under Tony Blair and then, after a period as a minister (also under Blair) and then on the back benches, had been recalled to government by his friend Brown, first as Deputy Chief Whip and then, for a second time, as Chief Whip from 2008. During his tenure as Leader of the Opposition from 1994 to 1997, Blair had pushed through rule changes which meant that the position of Opposition Chief Whip, which is one of the few paid posts in opposition, became his gift as leader rather than being elected by Labour MPs, as it had been up until 1995. Following the 2010 defeat, Nick Brown's many friends and allies in the parliamentary party had started lobbying other MPs to support a rule change to reverse this, making the Chief Whip's post once again elected by the PLP. Not only that, but unlike members of the shadow Cabinet (who at that time were also elected by Labour MPs for two-year terms) the proposed changes to standing orders would see the Chief Whip elected for a full five-year period.

The package of rule changes had been proposed by the party's *grande dame*, Margaret Beckett, and approved by MPs before the summer recess. By conference, the plans of the Brown supporters to install their man as an alternative power base to the leader's in the parliamentary party were well under way. As incumbent Chief Whip, Brown would be a difficult candidate for any challenger to beat.

Nevertheless, there was no shortage of volunteers willing to try. Blairite MPs in particular saw Brown as devious and conspiratorial, loyal to Gordon Brown and consequentially disloyal to Blair, who had first appointed him to that office. If there was to be an election for the job, it certainly wasn't going to be uncontested.

And then, with a devastating sureness of touch that his detractors might have expected from his older brother but never from him, Ed struck. On Wednesday 29 September, still basking in the praise for his conference speech and more relaxed now that this first big test of his leadership had been overcome, Miliband invited Brown to his suite to inform him that his services as Chief Whip had been appreciated but that it was time to stand down. Whether it was implied or stated explicitly, Brown was in no doubt about the consequences of defying the leader: had he insisted on standing anyway, Miliband would have made the ensuing contest a test of his own leadership; and were Brown to win, it would make him look disloyal. But he could not win, and Brown knew it. He dutifully agreed to Miliband's demands and later issued a letter of resignation. That same evening it was announced that Rosie Winterton, the former senior minister who represented the neighbouring seat to Miliband's, and who had been a vocal supporter of his leadership bid, would be standing for the post of Chief Whip. It was still an elected position, it was still for a term of five years. But Miliband made sure that rule change or no, he was the leader and he would decide who filled it and for how long.

Miliband made his first appearance at the despatch box as Leader of the Opposition on Wednesday 13 October 2010, during Prime Minister's Questions (PMQs). Miliband chose to open on an issue that would unite the House – the attempt earlier that month by American special forces to rescue British aid worker Linda Norgrove from the Taliban in Afghanistan, which left Norgrove fatally wounded – before moving on to the subject of child benefits.

During his first twenty-four hours as leader, Miliband had coined the phrase – and intended narrative of his leadership – 'the squeezed middle', those working and middle-class voters who felt their hard work wasn't offering the stability and security they deserved and with whom Miliband confessed, in an article in the *Sunday Telegraph* the day after he was declared the victor in the leadership election, his party had lost touch in recent years. He returned to that theme now in response to the government's recently announced (and controversial) plans to limit child benefit to households where no one paid income tax at the higher 40 per cent rate. Medium-earning families would be hardest hit by the change, Miliband told an excitable Commons. In David Cameron's replies was the clear Conservative strategy that would be deployed against Miliband in the years ahead: to attack the record of the previous Labour government of which he had been a member, and to attack Miliband personally as the 'wrong choice', the puppet of the trade unions who had secured him his recent victory and the pale shadow of his mentor, the unpopular and defeated Gordon Brown.

'The right honourable gentleman has suddenly discovered middle-income families,' Cameron began. 'We are now hearing about the squeezed middle, but who squeezed the middle? Who doubled the council tax and put up tax 122 times, and who taxed the pensions, the petrol, the marriages and the mortgages? Suddenly, having done all that to middle-income earners, Labour wants to stand up for them. That is a completely transparent political strategy to cover up the inconvenient truth that he was put where he is by the trade union movement. It is short-term tactics and political positioning: it is not red, it is Brown.'

It was an attack that was to prove effective, even if that was not immediately perceived in polling at the time. The (needlessly) extended period set down by Labour's NEC for the leadership contest had focused the party on its internal processes at a time, immediately following the formation of the Conservative–Liberal Democrat coalition, when ministers were making a concerted effort to blame Labour entirely for the creation of the £156 billion structural deficit they had inherited. Overgenerous spending by Labour ministers – the failure to 'fix the roof while the sun was shining', as Conservative MPs regularly put it – had created the current economic austerity, they repeatedly claimed with a strategic degree of discipline. The counter-argument – that the deficit had been created largely by a critical drop in tax revenue following the 2008 crash and subsequent recession, for which Labour was not to blame – was too rarely made by Labour during this period, distracted as it was by the leadership election. The irony for Labour was that George Osborne, as shadow Chancellor, had in fact made great play of his and his party's commitment to support the then government's spending plans up until November 2008, by which point the majority of the deficit had already been accumulated.

But by the end of the year, the argument had been all but won by the government; Labour's reputation as a well-meaning but financially incompetent party had been reinforced to an extent not seen since James Callaghan's unfortunate administration of 1976–79. It was against this backdrop that Miliband's fightback on behalf of the 'squeezed middle' had to be staged.

The early part of Miliband's leadership was undermined by a conflict which the leader himself was loath to confront or deal with. Since the government's announcement of a cuts programme in an attempt to reduce the deficit, various protest movements had emerged to challenge ministers' agendas. UK Uncut specialised in making life difficult for ordinary shoppers in stores owned by business interests which, in the eyes of the organisers, were not paying their fair share of taxes, thus avoiding responsibility for the austerity now being forced upon ordinary workers. Similarly the Occupy movement, active on both sides of the Atlantic, claimed to represent the '99 per cent, not the one per cent' and attracted headlines by attempting – before being prevented by legal action – to occupy the London Stock Exchange, switching their target to the area outside St Paul's Cathedral. Miliband cherished his reputation as being more left wing than his predecessors, but was conscious of the damage that he would suffer if he were to become too closely associated with these 'grassroots' protest movements, especially if, as is often the case, protests turned to violence.

Then, in late 2010, David Cameron's coalition partners, the

Liberal Democrats, committed an act of political cynicism rarely encountered in modern politics. Having campaigned hard on a pledge not to vote for any increase in higher-education tuition fees, Nick Clegg now ordered his MPs to vote for a massive increase in higher-education tuition fees. The policy of raising the maximum level of annual fees at English universities from the £3,375 limit in 2011/12 to £9,000 the following year was agreed following a review into university funding by Lord Browne. The Cabinet minister in charge of adopting the policy and pushing it through Parliament was himself a Liberal Democrat: the Business Secretary, Vince Cable.

The tuition-fee rise sparked fury, particularly among student groups and particularly aimed at the Lib Dems. On 10 November 2010, an estimated 50,000 took to the streets of central London to protest. Although largely peaceful and good-natured, the event took a violent turn when some forced their way into a tower block in Millbank, where Conservative HQ was located. While some protesters occupied the lobby area, others made their way to the building's roof where they flew an anarchist flag. One student was later sentenced to thirty-two months in jail after admitting throwing a fire extinguisher into the crowd below, narrowly missing protesters and police officers.

Two weeks later a second student protest led to more violence at Lib Dem HQ in Cowley Street, and police used their infamous 'kettling' tactics to corral the protesters into a narrow part of Whitehall. Six days later, more kettling tactics were used to hold protesters in Trafalgar Square. The last demonstration of the year took place in Parliament Square, directly opposite the Houses of Parliament, on Thursday 9 December, to coincide with the Commons debate authorising the rise in fees.

There was undoubtedly a high level of sympathy in the wider electorate towards students facing such a steep increase in fees. But much of that sympathy dissipated as TV news showed the more violent and newsworthy side of the protests. Labour's, and Miliband's, problem was in balancing a respect for law and order with the opportunity to capitalise on the students' anger. It was a difficult balancing act for a party that, during much of the 1980s, was seen as being too soft on crime, too frequently making excuses for criminal behaviour. The reluctance of Labour's then leader, Neil Kinnock, and the wider party to condemn violence on picket lines during the year-long miners' strike of 1984–85 caused lasting damage to Labour's reputation. Now, Miliband was accused of encouraging the student protests in an attempt to win public support against the fees rise. This accusation grew legs when, following violent outbreaks during the march of 24 November, Miliband told the Radio 4 *Today* programme that he had been 'quite tempted to talk to them'. Asked why he hadn't in fact done so, Miliband responded: 'I think I was doing something else at the time, actually.' He later added: 'I think that peaceful demonstrations are part of our society and, of course, as the Labour leader, I am willing to go and talk to people who are part of those demonstrations. It is an indication of what is happening to this country because I think people have a sense of anger and a lot of the anger is quite justified.'

If Miliband did wish to address some angry crowds, he didn't have to wait long. While he had been campaigning for the leadership he had, in fact, agreed to attend the TUC-organised anti-cuts rally in Hyde Park planned for 26 March 2011 (David, extended the same invitation, had reserved his position). Others close to the top of the party had been nervous about Ed's attendance, fearing that a Labour leader addressing large crowds of protesters might evoke images of Michael Foot's hapless attempts to avoid defeat by speaking to the converted at similar events in the early 1980s. Their fears were well founded. As Miliband addressed the peaceful crowd, other, less peaceful, individuals took the opportunity to attack shops and banks in nearby Oxford Street. TV news viewers were treated to images of the violence while Miliband's words provided the narrative. Even worse, the Labour leader, in his speech, chose to compare the fight against government spending cuts – cuts that were broadly similar to the cuts a re-elected Labour government had pledged to impose had the general election turned out differently – to the campaigns against apartheid in South Africa, for civil rights in the United States and for women's suffrage in the last century.

Miliband's critics within the Labour Party were quick to criticise this fashion towards seeking the adoration of the crowds at the expense of a more statesmanlike approach. In fact it was only the recent raw memories of divisions within the PLP under Brown that prevented MPs from speaking more publicly against the new leader. There had been a realisation, almost as soon as Miliband became leader in September 2010, that he would, if he chose, lead the party into the next general election, however badly he might perform in the interim. A party that had fought so hard to maintain Gordon Brown at the top of the party in the face of overwhelming evidence that he could not win an election was hardly going to depose Miliband before he got his chance at No. 10. This new self-denying ordinance meant simply that criticism was kept largely private, a subject of tearoom gossip rather than interviews with broadcast journalists. It didn't mean that the overwhelming conviction among those who had supported David

– that the party had made the wrong choice – disappeared. On the contrary, that conviction hardened, at least during the first half of the parliament. It wasn't just that Ed Miliband was too left wing, too ready to say what the crowds wanted to hear; there were also personal criticisms: his geeky looks, his odd, nasal voice, his seemingly over-rehearsed manner when it came to interviews. Miliband never quite managed to sound natural, like a 'normal bloke'.

From the end of 2010 and throughout 2011, Labour had managed, with a few bumps along the way, to maintain a modest polling lead over the Conservatives of about 5 per cent. The lead increased significantly during July of that year, largely in approval of Miliband's robust stand against Rupert Murdoch's newspaper empire, which had been accused of hacking the phones of celebrities and other public figures. This honeymoon ended when David Cameron's use of the national veto against an EU plan to tackle the euro crisis in December 2011 led to a narrowing in the polls and even a brief lead for the Conservatives.

Labour's electoral fortunes during the first full year of Miliband's leadership ebbed and flowed. The party held on to all five Labour seats in which by-elections were held, even in exceptionally difficult circumstances. In Oldham East and Saddleworth, the previous MP, Phil Woolas, had narrowly won re-election at the general election in 2010, only to have the result overturned by the Election Court in a rare ruling after his defeated Liberal Democrat opponent accused Woolas's team of making false statements about him during the campaign. These were difficult circumstances for Labour to fight another campaign. Nevertheless, the consequent by-election, held on 13 January 2011, was won by Labour's Debbie Abrahams who increased Labour's share of the vote by 10 per cent and was returned to Westminster with a majority of more than 3,500.

And just two months later, Labour faced another difficult challenge when Eric Illsley, the MP for Barnsley Central since 1987, pleaded guilty to expenses fraud after an investigation by the *Daily Telegraph* as part of its 2009 exposé. Illsley resigned from Parliament shortly before being sentenced to twelve months in prison. The by-election was therefore expected to be another difficult one for Labour. Instead, the new candidate, Dan Jarvis, increased the party's share of the vote by an impressive 13 per cent, winning easily with a majority of nearly 12,000.

In Leicester South, Labour had lost a by-election in July 2004 to the Liberal Democrats. But at the by-election held in May 2011, after Labour MP Sir Peter Soulsby resigned in order to contest the new post of mayor, Labour's Jonathan Ashworth was triumphant.

The next two by-elections – Inverclyde in June and Feltham & Heston in December – were sparked through more conventional circumstances, namely the deaths of the incumbent MPs, David Cairns and Alan Keen. Labour held on in both seats.

It is not unusual in British politics for the main opposition party to hold its ground and, indeed, to gain ground at by-elections, especially if the government is proving unpopular. But in previous periods of opposition, Labour had regularly lost out, even in its own 'safe' seats, to a resurgent third party. Following 2010 and the formation of the Conservative–Lib Dem coalition, polls showed a seemingly irreversible slide in the popularity of Nick Clegg's party, a trend magnified following its capitulation on tuition fees. Labour benefited in two ways from this – and suffered, albeit in the longer term, in a third way: at the local elections held in England in May 2011, Labour made more than 850 gains, mainly from the Liberal Democrats. Similarly, at by-elections caused by the bad behaviour of disgraced former Labour MPs, the Lib Dems found it impossible to capitalise and to pull off what had once been regular headline-grabbing victories. The downside of the Liberal Democrat slide, however, was that their coalition partners didn't seem to be suffering to the same extent. Yet in a first-past-the-post (FPTP) electoral system, it was the votes of Conservative supporters that Labour most needed to attract if it was to have a chance of defeating the Tories in 2015.

As well as the local elections, the Leicester South by-election and elections to the Welsh and Northern Ireland assemblies, two other votes taking place on 5 May 2011 were to form a significant part of the narrative of Ed Miliband's leadership.

The Liberal Democrats had, as was traditional, included a commitment to reform of the electoral system in their 2010 manifesto. Once ensconced in coalition negotiations with his future Conservative partners, however, Nick Clegg found this commitment was easily transmuted to a government pledge to hold a referendum on a new electoral system that neither he nor his party even wanted: the alternative vote (AV).

Miliband, keen to burnish his modernising credentials, was attracted to the idea of reform. He had played a central role in writing Labour's 2010 manifesto which also included a referendum on AV – the only party manifesto to do so. The party had also promised a free vote in Parliament on reducing the voting age to sixteen and (inevitably) to House of Lords reform. But Miliband also knew that a large swathe of his parliamentary party would refuse to countenance AV as a replacement to FPTP and MPs were free to campaign on the referendum, planned for 5 May, however they chose, though the leader made clear his own views that reform was necessary. Those urging reform were holed below the waterline from the start of the campaign. Few high-profile politicians wanted AV itself and saw the change instead as a way to inch towards the reform they actually wanted: true proportional representation in the form of the single transferable vote (STV) system. Their lukewarm support for the change on offer was easily exploited by the 'No to AV' campaign, which ran a series of effective posters and advertisements mocking the proposed change. The 'No' campaign won the day with nearly 70 per cent support. At a meeting of the PLP immediately following the local elections and AV referendum, Miliband was pressured by MPs to set the whole issue of electoral reform aside up to and beyond the next general election – pressure to which he readily succumbed.

But the other set of elections held on 5 May, to the Scottish Parliament in Edinburgh, signalled a sea change which would have genuinely catastrophic repercussions for Miliband and his party. Scottish Labour, despite having lost by a single seat to Alex Salmond's SNP in 2007, had been modestly optimistic about their chances of regaining power at Holyrood four years later. Under their new leader, Iain Gray, they had presented a united and coherent front to the SNP's minority Scottish Executive (now rebranded as the 'Scottish government') and looked like they had recovered from the trauma of losing power so unexpectedly in an institution that they, more than any other party, had been responsible for delivering.

But in the last few weeks before polling day, the opinion polls had seen a remarkable change: the SNP, over whom Labour had seemed to be enjoying a healthy advantage, now took a double-digit lead. On the evening of 5 May, as Miliband was being congratulated for delivering a modestly decent result south of the border, his party was being driven from its traditional strongholds in Glasgow, Lanarkshire, Ayrshire and Edinburgh. Labour's fall in representation at Holyrood, from forty-four in 2007 to thirty-seven now, was massaged by the hybrid FPTP and proportional list system used: having once reigned supreme in Scotland, Labour had clung on to just twenty-five of the seventy-three FPTP seats, winning another twelve seats through the additional member system. Salmond, meanwhile, achieved precisely what the electoral system for Holyrood had been devised to prevent: an overall majority. The SNP won sixty-nine seats out of the total of 129 (see Chapter Seven).

Labour in Scotland were thus thrown into disarray at a time when the SNP's most cherished policy – a referendum on Scottish independence – now seemed inevitable.

Throughout 2011, Labour's poll lead was modest, but in 2012 it became more consistent and wider. In his 2012 Budget, the Chancellor, George Osborne, reduced the top rate of tax levied on those earning more than £150,000 a year from 50 to 45 per cent. Following a series of reversals accompanied by almost universal criticism of some of the Budget's main measures, Miliband earned some valuable praise for an effective demolition of Osborne at Prime Minister's Questions on 18 April. He channelled Peter Capaldi's character, Malcolm Tucker, in the BBC political satire *The Thick Of It*: 'On charities, the reality is that the Prime Minister is not making the rich worse off, he is making charities worse off. Over the past month we have seen the charity tax shambles, the churches tax shambles, the caravan tax shambles and the pasty tax shambles, so we are all keen to hear the Prime Minister's view on why he thinks, four weeks on from the Budget, even people within Downing Street are calling it an omnishambles Budget.'

Miliband's constant championing of 'the squeezed middle' seemed to be cutting through to the general public. Whatever the reservations of parliamentary colleagues about his support for more obviously left-wing policies such as the 'Mansion Tax' (a tax on properties worth more than £2 million), the advances in the polls convinced them to keep their views to themselves.

In fact, during this period, Miliband believed he could be successful in moving the political debate – and the voters them-selves – leftwards. He believed that the 2008 financial crisis and the consequent austerity, and the perception that ordinary people, particularly those furthest down the wealth–distribution curve, were paying the highest price for the failure of the bankers and the establishment, had rendered the old arguments about New Labour and its deliberate appeal to Tory voters' interests irrelevant. Not only was New Labour dead and buried, but solidly left-wing policies and principle could now win the support of those who had voted for Cameron's Conservatives in 2010 and who were now rethinking that decision. Miliband's faith in his own persuasive powers emboldened him to make one of the most forthright at-tacks on consumer capitalism by any Labour leader in decades. During his annual conference speech in September 2011, he out-lined the distinction a future Labour government would make, between the hard-working 'grafters' and the parasitical 'predators' (Miliband was genuinely annoyed when a passage in the same speech, where he stated he was not Tony Blair, was greeted by cheers from a part of the audience – an event remarked upon by most of the media and which infuriated supporters of the former Prime Minister).

This philosophy was to lead directly, in the ensuing three years, to the adoption of left-wing but, Miliband hoped, appealing pol-icies like a freeze on energy prices (accompanied by exuberant attacks on the 'big six' energy companies), the reinstatement of the

50p rate of income tax for high earners, and the renationalisation of Britain's railways.

A Leader of the Opposition has three main jobs: to design an appealing future programme for government, to project himself (or herself) in a positive light to the electorate, and to manage the party. On the first task, Miliband was making progress. Whether that progress was in the right direction was a matter for private discussion, at least while the polls were holding up. On the second task, Miliband's personal appeal, he was still falling short. Many Labour MPs reported throughout the 2010 parliament that working-class voters in particular were critical of what they saw as the leader's act of betrayal of his older brother. Such disloyalty might be tolerated among middle-class metropolitans and intellectuals, but in working-class communities where familial bonds were of the highest value, Miliband's decision to snatch the crown from his older brother was, it was suspected, indicative of a deeper personal flaw. That the media at the time talked up the perception that David had undoubtedly been the more effective politician added to the 'treachery' narrative. Opinion polls and more qualitative surveys (focus groups) organised by both the Labour Party and the Conservatives were reported to have raised similar perceptions among key voter groups.

The third task, party management, might not have taken up quite so much of Miliband's time and energy had it not been for the Member for Falkirk.

CHAPTER SIX

SO THIS BLOKE WALKS
INTO A BAR...

E ric Joyce was that strangest of political creatures: an army
officer who chose to move into Labour politics. While in the
second half of the twentieth century there had been a proud and
established tradition of former servicemen and women entering
Parliament via the Labour Party, the further the Second World
War and national service receded into the past, and, crucially, the
more Labour allowed its anti-nuclear activists to drive it towards
an openly hostile approach to the military establishment in the '70s
and '80s, the rarer such a transition became. As the Conservatives
benefited from their reputation as the patriotic friend to the UK's
armed forces, Labour's pacifist wing was more often expressing
ambivalence towards the troops' enemies in terrorist organisations
such as the Provisional IRA.

Joyce himself had in fact served in Northern Ireland, as well
as in Germany and Belize, having trained at the Royal Military
Academy at Sandhurst in the late 1980s. It was therefore deemed
eminently newsworthy that he should write an essay for the Fabi-
ans in 1997 criticising the army for racist and sexist discrimination.
Such a breach of protocol resulted in his suspension from the

army, after which he served as a staff member of the Commission for Racial Equality in Scotland, while at the same time pursuing his political ambitions.

As something of a media celebrity among party activists and with a reputation as a Fabian intellectual, Joyce was initially successful in his application to Labour's list of pre-approved candidates for the first Scottish Parliament elections, planned for 1999, an achievement that proved beyond the reach of a significant number of more experienced and well-known politicians whose desire to move from the House of Commons to Holyrood was frustrated by the party's Scottish leadership. Nevertheless, it was Westminster, not Holyrood, where Joyce was to begin his career as an elected Labour politician. When the Labour MP for Falkirk West, Dennis Canavan, failed in his own bid to win the 'pre-approval' of his party to stand as a Scottish Parliament candidate in the seat he had represented at Westminster for twenty-five years, he decided to stand anyway, but as an independent. Against expectations dictated by the then established rules, Canavan not only won the seat at the first Holyrood election in 1999, but won it with a massive majority of 12,192 over the official Labour candidate, giving him the largest majority of any Member of the Scottish Parliament (MSP).

Even if Canavan had successfully won the Labour nomination for Holyrood, the fact of his standing at all would still have meant Labour needed to find a new candidate to fight the Westminster seat at the next general election, expected in 2001. Joyce won the nomination, and would no doubt have coasted to an easy victory had Canavan emulated other colleagues who were serving dual mandates as MP and MSP in the two-year interregnum between the Holyrood and the expected Westminster elections, by remaining in both posts until the general election. But Canavan, still resentful of his rejection by Labour, had no inclination to make life easier for his former party, and in November 2000, formally resigned as an MP. The timing of the subsequent by-election was in Labour's hands and they moved quickly to hold it before Christmas, setting Thursday 21 December as polling day. As had become customary in by-elections in Labour-held seats, the campaign was hard fought, with a robust and energetic challenge to Labour from the SNP. In the end, a swing of 16 per cent to the nationalists from Labour, and a low turnout of 36 per cent, meant the SNP fell just short of securing a headline-grabbing victory and Joyce was elected with a majority of 705 votes. The Labour majority in the seat at the previous general election had been nearly 14,000.

Although a popular and hard-working MP, Joyce was also something of a loner in a club where personal friendships and informal alliances were key to promotion, and failed to achieve the ministerial office that many – perhaps Joyce included – had expected. He had held a number of posts as a parliamentary private secretary (PPS), the lowest-ranking government position from which ministers are frequently drawn, but the call to ministerial office never came. Perhaps this was a consequence of what he himself later described as 'a bit of mixing in my life, since my teens', the 'mixing' in question including car theft and assault.

It wasn't until after the 2010 election, with Labour now in opposition, that Joyce was finally called to serve his party on the front bench as a shadow Minister for Northern Ireland. His critics' reservations about him were unfortunately confirmed when, in November 2010, just two months after his appointment by Ed Miliband, police were called to Grangemouth oil refinery near Falkirk, where Joyce had driven from Edinburgh Airport at the end of the parliamentary week. He refused, on request, to supply a sample of breath to the officers and was arrested, spending a night in the cells before appearing in court the next day. Joyce received a driving ban and a £400 fine. He also resigned from the front bench.

But it was another drink-related incident more than a year later that sealed the fate of Joyce's political career – and inadvertently sparked a chain of events that reshaped the Labour Party.

On Wednesday 22 February 2012, police were called to a disturbance in the Strangers' Bar in the Palace of Westminster. The source of the disturbance, the Honourable Member for Falkirk, had headbutted at least one Conservative MP in a fight that had involved, at one point or another, at least five other MPs. 'It wasn't a fight – it was me on the rampage,' is how the typically good-humoured Joyce was later to describe the scene. He claimed that an impromptu performance of a song from *The Barber of Seville* by a guest of his had provoked a complaint from a nearby Conservative MP, at which point a 'spat' ensued, involving tie-grabbing, the throwing of punches and the aforementioned headbutting; all by Joyce. A number of police officers (Joyce later claimed that eight were required) finally subdued him and carried him to a cell in nearby Belgravia police station. At a subsequent court appearance, Joyce escaped a widely expected prison sentence and was instead given twelve months' community service, fined £3,000 and ordered to pay £1,400 compensation to his victims.

Joyce had been suspended from membership of the Labour Party as soon as the news of the Strangers' Bar incident was reported. But in a personal statement to the House of Commons on Monday 12 March, he announced that he had resigned from the party. This meant that he would not and could not be a Labour candidate at the next general election. Indeed, Joyce made it clear that while he did not intend to resign his position immediately, he would serve out the rest of the parliamentary term as an independent MP and not seek re-election in 2015.

Joyce had secured a 7,800 majority in the constituency (renamed simply 'Falkirk' following the boundary review that took effect at the 2005 general election) and the seat, all things being equal, would almost certainly be retained by Labour at the next election. It was therefore considered a valuable political prize by those with ambitions to become a Labour MP. And now there was a vacancy.

Shortly after Joyce's public declaration that he wouldn't be seeking re-election, Stephen Deans, a shop steward for the Unite union at the nearby Ineos Grangemouth refinery, was elected chair of Falkirk Constituency Labour Party (CLP). Deans immediately embarked on a campaign to recruit new members to the local party, an activity which was, and remains, an entirely legitimate one. Members are a local party's lifeblood and national headquarters of all mainstream parties constantly encourage membership drives. However, it became clear that Deans, as well as successfully recruiting members of Unite to the local Labour Party, was also supporting the candidacy of another local member, Karie Murphy. Murphy, a close friend of the Unite general secretary, Len McCluskey, was also a staff member of Labour's general election co-ordinator and vice-chair, Tom Watson MP, himself a close friend and former flatmate of McCluskey's. Ranged against Murphy for the Labour nomination were Gregor Poynton – seen as the 'Blairite' candidate, the political director of communications consultant Blue State Digital and husband to Dunbartonshire Labour MP Gemma Doyle – and Linda Gow, a former leader of Falkirk Council.

Murphy's opponents became convinced that the recruitment

of Unite members to the Labour Party was part of a strategy to secure the nomination for her; while recruitment of new members is encouraged, such recruitment cannot, under party rules, be used to 'fix' selections (although mass recruitment drives of one sort or another pepper the history of Labour selection contests throughout the country).

Those supporting Murphy feared that Poynton, an experienced campaigner and personable former party staffer, was Murphy's most serious opponent. They also understood that the best way to neutralise his challenge would be to select the new candidate from an all-women shortlist. When the CLP, with the support of Deans, decided to consult the membership on whether or not to initiate an all-women shortlist, both Poynton and Gow wrote to the membership to demand an open contest instead.

It was the fear of a deliberate attempt to 'steal' the selection contest for Unite's favoured candidate that resulted, in May 2013, in the national party suspending the CLP and carrying out an internal investigation into the selection process. To head off any attempt to circumvent the party rules, the NEC imposed a retrospective 'freeze date' of 12 March 2012 (the date Joyce had announced his intention not to stand again), which meant that anyone joining the party after that point would not be able to cast a vote in the selection contest.

Deans dismissed the development as an attack on the union by 'a Blairite rump'. Later that same month, a sub-committee of the NEC confirmed that the new candidate would be chosen from an all-women shortlist. Murphy, however, would not be on it; she announced on 13 May that she was withdrawing from the contest to replace Joyce, denying that any of the allegations that had been made against her and Unite had any validity.

In June, Labour announced that the entire selection process would be overseen by national, not local, officials, and the row bubbled over for another few weeks until, at the beginning of July, it exploded. Ed Miliband, conscious of Conservative criticism that his election as leader put him in the pockets of the trade unions who had swung the electoral college vote in his favour, upped the ante to an unexpected degree. Facing calls from David Blunkett, the former Home Secretary, three days earlier that Labour should publish the internal report into Falkirk, Miliband infuriated McCluskey by announcing that he would be submitting it instead to the police, so serious was the evidence of 'machine politics' uncovered by the investigation. In a naked bid to reassert his independence from the unions, Miliband declared: 'I am going to be very clear about this. I will act without fear or favour on behalf of cleanliness, transparency and fairness when it comes to Labour Party selection and the way the party is run. I am defending the good name of hundreds of thousands of union members, hundreds of thousands of Labour members and Labour supporters all around the country.'

He went on: 'My message to Len McCluskey is clear: face up to your responsibilities, face up to what people within your union were doing. Stop defending this.'

At the same time, Labour suspended the memberships of both Murphy and Deans. This was the most confrontational message sent by any Labour leader in living memory to the leader of the party's biggest donor. McCluskey responded publicly by describing the party's actions as 'disgraceful'.

Tom Watson, Murphy's employer, and a former official of the AEEU, a forerunner to Unite, had had enough: he resigned from the shadow Cabinet, ostensibly to avoid embarrassing his leader, since he was now calling for the Falkirk report to be published, in opposition to Miliband's position.

All of this could already have been described as a very Labour-oriented scandal, even before it emerged that a scheme set up under Tony Blair, entitled 'Union Join' – through which unions could encourage their members to join Labour and have their fees paid by the union for the first twelve months – was only now being abolished by Miliband.

Now Miliband saw his opportunity to grasp his 'Clause IV moment'. When Blair, at the end of his first conference speech as leader in September 1994, suggested a redrafting of the party's principles, it quickly became obvious that what he meant was the ditching of the original Clause IV from the party's constitution. The clause, committing the party to the 'common ownership of the means of production' was seen as an outdated anachronism, but was fiercely guarded by the left of the party. It became an iconic issue and, when Blair succeeded in replacing the old Clause IV with his own, preferred wording at a special conference in March 1995, that too became an iconic moment for the young leader and future Prime Minister, the moment when he cast off the baggage of Labour's socialist past (although, ironically, the new Clause IV actually featured the word 'socialist' for the first time in the party's history).

Miliband would turn the Falkirk crisis into an opportunity: he would transform the party's democracy and establish himself anew as a great reformer in the Blair mould, escaping once and for all the accusation that he was a creature of the trade unions. Within three days of the announcement that the Falkirk file would, against the wishes of Unite, be passed to the police, Miliband announced a new deal for the relationship between Labour and the organisations that had given birth to the party at the turn of the nineteenth century. The central reform related to 'affiliated' trade unions, who counted their members as Labour supporters and paid the party the associated affiliation fees unless individual members 'opted out' of doing so. The reform was high risk: it could mean a massive drop in the amount donated by the unions if individual members had to choose to opt into the system rather than opt out. But Miliband was determined. 'In the twenty-first century it just doesn't make sense for anyone to be affiliated to a political party unless they have chosen to do so,' he told the *Birmingham Mail*.

There were other parts of the new deal that gained less coverage: open primaries for the selection of Labour's London mayoral candidate in 2016, for example, and a new code of conduct for new candidates. But it was the change to affiliated membership that was the most significant and radical. Not only might the party's coffers be depleted if a concerted effort to encourage individual trade union members' recruitment failed, but there would be another, under-reported consequence of the reform: the electoral college used in leadership elections since 1983 (and in deputy leadership contests since 1981) was based, at least in the trade union section, on mass affiliate membership. If automatic affiliation was to end, the electoral college could hardly continue, since the logical consequence of individual affiliation was surely one member, one vote in future leadership elections. MPs and MEPs, who currently enjoyed a third of the vote in the college as well as exclusive nomination rights, would retain the latter but forego the former, their influence reduced to no more than that of any ordinary member. The next leader of the party would be elected by party members, affiliated trade union members who had opted to become 'associate members' and a new category of 'supporting members', who could buy a vote in any future contest by paying a £3 subscription fee.

Blair had had his special conference to confirm the party's decision to ditch Clause IV, so Miliband would have his own special conference to approve his party's new relationship with the unions. Emily Maitlis, political editor of the BBC's *Newsnight*, reported on 29 January 2014 that Miliband was 'on the brink of making what could be the biggest decision of his leadership so far'. His reforms package, contained in a report compiled by former party general secretary, Ray Collins, was at that moment being studied by the NEC and would go before the formal committee the following weekend for approval, before being voted on by delegates at the special conference at the London Excel Centre on Saturday 1 March.

Despite the reservations of some Blairites who had hoped the Falkirk crisis could be used to sever the links between the party and the trade unions altogether, and those on the left who regretted the end of the 'opt-out' arrangement for affiliated trade unionists, Miliband won the day with a satisfactory 86–14 per cent vote for his reforms.

Maitlis reported that conflict existed even in the upper echelons of the party: 'One senior party figure described [the reform package] as "potentially bigger than Clause IV". Another, with serious concerns about Mr Miliband's proposals – and a taste perhaps for the dramatic – said "it could alter the course of history".'

Maitlis was surely correct: it was overly dramatic to suggest that future leadership elections could produce unexpected results, results that deviated radically from the pattern of previous contests. After all, the nomination threshold had been increased: candidates would now need to secure the support of 15 per cent of MPs and MEPs (the Collins Review had recommended an increase from 12.5 per cent in order to reduce the possibility that candidates who didn't enjoy broad support in the PLP might find their way onto the ballot paper). Provided parliamentarians in future didn't 'lend' their nominations to candidates they had no intention of supporting in the actual contest (as they had to Diane Abbott in 2010) then the new system would work exactly as expected.

In December 2013, the former Labour MSP Karen Whitefield was selected as Labour's candidate in Falkirk. At the 2015 general election, the SNP won the seat with a majority of 19,701.

CHAPTER SEVEN

REBELLIOUS SCOTS

The 1980s were an electorally desolate wasteland for the Labour Party. The civil war that had erupted between right and left in the aftermath of the party's eviction from office at the 1979 general election had been brewing for years, and now MPs, trade union leaders and activists gave full vent to the frustrations and demands of their respective positions. The schism affected Labour in Scotland as much as any other part of the country, but the electoral consequences were less severe. In 1983, as Michael Foot led Labour to a catastrophic defeat, his party north of the border suffered its share of the UK party's pain, losing three of the forty-four seats it had won four years earlier and dropping six points to a 35 per cent share of the vote. But in 1987, after a determined modernising effort by leader Neil Kinnock that saw a disappointing electoral reward in England (Margaret Thatcher's government was re-elected with a majority of 102), Labour in Scotland saw its representation leap to fifty out of seventy-two seats, accounting for almost half of the total Labour gains throughout the UK.

The relative success of Labour in Scotland was attributable to a number of factors. First, although it controlled much of Scottish local government, Labour rejected the divisive identity politics pursued in some London boroughs whose 'loony left' behaviour filled so many columns in the newspapers and did so much damage to Kinnock's efforts to make the party electable again. Similarly, no Scottish council followed the examples of Liverpool and Lambeth in defying the Conservative government's rate-capping policies by setting illegal budgets (although Edinburgh District Council, briefly under the leadership of the hard left in 1985, came perilously close).

This approach was underpinned by a second factor, the role of the trade unions. Organised labour had the most to lose from Labour's electoral irrelevance and worked extremely closely with party leaders in Parliament and in local government to guide the party along a moderate path. Whenever the hard left threatened to win policy victories at Labour's Scottish conference, party leaders could almost always rely on the trade unions' big battalions to ride to the rescue with a conveniently large block vote.

A third factor was the increasing perception that the Conservatives under Margaret Thatcher appeared less in touch with Scottish attitudes and could easily be painted as anti-Scottish, despite a disproportionately large representation of Scots in her Cabinet. And this, in turn, led to the fourth and decisive factor: the Conservatives' opposition to devolution.

Labour had, of course, been fatally divided in the late 1970s when Callaghan's government, seeking to stem the rise of the SNP, had proposed a Scottish Assembly in Edinburgh and subjected it to a referendum in March 1979. Scots voted for the measure, but not in enough numbers to meet the threshold that had been imposed by Parliament (against the government's wishes), that demanded that at least 40 per cent of all eligible voters should vote Yes. Back in opposition post-1979, Labour presented a more unified approach to devolution and resolved to support a more powerful devolved parliament, with tax-raising and legislative powers. For the next decade and a half, led through most of that period by the Glasgow Garscadden MP, Donald Dewar, Labour in Scotland exploited a fruitful – but ultimately disastrously self-defeating – strategy of portraying the Conservative government as undemocratic, even un-Scottish, for opposing devolution. Dewar would frequently repeat the claim that, particularly post-1987 when Scotland returned only ten Tory MPs, the government had no mandate to govern there. A devolved parliament in Edinburgh would, he believed, satisfy the longing of those who wanted more self-government while wishing to maintain Scotland's membership of the United Kingdom. It would also, Labour said, provide protection for Scots from some of the worst excesses of Thatcherism, specifically the poll tax (or community charge) that was included in the 1987 Conservative election manifesto.

Until the party returned to government in its 1997 landslide, Labour in Scotland (rebranded as 'the Scottish Labour Party' from 1995) maintained its unending invective of accusing first the Thatcher and then the Major governments of being anti-Scottish on the basis that they opposed devolution. It would be untrue to suggest there were no 'devo-sceptics' at any level of the party who might have expressed reservations about such a strategy. But such individuals managed to swallow their reservations in the hope that a united front might yet yield electoral dividends.

Once in government as Secretary of State for Scotland, Dewar set about producing a White Paper on devolution, closely modelled on the blueprint produced by the cross-party Scottish Constitutional Convention that met from 1989 to 1995. The proposals in the paper for a devolved, tax-raising parliament in Edinburgh were then put to a vote of the Scottish people in a two-question referendum in September 1997: the first question asking if voters supported the setting up of the parliament, the second question asking if such a parliament should have tax-raising powers. Following a campaign where a double 'Yes' vote was supported by Labour, the SNP and the Liberal Democrats, with William Hague's Conservatives fighting a lone, vain fight for the status quo, Scotland gave its verdict: on a turnout of 60 per cent, 74 per cent supported the parliament in principle, while 63 per cent supported giving it tax-raising powers.

Dewar himself decided to quit the House of Commons at the next general election in order to stand as a new Member of the Scottish Parliament (MSP) in 1999. He duly led his party to victory, falling short of a majority (an outcome the electoral system was designed to guarantee) and forming the first Scottish Executive in coalition with the Liberal Democrats.

Now that Scottish Labour had delivered the parliament it had promised and which its opponents had predicted it never would, it started to find its role increasingly difficult to define. Yes, it had played a defining role in delivering home rule, and was now governing Scotland from its democratically elected parliament. But to observers it now looked as if it had 'sorted' Scotland in order to be allowed to concentrate on more important matters, especially matters that remained the remit of the UK Parliament at Westminster.

It had always, without much supporting evidence, been claimed and blithely accepted that Scottish Labour's Achilles' heel was its cultural devotion to Westminster, even after devolution, epitomised by its alleged tendency to send its 'top team' of talented politicians to London and allow the Edinburgh parliament to be run by 'the B-team'. In contrast (so Scottish received political wisdom went) the SNP prioritised Holyrood by sending their most talented politicians there. There was certainly a wide range of abilities among the Labour representatives sent to both parliaments; perhaps the perception grew because, post-1999, the media paid significantly less attention to MPs than to MSPs, and TV viewers were able to see and hear more of those in the new (and expensive) horseshoe-shaped chamber at the foot of the Royal Mile, while less articulate MPs perhaps found it easier to avoid the glare of publicity that might highlight their insufficiencies. Whatever the truth of the perception, a perception it certainly was, and it took hold among the public and the media to a damaging degree. Almost from the start of the new parliament, Scottish Labour MPs – even those who had tried and failed to gain their party's approval to stand as a candidate for Holyrood – were privately scathing of their comrades in Edinburgh. Tearoom jokes about an amendment to the Scotland Act ('Line 1, between "There shall" and "be a Scottish Parliament", insert "not"') were repeated to much hilarity. Defensive about their continuing role in the Commons and the removal from them of responsibility for policy in the areas of health, education and transport, among others, Scottish Labour MPs barely tried to hide their resentment at their Holyrood colleagues, and were never slow to point out the significantly larger voter turnouts for general elections in Scotland versus Holyrood elections.

A particular fault line emerged when, following Labour's re-election as senior partner in the Scottish Executive in 2003, then First Minister Jack McConnell struck a deal with the Lib Dems that would mean the abolition of the first-past-the-post (FPTP) electoral system for local authorities in Scotland. This change had been discussed in 1999 but a resolution had been deferred; it could be deferred no longer if Labour wanted to avoid becoming a minority administration. MPs – and, to be fair, the majority of Scottish Labour activists – were appalled at the change which would see hundreds of Labour councillors removed from town halls across the country without a single vote changing hands. At a time when SNP parliamentarians, previously usually limited to two or three in the House of Commons in recent decades, now numbered thirty-five MSPs and six MPs – plus a much larger number of full-time support staff – McConnell's Westminster colleagues had real fears about the erosion of the party's activist base at the next local authority elections.

Adding to the sense of Scottish Labour's aimlessness was the revelation that the party had never planned for a post-Dewar strategy, perhaps hadn't even considered such a need. But when Dewar collapsed and died in October 2000, he was replaced by his enterprise and lifelong learning minister, Henry McLeish, following an internal election by members of the party's Scottish Executive Committee. McLeish proved an uninspiring and accident-prone First Minister, forced out of office after just a year when various complicated and opaque financial arrangements surrounding his constituency office were exposed. He was replaced by McConnell, who had served Dewar as his finance minister and who had replaced McLeish at education a year earlier. McConnell therefore became the first First Minister never to have held office as an MP.

It is never easy for a relative political unknown to follow a political giant, but McConnell, at the subsequent 2003 Holyrood elections, was helped by the fact that the SNP were experiencing exactly the same problem: after ten years leading his party, Alex

Salmond had decided to resign, and was succeeded by the popular but uninspiring figure of John Swinney. Labour emerged from polling day once more as the biggest party, with fifty-six seats to the SNP's thirty-five.

Still Scottish Labour looked and sounded like it felt it had a right to rule, that it had regarded the establishment of devolution as a box-ticking exercise and, now that the box was ticked, felt little need to do much more other than keep the show on the road. Perhaps the party's continuing competent but unimpressive performance at Holyrood could have succeeded in winning another term, were it not for the re-emergence of McConnell's and Scottish Labour's nemesis.

Alex Salmond had decided, after it became clear he would not be First Minister following the first elections to the Scottish Parliament in 1999, to call it a day as far as the leadership of his party was concerned. He would give up his Holyrood seat and stand instead for re-election to the House of Commons. To those who know Salmond well, this was no surprise. Despite being a fierce and effective advocate of Scottish independence, Salmond had always, since he was first sent there by his electors in the northeast seat of Banff and Buchan in 1987, enjoyed life at Westminster. The confrontational design of the chamber itself suited him, but so did the relaxed atmosphere in the bars and restaurants, both within and beyond the palace. Even political opponents reported long enjoyable nights sharing whisky and political gossip in equal measure in Salmond's company. And when Swinney, humiliated by a particularly poor SNP showing at the 2004 European Parliament elections, announced his resignation, Salmond made it clear he would not be a candidate. Echoing the words of American Civil War general, William Tecumseh Sherman, he told reporters in June: 'If nominated I'll decline. If drafted I'll defer. And if elected I'll resign.' Nevertheless, a month later he announced his candidacy, perhaps spurred on by the realisation that his preferred candidate, Nicola Sturgeon, would be unlikely to beat Roseanna Cunningham, the party's current deputy leader. Instead Sturgeon agreed to withdraw her candidacy for the leadership and stood on a joint ticket with Salmond as his deputy. Both were elected at the party's conference that September.

A triumphant Salmond told delegates at the conference: 'It is often said that Mr McConnell is no Donald Dewar. Donald Dewar? Jack McConnell is no Henry McLeish!' In one deftly delivered remark, Salmond managed to praise a respected and late First Minister while using his reputation to dismiss both his successors. McConnell faced a tough fight for his job.

It was a fight he almost won. When the results of the 2007 Scottish Parliament elections were announced, the SNP had won a total of forty-seven seats to Labour's forty-six. Close as the result was, even if Labour and Lib Dems numbers had been combined, they would fall two seats short of an overall majority. And when the Lib Dems, having refused to entertain coalition talks with the SNP, nevertheless made it clear they would support Salmond's claim to be the new First Minister, McConnell accepted defeat.

Within four years, Salmond had transformed himself into something closely resembling a statesman. Pursuing an unashamedly populist, rather than progressive, agenda, he embarked on a policy platform that included the reduction and then removal of prescription charges. Inevitably, the SNP's agenda also included a commitment to their manifesto promise to hold a referendum on Scottish independence. The Bill was defeated in 2010 by a combination of Labour, Lib Dems and Conservative MSPs, although no one doubted that the issue would be resurrected if the SNP managed to stay in power beyond the May 2011 elections.

For most of the year leading up to polling day, Scottish Labour, now led by former minister Iain Gray, enjoyed a lead in the polls of between one and fifteen percentage points. Even as late as 2 March 2011, a TNS-BMRB poll for the *Herald* newspaper put support for Labour at 44 per cent in the constituency ballot – fifteen points ahead of the SNP. But at the beginning of April, the polling suddenly performed a dramatic reversal. On 9 April, a poll by Scottish Opinion for the *Sunday Mail* gave the SNP a ten-point lead, after which Scottish Labour never regained the lead. The results of the 5 May poll were, by any measure, a political earthquake.

The 'additional member system' for Holyrood had been devised with the aim of denying any one party an overall majority – essentially to quell the fears of Labour's partners on the Scottish Constitutional Convention that Labour might take permanent control of the new parliament in the same way it had managed over decades with a number of local authorities. The new system would see MSPs elected by FPTP in seventy-three constituencies, with an additional fifty-six MSPs elected on a proportionate basis from regional lists. Voters therefore had two separate votes, one for the constituency in which they lived and a second one for their regional list. This system assumed – entirely wrongly, as it turned out – that the vast majority of voters would support their party of choice using both their votes. In 2011 Salmond cleverly rebranded his party on each of Scotland's eight regional lists as 'Alex Salmond for First Minister', thereby achieving the top spot (parties were listed alphabetically on the ballot paper) while encouraging voters who had voted for another party in the first ballot to switch to the SNP in the second.

And by this method, by encouraging voters to split their party allegiance, Salmond achieved what had been assumed to be impossible: an overall majority of MSPs, sixty-nine out of 129. Labour, meanwhile, were decimated, winning just twenty-five constituencies. And with no strategy in place for maximising their list vote, Labour's total was a miserly and unimpressive thirty-seven. Seats across the country, and in Labour's traditional heartlands, seats that had been Labour since the beginning of the Scottish Parliament – and which as Westminster seats had returned Labour MPs for much longer – fell to the SNP.

The shock for Labour was even more unexpected and painful because of its healthy result at the UK general election a year earlier, when it returned forty-one MPs – exactly the same result as in 2005 – with traditionally healthy majorities. But by May 2011, the UK Prime Minister was once again a Conservative, David Cameron, a fact Salmond exploited during the campaign: only an SNP Scottish government could protect Scotland from the party of Thatcher.

Whatever turmoil Scottish Labour was now experiencing, attention was turning to the more important matter of Scotland's constitutional future. A strand of Unionism had long argued that holding a referendum on independence would help destroy the independence cause as well as the SNP itself, provided, of course, voters behaved as the vast majority of opinion polls on the matter predicted. Such a referendum was designated in the Scotland Act as a reserved matter over which Westminster rather than Holyrood had express authority. Cameron decided to call Salmond's bluff, announcing in January 2012 that he would authorise the Scottish Parliament to legislate for a binding referendum.

In October 2012, after months of negotiation between the two governments, Salmond and Cameron met in Scotland's capital to sign what the media would christen 'The Edinburgh Agreement', setting out the principles that the referendum would be legislated for by the Scottish Parliament, command the confidence of the Scottish public and deliver a fair exercise whose result would be respected by all sides. Polling day was set, by Salmond and the SNP, for Thursday 18 September 2014, nearly two years away and, crucially, just six months before the start of the 2015 general election campaign. Salmond was also allowed to set the question ('Should Scotland be an independent country?') and the franchise to be used (he insisted on allowing EU nationals and residents aged sixteen and over to take part).

For Scottish Labour under its new leader, Johann Lamont, participation in the cross-party Better Together campaign presented few political or ideological difficulties. For the SNP-led Yes campaign, however, it provided an opportunity to depict their chief opponents as 'Red Tories', in cahoots with the hated UK government in defence of the establishment. This was simply a tactic to try to split the Better Together campaign and render it less effective; it is questionable (to say the least) to assume that, had Labour campaigned exclusively within its own party campaign, it would have been immune from nationalist taunts that it was working on the same side as the Tories, if not in the same campaign.

And now, as polling day in the most important constitutional referendum in the UK's history inched closer, Scottish Labour found itself the target of the same arguments deployed by Donald Dewar in the '80s and '90s: if the Conservatives had been anti-Scottish for opposing devolution then, weren't Labour anti-Scottish for opposing independence now?

At the start of 2012, as Cameron prepared to announce his decision to allow Salmond to go ahead with his referendum, opposition to independence, according to one poll, enjoyed a clear twenty-point lead over support. In January of 2014, that number was oscillating between seven and twenty points. In the final few weeks, a YouGov poll for the *Sunday Times* revealed, for the first time, a 2 per cent lead for Yes, followed a week later by a seven-point lead in an ICM poll for the *Daily Telegraph* (the latter using a much smaller sample). Overall, however, the polling numbers for No looked healthy. Senior figures at No Thanks (the brand had been changed from 'Better Together' 100 days before polling day) had warned their political leaders in advance that the polls would narrow and even go into deficit before polling day. But this had been factored into their calculations and No would still prevail, they assured advisers to both Cameron and the former Prime Minister, Gordon Brown. Nevertheless, panic was the order of the day, and three days before polling, the *Daily Record*, Scotland's second biggest-selling newspaper, duly carried a front-page splash declaring 'The Vow', a dramatic intervention by Cameron, Miliband and Nick Clegg promising 'extensive new powers' for the Scottish Parliament if Scots voted No.

Debate still surrounds the effectiveness and, indeed, the very meaning of 'The Vow'. Whether or not it had the impact its creators later claimed, the votes on referendum night told their own story: No had won by a clear margin of 55 to 45 per cent.

The following day, declaring that 'the dream [of independence] shall never die', Alex Salmond announced his resignation as First Minister.

It should have been a day of celebration for Scottish Labour. It had worked hard and with a united front to secure the Union, and it had won. Salmond had been defeated in the only fight his party saw as worth fighting. And yet...

Voters in Labour strongholds of Glasgow, North Lanarkshire and West Dunbartonshire, as well as in the former stronghold of Dundee, had voted heavily for Yes. Polls showed that up to 30 per cent of Labour voters had decided to support the nationalist cause. Would those voters return to the Labour fold now that the referendum was over?

And lest Scottish Labour might start celebrating, David Cameron, in his early morning comments from Downing Street on the Friday after the result was declared, delivered a punch to the solar plexus of his former Unionist allies before they even had time to put the champagne on ice: welcoming the referendum result with relief, he added triumphalism to the mix with a sop to English nationalism. 'We have heard the voice of Scotland and now the millions of voices of England must be heard,' he told a surprised audience of reporters. And blindsiding the Labour Party, with an eye to the oncoming general election campaign, he challenged the opposition to accept the principle of 'English votes for English laws' in the House of Commons. At a time of maximum tension and fragility for the 307-year-old Union, David Cameron had just resurrected the West Lothian Question. All talk of a united Britain suddenly died; it looked to many people as though Cameron had just used the referendum result to silence – or at least curtail – the voice of Scotland in the parliament to which it had just voted to continue sending representatives.

Meanwhile, tensions and divisions within Scottish Labour that had remained largely hidden during the two and a half years of campaigning surfaced in a dramatic and catastrophic way. Johann Lamont, the MSP who had succeeded Gray as party leader following Labour's dismal performance at the 2011 Scottish Parliament elections, had never been highly rated by her Westminster colleagues. While she had performed effectively in the chamber at Holyrood, providing feisty and often humorous criticism of Alex Salmond at First Minister's Questions each Thursday, she was nevertheless accused – by the traditional Labour Party method of anonymous briefings – of failing to offer the vision the party needed if it was ever to wrest control of government at Holyrood again. Lamont's former close friend, Margaret Curran, now the shadow Scottish Secretary, and former Scottish Secretary Jim Murphy, were accused of undermining her in the hope that she would step aside before the general election so that an alternative, more voter-friendly figurehead (i.e. Murphy) could take charge in Scotland.

The leadership crisis came to a head when, on Friday 17 October, Lamont received a call from Tim Livesey, Ed Miliband's chief of staff, informing her that Ian Price, who Lamont herself had appointed as Scottish Labour's general secretary in 2013, had been sacked by party HQ in London. Lamont was understandably furious at such high-handed behaviour. A week later Lamont announced her resignation.

Obviously hurt by the briefings against her by people in the party she had regarded as friends as well as colleagues, Lamont's choice of language, contained in an interview she gave to the *Daily Record* on the afternoon of Friday 24 October, could not conceivably have been any more explosive or damaging to Scottish Labour: 'Just as the SNP must embrace that devolution is the settled will of the Scottish people, the Labour Party must recognise that the Scottish party has to be autonomous and not just a branch office of a party based in London.'

This was a gift to the SNP, who would continue to throw the 'branch office' label at their opponents for a long time after the dust from the referendum had settled. Lamont also encapsulated the long-running rivalry between the Holyrood and Westminster tribes of Scottish Labour by stating: '[Westminster] colleagues need to realise that the focus of Scottish politics is now Holyrood, not Westminster.'

Immediately speculation about who might replace her began, and for a few days it was even suggested that Gordon Brown, who remained Labour's most popular character in Scotland, might step up. But the former Prime Minister had already made up his mind to step down from the Commons at the general election – and from frontline politics altogether – and was planning to announce his decision at the start of December. He was not tempted by the vacancy.

The other obvious candidate to replace Lamont was Jim Murphy, the Eastwood MP who had earned respect – and a great deal of publicity – for his audacious crowd-baiting speeches in support of a No vote during the referendum from the top of a pair of Irn-Bru crates. Seen as a 'big beast' in Scottish politics, Murphy had been demoted by Miliband from the post of shadow Defence Secretary to shadow International Development Secretary, and was known to be unhappy about the prospect of continuing to serve Miliband (especially after working as campaign manager to Miliband's older brother, David, in the leadership election of 2010). Murphy duly resigned from the shadow Cabinet the following month and announced his candidacy. He was elected leader on 13 December 2014, becoming the first Scottish Labour leader in the devolution era not to have been elected as an MSP first. His duties holding the new First Minister, Nicola Sturgeon, to account in the chamber at Holyrood would be undertaken by his new deputy, Kezia Dugdale MSP. This was an identical arrangement to that adopted by Alex

Salmond when he returned as SNP leader in 2004, but without a seat at Holyrood at the time; until 2007 his deputy, Sturgeon, led for the SNP at FMQs.

Even before Lamont's resignation, the polls in Scotland had started moving against Labour. Before the official referendum campaign began, in January 2012, a Survation poll for the *Mail on Sunday* had put support for Scottish Labour at 40 per cent, nine points clear of the SNP. On 5 October 2014, even following two and a half years of solid campaigning on, and saturation media coverage of, a controversial and divisive issue, Survation for *Scotland on Sunday*, gave Labour some hope that it might yet maintain its dominant position, at least in Westminster voting. The poll suggested it enjoyed the support of 39 per cent (just three down on its 2010 showing) to the SNP's thirty-five. But throughout the month there was an inexorable reversal in the historic position Labour had enjoyed for decades. By the end of October, a number of polls were reflecting the sea change brought about by three solid years of campaigning in the referendum. On 30 October, a YouGov survey for *The Times* showed the SNP on 43 per cent and Labour on 27. By the year's end, no poll indicated a return to 'normal' for Scottish Labour.

With UK polls showing a tightening race for Downing Street at the general election the following May, Scotland's traditional tranche of Labour seats was vital to the party's – and Ed Miliband's – election hopes. But there were still six months before the campaign starting pistol was officially fired. Surely that was plenty of time for Scottish Labour's new leader, Murphy, to turn things around?

CHAPTER EIGHT

'HELL, YES!'

It was all David Cameron's fault. Initially an outsider in the race to succeed Michael Howard as Conservative leader in the second half of 2005, the Witney MP suddenly and unexpectedly assumed frontrunner status on the back of a single fifteen-minute speech to the Tory conference in October. It stood out from the other candidates' efforts because, unlike his rivals, Cameron adopted an informal tone and, crucially, didn't use an autocue or a prepared script. Although he had meticulously rehearsed and memorised his pitch, it looked to the assembled delegates – and to the outside world – as if he was making it up on the hoof, and making up a very effective message. Having set the standard for conference speeches, others followed his example, including Gordon Brown and Nick Clegg. Speaking 'off the cuff', or at least appearing to, became the touchstone by which a political leader's speeches would be judged.

Miliband almost perfected this approach. At his party's 2012 annual conference in Manchester, he earned widespread (though not universal) praise for his 'One Nation' speech that he recited, seemingly effortlessly, without notes. But two years later, back in Manchester, he came unstuck precisely because of this new – and unnecessary – fashion for rejecting the aid of the autocue. Aides subsequently blamed the Scottish independence referendum – which had concluded less than a week earlier – for the absence of the usual intense preparation that would normally have gone into constructing the speech and then, in Miliband's case, memorising it. Nevertheless, when it transpired, even before the leader finished speaking, that he had missed out large parts of the speech – and worse, those parts that dealt with the controversial issue of the deficit and how Labour planned to deal with it – the criticism was swift and came from unexpected quarters. Miliband's most important trade union ally, Len McCluskey, the general secretary of Unite, told Sky News: 'I know people think it is impressive to talk for sixty minutes or eighty minutes without notes. It is not something I'd do. I much prefer to have notes in front of me. Of course it was a glaring omission.' And former Home Secretary David Blunkett was reported as believing it 'fell short of the standard expected of a prime ministerial candidate'. Blunkett said: 'Prime Ministers do autocue.'

It was a messy, unsatisfying and disquieting end to that year's last – and therefore the most important – party conference.

And before the official start of the 2015 general election campaign, before even the end of the year, there was still the by-election in Rochester to come.

It's easy, with hindsight, to read too much into past events and apply a significance that helps to explain subsequent events. It is difficult, however, to analyse Emily Thornberry's behaviour as anything other than an illuminating example of what, under Ed Miliband's leadership, the Labour Party had become.

The Rochester and Strood by-election had been called when the sitting MP, Mark Reckless, had defected to the UK Independence

Party (UKIP) and, following the example of his party colleague, Douglas Carswell, had duly resigned from the Commons in order to stand under his new party's colours. Reckless's victory on 20 November 2014 was overshadowed by unnecessary and self-inflicted damage to the Labour Party, allowing David Cameron to shrug off the second loss of a seat to UKIP in little over a month.

The drama began – as political dramas often do – with a tweet, sent from Thornberry's account on polling day. Although the text merely read: 'Image from Rochester', the attached photograph spoke volumes. It showed a white van parked in the driveway of a modest mid-terraced house from whose windows hung two St George's flags. The intended political message was clear: if UKIP were going to win the seat it would be thanks to the (to Thornberry) inexplicable and tasteless affection for English nationalism. On top of which, the then shadow Attorney General's inclusion of the white van suggested a snobbish attitude to working-class voters.

Miliband immediately saw the danger of the narrative that, within hours, engulfed social media and was threatening to dominate the TV news headlines and the front pages of the next day's newspapers. He called Thornberry the same evening to inform her that her services were no longer required.

The swiftness and ruthlessness with which Miliband took action impressed and surprised many – and angered many of Thornberry's allies. In a subsequent TV interview, however, Miliband merely reinforced the impression that if his frontbench colleagues appeared out of touch with working Britain, Miliband was cut from the same cloth. When asked by an interviewer what he thought when he saw a white van, he replied, 'I think, respect.' The reply raised smirks and eyebrows throughout Westminster and was widely mocked as just as patronising and clueless as Thornberry's attitude had been.

Jamie Reed, the Copeland MP, made matters worse for Miliband when, at Prime Minister's Questions six days later, in a preamble to a question about cuts to council funding, said, 'The first thing I think of when I see a white van is whether or not my father or my brother is driving it.' The quip provoked much laughter on both sides and, by presenting a funny and down-to-earth approach to the issue, exposed Miliband's own contortions on the issue as insincere and manufactured. It also unhelpfully evoked memories of another self-inflicted media 'incident' in which Miliband's determination to broadcast a single, disciplined message and his strangely unnatural speaking style caused a high level of embarrassment. Three years earlier, an ITV pooled camera (a crew with exclusive rights to carry out the interview on condition they distributed the recording to other broadcasters) asked Miliband about his attitude to recent industrial action in the public sector. Despite being asked the question five or six times, Miliband repeated almost exactly the same sentences verbatim each time. The reporter, Damon Green, was so incensed at Miliband's attempt to use him as a 'recording device for a scripted sound bite', that he thought it 'perfectly proper' that the full unedited video found its way on to the YouTube video-sharing platform. The columnist and broadcaster Charlie Brooker described it as 'an interview with a satnav stuck on a roundabout'. The criticism was arguably unfair: other politicians had used the same trick to get a central point across, making it deliberately difficult for editors subsequently to remove the main point the politician was trying to make. But Miliband's performance was particularly damaging due to his stilted, rehearsed delivery and his unfortunate nasal tone. And although the recording was made in 2011, it was to become one of the most-watched political videos during the 2015 general election.

In reference to claims made by some of Miliband's more enthusiastic supporters during the 2010 leadership election (see Chapter Four) a former backbencher said after the video became an internet sensation for the second time: 'It turns out that Ed does indeed "speak human", but only as a second language.'

* * *

The 2015 general election was the first whose date was known more than four years in advance. The Conservative–Liberal Democrat coalition government had agreed, during the talks which thrashed out a programme of government in the days following the 2010 election, to introduce fixed-term parliaments. It had long been a demand of the Liberal Democrats and their predecessors that the Prime Minister of the day should be deprived of the advantage of choosing the date of the general election, a constitutional quirk that gave the incumbent government a distinct advantage. Whereas the Liberal Democrats had usually offered four-year terms as the standard at which the Commons should aim, once offered the prospect of Cabinet positions, they were easily persuaded that five-year terms would be preferable. The parties were therefore able to prepare poster and newspaper advertising campaigns and leaflets well in advance, confident that the polling date was guaranteed in law.

On 26 March 2015, four days before Parliament was officially dissolved, signalling the official start of campaigning, Ed Miliband appeared as a guest on *Channel 4 News*, interviewed by Jeremy Paxman. Miliband affected a bullish, confident swagger, making jokes with the feared interviewer. When Paxman related an anecdote about having met a man on the Tube who told Paxman that Miliband would be a walkover for any world leader he might meet as Prime Minister, Miliband responded with a prepared defence. In the summer of 2013, he reminded viewers, he had stood up to pressure, not only from Cameron and his deputy, but also President Obama (and for emphasis, Miliband relished giving the President his title of 'Leader of the Free World') and had refused to promise Labour support for military intervention in Syria, where President Assad stood accused of having used chemical weapons against his civilian population. 'I made up my mind and we said "no", right?' Miliband told Paxman belligerently. 'Standing up to the Leader of the Free World [the second time he had invoked the title in less than a minute] I think shows a certain toughness.'

Not only did Miliband take credit (rightly) for the government's defeat in the Commons vote in September of that year, he carefully and forcefully contrasted his own actions with those of Blair (without naming the former Prime Minister) in the run-up to the invasion of Iraq by allied forces in March 2003. Blair's decision had come about as a result of 'a rush to war, without knowing what your strategy is and without being clear about what the consequences would be'.

The decision not to support military action against Assad had not been a universally popular one within the Labour Party. While the hard-left, anti-war wing of the party had welcomed it, there was significant criticism and dismay from Labour's right-wing and Blairite factions, for whom 'liberal interventionism' was a moral touchstone of foreign policy.

Miliband ended his argument by posing Paxman's own question to himself: 'Am I tough enough? Hell, yes, I'm tough enough!'

The remark, coming from Miliband, sounded forced, rehearsed, staged, stilted and completely unnatural.

For Miliband and his team, it was essential that the impression of being a pushover – by the trade unions who put him in his job, or by the SNP who threatened to be a decisive factor in the event of a hung parliament – had to be dealt with. What better way than to distance himself from the toxic legacy of Iraq (and, by inference, from Blair too)? Whether the nationwide TV audience were suitably convinced by the gambit would not be known for another six weeks.

Parliament was officially dissolved on Monday 30 March, marking the official start of the campaign. Between then and polling day, the results of ninety-five different polls were published. Of these, forty put Labour in the lead, thirty-six put the Conservatives ahead and nineteen – a historically high percentage – predicted a dead heat between the two main parties.

The overwhelming number of pundits, commentators and politicians expected another hung parliament, with no party commanding an overall majority. The odds were particularly against David Cameron; no sitting Prime Minister had managed to serve a full term in office and then increase his party's share of the vote since 1900. And despite Labour's difficulties in Scotland, where every poll predicted a significant advantage in seats for the SNP over Labour, Miliband strongly believed his pitch to the nation would result in him entering Downing Street, either by virtue of a Labour minority administration or by a coalition deal with his preferred partners, the Liberal Democrats.

In the weeks leading up to dissolution, Miliband found himself under pressure from his Scottish MPs to rule out publicly any possibility that Labour would consider forming a coalition, after polling day, with the SNP, however many seats they were to win north of the border. This appeal was made by MPs nervous that the SNP's electoral appeal was based on an assumption by voters that voting SNP rather than Labour would make no difference to the likelihood of a Labour government being elected. Miliband at first demurred on this advice, opting for caution in his public remarks. However, once the campaign proper was under way, he made clear that a deal between his party and the nationalists was indeed not on the agenda, regardless of how the parliamentary arithmetic added up after 7 May.

For the media, the most significant events of the campaign were those that the media itself had created five years earlier: the leaders' debates. But this time it proved more difficult to get the three main party leaders in the same studio. Negotiations among parties organising in Great Britain (excluding Northern Ireland) led, on 2 April, to a seven-way leaders' debate broadcast on ITV: Cameron, Miliband and Clegg, plus Nigel Farage of UKIP, Nicola Sturgeon of the SNP, Natalie Bennett of the Green Party and Leanne Wood of Plaid Cymru. The format was widely seen as less satisfying than the three-way debate of the previous campaign, and of benefit to David Cameron, who had made the inclusion of all seven leaders more likely by threatening not to take part unless the Green Party was included.

A further 'challengers' debate', hosted by David Dimbleby and broadcast on BBC1 on 16 April, involved only five leaders representing those not currently in government: Miliband, Farage, Wood, Sturgeon and Bennett.

A third 'main event' was a special edition of the BBC's *Question Time* on 30 April, exactly a week before polling, when each of the three main party leaders were separately interviewed by Dimbleby and were also asked questions by the studio audience. An instant poll by ICM for *The Guardian* concluded that Cameron had performed the best of the three. However, this may have been helped by the unfortunate and clumsy trip performed by Miliband as he left the stage and which was subsequently broadcast repeatedly.

That trip – perhaps channelling the famous pratfall of Miliband's earliest champion, Neil Kinnock, on the beach at Brighton shortly before he was elected leader in 1983 – was a highlight of the campaign compared to Labour's main campaign event in Hastings on Sunday 3 May.

The party leader, the man who genuinely expected to be in No. 10 within the week, stood before the assembled media, flanked by local party workers, including Sarah Owen, Labour's hopeful in this marginal seat. This was a proud day, a day when the next Labour Prime Minister would not only remind a watching nation of the six key pledges that would guide his administration, but would do so in such a way that the relevant words would be carved indelibly on the nation's consciousness as well as on a more permanent edifice.

But first to those pledges.

Eighteen years earlier, the last time that Labour had successfully moved from opposition to government, Tony Blair had made much campaigning and propaganda use of the 'pledge card'. Aware that voters' attention spans are limited, he could not rely on their willingness to read the party's manifesto in full, and sought instead – as befitted New Labour's approach in other areas – to condense the party's policy message into five neat 'sound bites', which were then printed on laminated credit-card-sized pieces of cardboard and distributed to local campaigns and candidates throughout the country. The five pledges were attractive without being particularly radical, yet were also specific ('cut class sizes to under thirty for five-, six- and seven-year-olds by using money from the assisted places scheme'), giving the (intended) impression that Blair's shadow team knew exactly what they were doing and what they wanted to achieve.

Miliband's Labour attempted a version of this successful tactic, with the bold difference that none of the six pledges in 2015 were specific or radical. Indeed one of them – 'controls on immigration' – was merely a statement that such things do exist under any government, the equivalent of simply saying 'income tax'. Yet it still managed to infuriate a large proportion of social media users who naturally interpreted the very words as a statement of intent to increase border controls, especially once this 'pledge', along with the five others, was emblazoned on a series of colourful mugs that went on sale during the campaign.

Another of the pledges was 'an NHS with the time to care', an undoubtedly sincere attempt to place the party on the side of patients, but one so lacking in detail that it might have been better written on the inside of a Hallmark greeting card.

On 3 May, that day's photo opportunity was the unveiling by Miliband of the party's pledges carved into an eight-foot-tall slab of granite, a monument that would, following Labour's victory the following Thursday, be erected in the garden at Downing Street to serve as a daily reminder to the new Prime Minister of his promises to the electorate. Given the reaction of the media to the stunt – a cruel mix of ridicule and anger – it is hardly surprising that the apparatchik whose brainchild the 'Ed Stone' was has yet to identify themselves. If success has many fathers and failure is an orphan, then the 'Ed Stone' was a bastard child whose birth certificate had been shredded before being incinerated.

John Rentoul, *The Independent*'s chief political commentator and biographer of Tony Blair, described the stone as the 'most absurd, ugly, embarrassing, childish, silly, patronising, ridiculous gimmick I have ever seen'. The columnist Chris Deerin tweeted: 'The heaviest suicide note in history'.

Another unhelpful comparison with Neil Kinnock was made, this time with the former leader's 'Sheffield moment' when, with a week to go until polling in the 1992 general election, Kinnock got carried away with himself and repeatedly shouted 'All right!' at his screaming audience using a strange (and decidedly un-prime ministerial) mid-Atlantic accent.

Miliband wasn't screaming, although columnist Dan Hodges reported the reaction of one Labour press officer, on seeing the live coverage of the stone's unveiling. When it appeared on TV, Hodges wrote, the press officer 'started screaming. He stood in the office, just screaming over and over again at the screen. It was so bad they thought he was having a breakdown.'

The fallout from this particular farce might have barely infringed on the local campaigns of many Labour candidates, who were not finding their own hurdles hard to encounter. Anticipating a good performance by the SNP, the Conservatives had released a campaign poster depicting a tiny Ed Miliband in the pocket of a towering Nicola Sturgeon, reinforcing the message that a vote for Labour was a vote for a government that would put Scotland's interests before those of England. The theme worked just as effectively for the SNP in Scotland, where former Labour voters were reassured that their switch to the SNP would still result in a Labour-led government, notwithstanding Miliband's denials during the campaign. In shipbuilding towns such as Plymouth, but also in more dispersed areas such as Derby and Telford,

Labour activists found themselves having to deny that Sturgeon would have any say over Prime Minister Miliband.

At 10.00 p.m. on Thursday 7 May, the BBC announced the results of its exit poll. The Conservatives were on course for 316 seats – ten short of an overall majority; Labour were predicted to win 239 – nearly twenty fewer than in 2010; the Lib Dems would drop from fifty-seven in 2010 to just ten; and the SNP would win all but one of Scotland's fifty-nine seats.

The immediate reaction from Labour HQ was genuine disbelief; for hours afterwards those around Miliband maintained their strongly held – and in their view, evidence-based – view that Labour would still prevail, that the polls were wrong. Dan Hodges reported one Labour MP telling him: 'Up until 2.30 a.m. on Friday morning we were still being told we were going to win the election. I was told, "Don't worry, we're getting the samples from the counts fed back, and they're showing it's okay. The exit poll is wrong. Our numbers are still holding up."'

The numbers did not hold up. Against all expectations, not only did the Conservatives emerge as the single largest party, Cameron became the first Tory leader since John Major to win an overall majority, albeit a relatively narrow one of twelve. The final declared results showed that the BBC's exit poll had in fact been devastatingly accurate: the Conservatives won 330 (fourteen more than predicted), Labour 232 (seven fewer than the exit poll suggested) and the Lib Dems eight (two short of the exit poll prediction). The SNP took fifty-six out of fifty-nine seats in Scotland, leaving Labour, the Conservatives and the Lib Dems with a solitary seat each.

Labour had performed especially badly compared with virtually every published opinion poll. Its 30.4 per cent of the vote was well below the average poll rating throughout the campaign; of the ninety-five polls published, only seven had put Labour on 30 per cent or less. And yet the final tally told its own story: with barely more seats than the party had won at the 1987 general election, and a virtually identical share of the vote, Labour had suffered a brutal defeat. The shadow Chancellor, Ed Balls, lost his West Yorkshire seat of Morley and Outwood. The shadow Foreign Secretary, Douglas Alexander, was gone too, as was Jim Murphy, the leader of Scottish Labour. In fact the party's entire Scottish heartland was gone – and not even marginally. Glasgow North East, seen as one of the safest Labour seats in the UK, let alone Scotland, experienced a two-party swing to the SNP of a colossal, genuinely unprecedented 39.5 per cent. Five-figure majorities enjoyed by Labour MPs for decades were replaced by similarly sized SNP majorities. Even the Kirkcaldy seat of retiring MP and former Prime Minister Gordon Brown fell victim to the nationalist tsunami. In the aftermath of the independence referendum, those Scots who had voted Yes, irrespective of their previous party alignment, had voted uniformly for the local nationalist candidate, while the support of the majority who had voted to preserve the Union was split three ways.

One defeated Scottish Labour MP, who had been in office since the 1980s, had had enough public humiliation for one lifetime and decided to travel to London the day after the election in order to clear out his House of Commons office, believing a clean and quick break would lessen the pain. He was therefore not best pleased to discover that another passenger on the plane that day was First Minister Nicola Sturgeon. As she entered the aircraft, she was greeted by a spontaneous and enthusiastic round of applause and cheers from the other passengers. The former MP's reaction to this public display of support is not recorded.

The nationalist effect took its toll in England too, with defeated and near-defeated MPs relaying the same message: English voters did not warm to the idea of a Labour government, especially one at the beck and call of the nationalists.

The victory was Cameron's. As Prime Minister in his own right for the first time, he would surely ride out the next four or five years as master of the political landscape, having earned the gratitude of a party now returned to what it regarded as its natural birthright: government.

But the defeat was Miliband's.

The next day, in front of an audience of Labour activists and journalists in Westminster, Ed Miliband announced his resignation that same day as leader. 'This is not a speech I ever wanted to make,' he told his tearful audience. 'I take absolute and total responsibility for the result.'

Taking the lead from his predecessor, Miliband wasn't hanging around. His deputy, Harriet Harman, would, for the second time in her career, step up as acting leader until a replacement for Miliband was elected.

Nominations for leader of the Labour Party opened on Tuesday 9 June 2015.

CHAPTER NINE

OUTSIDE LEFT

It is not possible to understand the difficulties of the Labour Party from 2015 without understanding the nature of the British far left and the Labour Party's relationship with it.

British socialism has, since the nineteenth century, split along two separate paths. The first, the larger movement, dominated by the trade unions which gave birth to the Labour Party at the very start of the twentieth century, was committed to working within the parliamentary system in which it found itself. This vein of socialism had little time for Marxist theory and was, most of the time, wholly committed to achieving the 'New Jerusalem' following a democratic vote in the House of Commons by a duly elected majority comprised of Labour Party MPs. Although the 'broad church' the party was said to be included individuals on the left who occasionally sought common cause with more radical remnants beyond the party, and although such ecumenism was frequently the cause of internal party strife, Labour was democratic first, socialist second.

The other vein of socialism was advocated by those who read Marx, Engels, Lenin and Trotsky. They were inclined to the view that the Russian revolutions of 1917 had swept away an aristocracy and a system that couldn't be dealt with any other way, and hoped that history might repeat itself everywhere else on the globe, including in Britain. Ideological purity among such activists led to frequent and sometimes violent splits over the years, between those who wholeheartedly supported Stalin's ruthless purges and encroachments on other nations' sovereignty, and those who condemned the same leader for betraying the revolution. This latter group found comfort and inspiration in the writings of Leon Trotsky, Stalin's bitter enemy who had fled to exile rather than risk execution in Russia. It was Trotsky who advocated the tactic of entryism by his followers in mainstream political parties of the left operating in democratic countries beyond the Soviet Union. By the 1960s and 1970s, debates and conflicts between and among all the various splinter groups of the Trotskyite and Marxist left were raging across university and college campuses in the UK. While most Trotskyists cultivated their own ideological purity in their own parties such as the Socialist Workers' Party, the International Socialist League the International Marxist Group, the Revolutionary Socialist League and the Spartacists, others started to view the Labour Party as ripe for infiltration.

Ever since Ramsay MacDonald, Labour's first Prime Minister, abandoned the party in 1931 to form a national government with the Conservatives, the narrative of betrayal has played a central role in the relationship between the broader left and the Labour Party. The accusations from student demonstrators and even some left-wing Labour MPs would begin early in each Labour administration's life: anything short of a complete restructuring of the economy and the nationalisation of every private company – including the hated banks and the newspapers – was conceding to the capitalist system. Harold Wilson, who led Labour to four general election victories over the space of a decade from 1964, was a hate figure among the radical left, both beyond the party and within it. During the 1960s, Labour Party branches and general management committees (GMCs) of local constituency parties started to notice the arrival of angry, articulate and revolutionary elements signing up as members, many of whom quickly assumed positions of influence among the office bearers. This trend accelerated in the 1970s, and although there was never a point at which a majority of local parties found themselves under the influence of the Trotskyites, their commitment and their organisational abilities gave them more influence than their actual numbers justified. Chief among the entryist groups was Militant, named after the newspaper its members sold religiously, founded in 1964. Throughout the 1970s and into the early 1980s, Militant organised relatively openly in the Labour Party, thanks either to the tolerance of other more mainstream members or to their tendency to stop attending meetings as the Militant presence made meetings less attractive, more confrontational and, in many cases, simply more boring. These tactics were used deliberately to gain a foothold in hundreds of local parties throughout the country. Bullying and intimidation were the standard weapons to be used by the comrades for the greater good of the people's revolution, whenever it may come.

Once ensconced within a local Labour Party branch, activists would focus on making life difficult for the sitting Labour MP, if there happened to be one representing the constituency. National influence for Militant could best be achieved by the replacement of sitting Labour MPs – many of whom were, in fact, lazy and complacent in their sinecure – by committed members of Militant who would use their position in the Commons to fight the workers' corner and would never, ever compromise with the bosses. The only problem in the way of such a strategy was that until the early 1980s there were no systems in place to get rid of MPs as Labour candidates in between elections. Unless a parliamentarian was caught publicly in some devious and egregious behaviour, he or she (mostly he) could expect to remain as candidate, and therefore as MP, until they retired at a moment of their own choosing.

The Campaign for Labour Party Democracy (CLPD) was formed in 1973 to bring about exactly the kind of change to the party's rules and culture that Militant and its fellow travellers wished. Its aim was not only to introduce mandatory reselection of MPs between general elections, but to change the party's rules so that the leader himself would no longer be elected exclusively by Labour MPs, but by the Labour conference as a whole, with trade union and constituency delegates having a say. Only by securing such a change could the party feel confident that its leaders would think twice before obeying their natural instincts and betraying the workers once safely in office.

The catalyst for CLPD's advance came in 1979, with Jim Callaghan's ejection from office and his administration's replacement by Margaret Thatcher's Conservative government. The 1980 Labour conference agreed to create an electoral college to replace MPs' exclusive franchise for electing the leader and agreed that a special conference, to be held early the following year, would determine the precise share of the vote each section of the party would have in future leadership elections. The decision prompted Jim Callaghan, still leader at the time, to announce his resignation shortly afterwards, in order to avoid his successor being chosen by the new system. Unexpectedly, Callaghan's preferred candidate, the shadow Chancellor Denis Healey, was beaten in the final round by the left-winger, Michael Foot, giving encouragement to those who sought a more red-blooded and truly socialist election platform.

At the special conference at Wembley on 24 January 1981, thanks to last-minute confusion and failures of co-operation between the largest trade union players, the final deal reached on the electoral college was less than satisfactory and was itself the cause of much negative news coverage. Instead of a college where MPs retained up to half of the share of the vote for leader, parliamentarians were relegated to just 30 per cent. Labour party members – represented through their GMCs – held another 30 per cent, while trade unions were given the lion's share of 40 per cent. It was a presentational nightmare and was greeted with jubilation by the CLPD, Militant and the Conservative Party.

Foot, despite being a man of the left, found himself forced into a position of having to take strong action against the central players in Militant, forcing their expulsion from the party in 1982. Nevertheless, many of their followers remained active in constituency parties and in local Labour-controlled councils. Ironically, the first Labour leader to have been elected for the first time by the electoral college process (Foot had himself been re-elected unopposed throughout his tenure, ostensibly via the college), Neil Kinnock, also proved to be Militant's nemesis. Impatient for a Labour victory after two devastating general election defeats, Kinnock recognised that Militant were not friends but parasites. His dramatic intervention, in 1985, against the Militant group that had taken control of Liverpool City Council and which had risked the livelihoods of thousands of workers in order to make a political point about the government's rate-capping regime, became an iconic moment for the party. Kinnock's conference speech, in which he condemned the far left's 'far-fetched resolutions', which are then 'pickled into a rigid dogma, a code', transformed his reputation in a wholly positive light and had the added bonus of forcing hard-left apologist Eric Heffer to flounce off the platform in support of the council's leaders, Derek Hatton and Tony Mulhearn. Kinnock followed the speech with a campaign to rid the party of the Trotskyites once and for all – inevitably labelled a 'witch hunt' by Militant and their supporters inside and outside the party.

Throughout the rest of the decade, emboldened by Kinnock's leadership and supported by party headquarters, Labour members conducted local investigations throughout the country with the aim of expelling those who were found to be members of Militant which, from the early 1980s, was deemed by Labour's National Executive Committee (NEC) an organisation 'ineligible for affiliation to the party nationally' because it pursued its own separate and incompatible political agenda and policies.

And throughout this period, as courageous individuals at local and national levels of the party stood up to Militant and their many fellow travellers, enduring intimidation and even legal action in pursuit of their aim of cleaning up the party, there were those who stood by and condemned such actions, who defended the right of Militant members to remain in the Labour Party. Chief among the Militant apologists was Tony Benn, the leading supporter of the CLPD's aims and the man who needlessly exposed the almost precisely 50/50 split between right and left in the Labour movement by insisting on challenging Healey for the deputy leadership in 1981. But Benn was not alone. Other members of the Socialist Campaign Group of MPs (normally shortened simply to 'Campaign Group') shared Benn's tolerance for the entryists and reserved their criticism for Labour's leadership, rather than those who had sought to subvert the democratic aims and principles of

the party. Throughout the years, the Campaign Group's membership has varied from election to election, but at various times has
included Benn, Dennis Skinner, Diane Abbott, John McDonnell
and Ken Livingstone as well as self-confessed Militant members
Pat Wall, Terry Fields and Dave Nellist. While tolerating and even
welcoming those Militant members who used the Labour Party to
win election to Parliament, the Campaign Group itself had never
overtly supported the Trotskyite aim of socialist revolution, even
if it had frequently supported some of the same individual policies
espoused by Militant.

In 1983, the Campaign Group welcomed the new MP for Islington North, Jeremy Corbyn, to its ranks. Corbyn, then thirty-four
years old, had played an active role in Benn's deputy leadership
campaign two years previously, was a member of the executive of
the CLPD and a prominent supporter of the 'Defeat The Witch
Hunt' campaign that opposed the party leadership's expulsion of
Militant. As chairman of his local Constituency Labour Party
(CLP) in London, Corbyn had also supported the campaign by
the Marxist writer Tariq Ali to have his exclusion from membership of the party reversed.

Born on 26 May 1949, the fourth son of comfortably well-off
middle-class parents, Corbyn was raised in Wiltshire and then
Shropshire, where he attended the independent Castle House
Preparatory School and Adams' Grammar School. He inherited
his radical instincts from his parents, Naomi and David, who
had met while attending a meeting in support of the republicans
during the Spanish Civil War.

Corbyn was not of an academic bent, and although he started a
college degree in trade union studies at North London Polytechnic,
he left before the end of the course and without a qualification. He

was active in the Campaign for Nuclear Disarmament (CND) and spent the early part of his working life as a full-time organiser for the National Union of Tailors and Garment Workers, then later for the National Union of Public Employees (NUPE) and the Amalgamated Engineering and Electrical Union (AEEU). He was elected to Haringey Council in 1974, a post he held until his election to the Commons in 1983. Like the rest of the hard left, he was a critic of both Wilson's and Jim Callaghan's governments of the 1970s.

Throughout the 1980s, including the period while he was an MP, Corbyn was closely associated with *London Labour Briefing* (shortened, following its launch in 1980, to *Labour Briefing*), a left-wing magazine whose parliamentary supporters included Benn and which promoted an assortment of left-wing causes, as well as support for a united Ireland and the Provisional IRA. Corbyn, during the 2017 general election, denied what had been widely reported without previous challenge: specifically that he had served as a member of the *Labour Briefing* editorial board. He was certainly closely involved in its production and distribution, a fact he never felt necessary to contradict until after he became leader of the Labour Party. The hard left had long supported the 'Troops Out' movement, dedicated as much to landing a blow against the UK as part of the hated 'imperialist' Western powers as it was about democracy on the island of Ireland. It was a cause with which Corbyn had been associated throughout his public life; he could have chosen to support the constitutional Irish nationalists of the Social Democratic and Labour Party (SDLP), with its links to the Labour Party via the Socialist International, the umbrella group for the world's progressive democratic left. Instead, Corbyn chose to lend his public and political support to Sinn Féin, the political wing of the IRA. Just weeks after terrorists had attempted to assassinate the British Prime Minister and her government by detonating a bomb at the Grand Hotel in Brighton in October 1984 – an attack that left five people dead and many others injured, including Margaret Tebbit (the wife of the then President of the Board of Trade, Norman Tebbit) who was left permanently confined to a wheelchair – Corbyn played host to Sinn Féin members, including its leader, Gerry Adams, in the Commons. This was followed in December of the same year by a statement published in *Labour Briefing* reaffirming the magazine's 'support for, and solidarity with, the Irish republican movement' and to 'fight for and secure an unconditional British withdrawal' from Northern Ireland. It added: 'It certainly appears to be the case that the British only sit up and take notice when they are bombed into it.' As Alex Massie of *The Spectator* reported in 2016, this statement had been preceded by another in *Labour Briefing* that crystallised the chasm between the magazine and mainstream Labour as represented by the party's then leader, Neil Kinnock: 'We refuse to parrot the ritual condemnation of "violence" because we insist on placing responsibility where it lies … Let our "Iron Lady" know this: those who live by the sword shall die by it. If she wants violence, then violence she will certainly get.'

Massie wrote:

There is no room for doubt about this and no place for after-the-fact reinterpretations of Corbyn's 'role' in the Irish peace process. That role was limited to being a cheerleader for and enabler of the republican movement. No one who was seriously interested in peace in the 1980s spoke at Troops Out rallies. The best that could be said of those people was that they wanted 'peace' on the IRA's terms. In other words, they wanted the IRA to win.

Three years after the Brighton bombing, during the 1987 general election campaign, Corbyn was reported to have stood in respectful silence during an event at Conway Hall in London, in tribute to an IRA gang that had been attempting to blow up a Northern Ireland police station when they were ambushed and killed by British soldiers.

Corbyn's choice of causes in the next thirty years as a Labour MP reflected those supported by the broader left: he insisted he was not a pacifist, yet opposed every military conflict in which Britain found itself involved, including the first Gulf War in 1991, Afghanistan from 2001 and, of course, the second war in Iraq in 2003. He maintained his early support for CND and strongly opposed the abandonment of Labour's unilateral disarmament policy by the party's annual conference in 1989. And in his long-term opposition to Israel, he found himself in common cause not only with Yasser Arafat's Palestinian Liberation Organisation (PLO) but also, in later years, with the Islamist terrorist organisation Hamas.

And Corbyn's advocacy in support of such groups and causes was not limited to addressing rallies and sharing cups of tea on the Commons Terrace; as a backbench MP he became a regular guest on Press TV, the UK-based broadcaster owned and controlled by the Iranian state and deprived of its broadcast licence in 2012. Corbyn's placid acceptance, without demur, of the description of Israel as 'the Zionist entity' by one Press TV presenter while the MP sat behind her politely listening, obviously endeared him to the station's bosses.

It is not quite true to suggest that, because Corbyn is reported to have rebelled against the Blair and Brown governments on more than 500 occasions, he was unable to respect a party whip; in fact he was an enthusiastic supporter of collective action, provided the collective in question was the Campaign Group, whose decisions and policy positions he faithfully supported throughout his time in Parliament.

The Campaign Group, while its composition and size – both proportionately and absolutely – had changed over the years, had never been as influential within the wider PLP as its members would have liked. In the early 1980s, it was certainly a force to be taken account of by the leadership, if not necessarily one that had to be reckoned with. But in later years, as the modernisation of the party progressed under Kinnock, Smith and Blair, and as popular support for, and acceptance of, the Labour Party grew, the Campaign Group virtually disappeared off the radar in terms of influence and credibility. When, in May 2003, John McDonnell spoke at a commemoration event for the late IRA terrorist Bobby Sands, he told the audience: 'It's about time we started honouring those people involved in the armed struggle. It was the bombs and bullets and sacrifice made by the likes of Bobby Sands that brought Britain to the negotiating table. The peace we have now is due to the action of the IRA.'

The remarks provoked an inevitable storm of protest from the Conservatives and from Unionist politicians in Northern Ireland. But whereas the Labour leadership took action against prominent anti-war MP George Galloway when, in 2003, he called on British soldiers serving in Iraq not to obey 'illegal orders', and asked why other Arab nations were not coming to the aid of the Iraqi people, no such action was forthcoming against McDonnell. It is perhaps an indication of how irrelevant and marginalised the Campaign Group and its members had become that Peter Watt, then heading up the party's constitutional unit and therefore responsible for enforcing the party's rulebook, cannot even recall the event happening. 'I can't remember anything at all about the McDonnell comments,' he says. 'But I remember exactly where I was when I heard what Galloway said.'

At each leadership election, it was expected that the group would nominate one of its number as the ritual sacrifice to the electoral process in order to 'make its voice heard' and 'give the membership a real choice'. While the group was occasionally successful in getting one of its number onto the ballot paper – Diane Abbott in the 2010 contest made it after securing the nomination of colleagues who had no intention of following through and actually supporting her, one of whom was the then favourite to win the contest, David Miliband – there were other times when the strategy was less successful (see Chapter One).

While Labour was a broad movement as well as a political party, incorporating the grassroots volunteer party and the trade union movement as well as the parliamentary party, its constitution demanded it be led by an MP in acknowledgement that its first political priority was to form a government and to elect a Prime Minister. And in any parliamentary system, it's vital that the leader enjoys the support of his or her MPs. This is why MPs rather than local parties have exclusive nomination rights. Local constituency parties, trades unions and affiliated socialist societies may offer supporting nominations, but only after MPs have decided which candidates are to be placed on the ballot paper. And following the Collins Review initiated by Ed Miliband (see Chapter Six), the nominating threshold had been increased from 12.5 to 15 per cent, in acknowledgement of the importance of this principle, even as the decisive 'block vote' previously enjoyed by MPs in the electoral college had been abolished.

As the Labour Party came to terms with its defeat at the 2015 general election, attention started to turn to the question of who would replace Miliband, and the Campaign Group met to decide who it should support.

CHAPTER TEN

BROADENING THE DEBATE

F ive years earlier, the assumption had been that David Miliband would succeed Gordon Brown. In 2015, the (admittedly
less widely held) assumption was that the Leigh MP and shadow
Health Secretary, Andy Burnham, would win the crown.

Burnham was known to be ambitious. He was also known
to have been bitterly disappointed by his fourth-place result in
2010. This time, his supporters believed, the omens were far more
propitious. A former special adviser to Chris Smith, the Culture
Secretary under Tony Blair, Burnham had been elected to the
Commons in 2001 and won promotion to the government in
2005, first as a junior minister at the Home Office and then, a
year later, as minister of state at the Department of Health. Under
Gordon Brown he had served as Chief Secretary to the Treasury, Culture Secretary and latterly as Health Secretary. Having
been roundly defeated for the leadership in 2010, Burnham spent
the next five years – mostly as shadow Health Secretary – cul-
tivating a left-wing image that was at odds with his earlier life
as a Blairite, generally opposing private-sector involvement in
the NHS.

When Miliband announced his resignation as leader the day

after the 2015 general election, Burnham was ready to make his second bid. But he was not the first out of the trap.

Liz Kendall had been elected to the Commons representing the Leicester West seat of her former boss, the Health Secretary, Patricia Hewitt, for whom Kendall had worked as a special adviser under Tony Blair. She had performed well as an MP but as shadow minister for Care and Older People, her immediate boss was Burnham. Rumours of behind-the-scenes friction between the two were rarely denied with any level of conviction. Even before the general election, Kendall had been talked of as a potential leader in the event of a Labour defeat at the polls, talk that Kendall did little to discourage. She was known to be impatient with the left-wing, anti-business direction in which Miliband was taking the party and in which her boss, Burnham, acquiesced in and encouraged, despite his recent past as a Blairite moderniser. Kendall also felt, with some justification, that she had been unfairly excluded from the shadow Cabinet at the expense of less capable colleagues who had entered Parliament at the same time as her.

On 10 May, she became the first candidate officially to announce her candidacy. A total of 232 Labour MPs had been elected the previous week. In order for Kendall (and any other candidate) to secure a place on the final ballot paper that would be sent out to all members, she had to be nominated by 15 per cent of that number: thirty-five.

Two days after Kendall announced she would stand, the man whom many tipped as a potential frontrunner made his own declaration of intent. Chuka Umunna had been the MP for Streatham since 2010 and had quickly been promoted to the front bench as shadow Business Secretary. An able and articulate parliamentarian, Umunna also hailed from the right wing of the party, and launched his leadership bid with an unashamed call for Labour to target the better-off middle classes as well as the poorer in society.

The next day, on 13 May, via a slick, professionally produced YouTube video, Burnham announced his candidacy, telling members he wanted to 'rediscover the beating heart of Labour'. On the same day, Yvette Cooper, the shadow Home Secretary, announced, via the *Daily Mirror*, that she too would stand.

And then there were three: on 15 May, just three days after his original announcement, Umunna unexpectedly and, to many people, inexplicably withdrew from the campaign, citing concerns over media intrusion and family pressures for his swift change of heart.

Three other candidates had publicly expressed an interest in standing, provided they could secure the nominations. Tristram Hunt, the historian and MP for Stoke Central, another of the 2010 intake, perhaps timed his intervention badly and found the field already crowded with candidates representing the Blairite wing of the party. Similarly, the shadow International Development Secretary and Wakefield MP, Mary Creagh, initially declared her desire to be a candidate, but conceded defeat when the required number of nominations proved unattainable.

The third candidate was Jeremy Corbyn.

The Campaign Group had held its traditional post-election defeat meeting at the Commons, at which a volunteer was sought to represent the true socialist tradition of the party in the forthcoming contest. Even at this stage, there was a lack of awareness of just how profoundly the nature of Miliband's reforms to the party rulebook had changed things. The scrapping of the electoral college and the introduction of one member, one vote (OMOV), with neither the unions nor the party's MPs having a weighted, decisive block, was, at the start of the leadership contest, not considered particularly important, especially as MPs retained their exclusive right to nominate.

Corbyn later told *The Guardian* what made him decide to run: 'Well, Diane [Abbott] and John [McDonnell] have done it before, so it was my turn.' He added: 'At my age I'm not likely to be a long-term contender, am I?' Corbyn was sixty-six.

And if there hadn't been a selection contest for another vital Labour Party position – that of candidate for the 2016 London mayoral election – the leadership election might have taken an altogether different course.

Boris Johnson, the colourful Tory mayor, had sought and won election as an MP at the recent general election and would occupy both positions until the following year when a new Tory candidate would stand in London. Labour had always considered the capital as its territory and felt the loss to Johnson in 2008 keenly. With Labour set for at least another five years in opposition at Westminster, the prospect of an elected position with actual, real executive power was an attractive one to ambitious and frustrated London MPs.

Applications for the post opened on 13 May, four days after nominations for Labour leader opened. Of the six candidates who made it onto the final ballot paper, four were serving MPs: Sadiq Khan (Tooting), Diane Abbott (Hackney North & Stoke Newington), David Lammy (Tottenham) and Gareth Thomas (Harrow West). Two other candidates made the final ballot paper: Dame Tessa Jowell, a former MP and Cabinet Minister, and Christian Wolmar, the transport expert and writer.

Nominations for Labour leader were required to be submitted to the Parliamentary Labour Party (PLP) office in the cloisters, in the lower levels of the Commons, near the entrance to the Members' cloakroom. Deadlines were usually strictly adhered to: if a candidate tried to submit a last-minute nomination at any point beyond the agreed cut-off point, party staff were authorised to refuse them. The deadline in 2015 was 12.00 noon on Monday 15 June.

On 12 June, it was reported that Corbyn had managed to secure a total of seventeen nominations – eighteen short of the thirty-five necessary. But, according to a report on the Total Politics website, the Islington North MP repeatedly emphasised his motivation for standing: 'I want to see a proper debate within the party. Essentially there's going to be that debate anyway because there are many in the party, and many members who joined the party, because they want something different. So that debate's going to happen and I will certainly be part of that debate whatever the outcome.' But in response to the suggestion by Andy Burnham that, magnanimously for an assumed victor, the Leigh MP might consider offering a 'helping hand' to those who cannot otherwise raise the number of nominations needed, Corbyn replied: 'I want people to choose of their own volition, I don't want charity.'

But charity is what he got. With barely five minutes to go until the close of nominations, Corbyn arrived, triumphantly, at the PLP offices with his nomination papers containing the names of thirty-six colleagues, including his own. Among them were David Lammy, Gareth Thomas and Sadiq Khan, none of whom were known to be remotely sympathetic to Corbyn's far-left political agenda. Nevertheless, from this point onwards, they could (and would) use their comradely gesture as part of their appeals to activists in whose hands the decision of who would represent the party in the mayoral election the following year rested. If just two of those thirty-six MPs had declined to support Corbyn, the future history of the Labour Party would have been very different.

Corbyn's confirmation as a candidate was greeted with delight by his supporters (in the Labour Party and far beyond it) and with fury and despondency by others. John Mann, the MP for Bassetlaw, said Corbyn's candidacy illustrated the party's lack of desire ever to win a general election again. Jonathan Reynolds (Stalybridge and Hyde), a supporter of Kendall's, said it showed Labour was not taking itself seriously.

Immediately, the centre of gravity of the contest shifted decisively to the left. Kendall, who had made an early positive impression, at least with the media, found herself increasingly isolated, bravely refusing to say what her audiences wanted to hear but increasingly incapable of reaping the benefits such courage might otherwise have delivered. Burnham, whose left-wing credentials had been brought into question since he first declared, now found himself outflanked on the left to a degree he could never have anticipated. Cooper, who had planned to present herself as the compromise candidate between Kendall's Blairism and Burnham's born-again leftism, found such triangulation pointless once Corbyn had entered the race with his well-known positions on disarmament, nationalisation and anti-establishment rhetoric.

Even before Corbyn's arrival on the ballot paper transformed the contest, worried attention was being turned to the new electoral system, a system that had never before been tested. The Collins reforms endorsed by Miliband and subsequently by special conference, not only introduced OMOV, but gave a vote to newly enrolled 'registered' and 'associate' members as well as to longer-term party loyalists. Associate membership was open to any member of an affiliated trade union or other organisation, while anyone who wished to have a vote in the forthcoming election could sign up before 12 August in order to do so, provided they paid a fee of £3. It was a system which, in hindsight, its creators might have identified as ripe for exploitation by individuals without the best interests of the Labour Party at heart. Conservative-supporting journalists such as Toby Young made great sport of his application to become a supporting member, and helped found the tongue-in-cheek 'Tories For Corbyn' campaign; when asked during the online sign-up process why he wished to become a registered member, he reportedly replied: 'To consign Labour to electoral oblivion.' His membership was subsequently revoked by media-aware Labour Party officials.

But despite reassurances by deputy leader Harriet Harman that 'due diligence' would be applied to make sure that only genuine Labour supporters took part in the election, there was little doubt that those who wished, for whatever reason, to buy a vote would be able to do so.

From the very early stages of the campaign, perhaps because of the sudden awareness of the unpredictability of the new electoral system, Corbyn's campaign began noticeably to get traction. His campaign meetings were by far the best attended of all the candidates' events, and they quickly became rallies rather than meetings. The energy and enthusiasm of Corbyn's supporters, and the large numbers of younger people in their ranks, made the campaigns of Kendall, Burnham and Cooper look stale, managerial and conventional by comparison. The latter three had become used – perhaps too used – to defending the harsh realities of government, to the need to accept the inevitability of compromise in order to win general elections. But this was not a general election, and this electorate was miles away from the voters whose judgement every four or five years decided who would govern the country. Labour had changed in the five years since the rank and file mirrored their parliamentary representatives and voted for David Miliband to be leader. The reality of politics was no longer the order of the day; that was what was on offer from Burnham, Cooper and Kendall. What was on offer from Corbyn was what the left-winger had told audiences throughout his career as a backbencher: whatever they wanted to hear.

As fears among moderate centrist and right-wing MPs grew over Corbyn's apparent popularity and momentum, they maintained a belief that the left-winger's many injudicious comments recorded in the past would yet derail his campaign. One such opportunity arose during an interview with Krishnan Guru-Murthy for *Channel 4 News* on 13 July. In March 2009, Corbyn, in his capacity as chair of the Stop the War Coalition, had addressed one of its events entitled 'Meet The Resistance', the 'resistance' in question being the opposition to Israel. In his remarks at the beginning of the meeting, Corbyn told an admiring audience: 'Tomorrow evening it will be my pleasure and my honour to host an event in Parliament where our friends from Hezbollah will be speaking. I've also invited friends from Hamas to come and speak as well; unfortunately the Israelis would not allow them to travel here, so it's going to be only friends from Hezbollah. As far as I'm concerned that is absolutely the right function of using parliamentary facilities...'

Both Hezbollah and Hamas are recognised internationally as terrorist organisations. When challenged on his use of the term 'friends' to describe them, Corbyn became aggressive and defensive. 'What I did was I spoke at a meeting in which I said I wanted all people involved in the Middle East issue to come together and be able to have a discussion, to be able to ...' At this point,

Guru-Murthy attempted to interject a supplementary question, at which Corbyn, known for his placid and courteous demeanour, erupted: 'Can you allow me to finish? Do you mind?'

The interview, bad-tempered throughout, at least on Corbyn's part, continued, with the leadership candidate offering as a defence his view that peace in the Middle East could only be achieved with dialogue involving all sides. On the question of the use of the term 'friends' to describe Hamas and Hezbollah, he said: 'I use [the term] in a collective way saying our friends are prepared to talk. Does it mean I agree with Hamas and what it does? No. Does it mean I agree with Hezbollah and what they do? No. What it means is that I think to bring about a peace process you have to talk to people with whom you may profoundly disagree.' Further challenged on his use of the term 'friends', Corbyn lost patience with his interviewer. 'You're trying to trivialise the whole issue of the Middle East, you're trying to trivialise the whole discussion about how you bring about a long-term peace process. And you know that!'

And as the interview left that particular subject behind, Corbyn told Guru-Murthy, 'Thanks for the tabloid journalism.'

It sounded – and was – petty and childish behaviour. A fundamental characteristic of the British left is its antagonism towards, and suspicion of, the mainstream media which, in its eyes, constantly fails to offer fair, balanced reporting of the issues dear to its heart. This initial, uncomfortable confrontation would set the tone for much of Corbyn's relations with journalists in the future.

As to his defence itself, it was becoming apparent that even a politician of such perceived purity was capable of rowing back on some of his previously expressed views, of dissembling in order to achieve electoral advantage, something which he and his comrades had regularly poured scorn on others for doing. More substantially, Corbyn was now rewriting his own history, with the Middle East as well as with Northern Ireland: friendly chats in the House of Commons with people who represented organisations that bombed hotels at seaside resorts in the UK or who organised suicide bombers in Tel Aviv restaurants were reframed as efforts to achieve peace.

At the beginning of August, Corbyn's past threatened to catch up with him again, during a phone interview with the broadcaster Stephen Nolan on BBC Radio Ulster. Asked repeatedly to condemn IRA bombing in Northern Ireland, Corbyn pointedly refused, falling back on his tried and tested 'I condemn all bombing.'

When Nolan persisted, asking if Corbyn specifically condemned the IRA, the leadership candidate replied: 'Look, I condemn what was done by the British Army as well as the other sides as well. What happened in Derry in 1972 [Bloody Sunday] was pretty devastating as well.'

The *Telegraph* reported:

When the question was put to him a third time, he said: 'Can I answer the question in this way? We gained ceasefires, they were important and a huge step forward. Those ceasefires brought about the peace process, brought about the reconciliation process which we should all be pleased about. Can we take the thing forward rather than backward?'

Nolan again asked: 'Are you refusing to condemn what the IRA did?' At which point railway noise could be heard in the background. Corbyn said that he could not hear the question because he was travelling on a train and had a poor signal. Asked the question a fifth time, Corbyn said: 'I feel we will have to do this later...', before the line went dead.

Corbyn's past – and his determination not to resile from it – seemed to cause the electorate in the 2015 Labour leadership election little cause for concern. A private survey, leaked to the *New Statesman* on 15 July, showed that, based on the nominations received by each candidate from local constituency Labour parties at that stage, Burnham led with 39 per cent, with Corbyn in second place at 33, Cooper on 20 and Kendall on 4 per cent. But the headline was generated when second preferences were redistributed: the survey put Corbyn fifteen points ahead of his nearest rival, Burnham.

The narrative of the contest was now decided. The momentum was Corbyn's and, helped, ironically, by the media he despised, a media that recognised a 'man bites dog' story when it saw one, his energetic campaign continued towards the finish line on 12 September, when the result would be declared.

A week after the *New Statesman* story, a decisive moment in the campaign arrived; decisive for much of the membership, at least. Cameron's government, determined to continue its reforms of the benefits system, had introduced a Welfare Bill, whose measures included the scrapping of the obligation on the government to report on progress towards abolishing child poverty, and included a reduction in support for poorer workers in the shape of cuts to tax credits. Shadow Work and Pensions Secretary Stephen Timms told the House of Commons that while Labour supported a benefits cap and other measures in the Bill, it could not support it at Second Reading because the Bill 'breaks promises that the Conservative Party made before the election to protect sick and disabled people'.

But Labour would not oppose the Bill outright. Harriet Harman, still in charge as acting leader, had decided that Labour would move an amendment to the Bill but, on the (correct) assumption that such an amendment would fail, would abstain on the actual Second Reading vote. *The Guardian* had reported, a week earlier, that Harman believed the party 'simply could not tell the public they were wrong after two general election defeats in a row ... adding it had been defeated because it had not been trusted on the economy or benefits.'

Her view was not unanimously welcomed by Labour MPs, however, and forty-eight of them – including Corbyn – rebelled and joined the SNP, the Liberal Democrats, the Democratic Unionists and the Green's sole MP in voting against. As the media narrative about Labour's alleged failure to take a stand in support of the most vulnerable gained ground, Andy Burnham released a statement: 'Tonight I voted for a Labour motion to oppose the Tories' welfare reform bill. It was a motion I had been calling for, because I have been clear all along – we cannot simply abstain on a bill that will penalise working families and increase child poverty.' Burnham also had abstained on the Second Reading vote, as had Cooper and Kendall.

Corbyn's stance was arguably populist, but it was also entirely consistent with his approach throughout his career. For him, welfare reform was, like nuclear disarmament, the Middle East conflict and nationalisation, a binary choice between good and bad. And if, on this welfare bill, Corbyn had voted for the side of Good, that meant his three opponents had supported Bad. On social media his supporters took a leaf out of the playbook of the Scottish Nationalists, who had helped turn the tide against Scottish Labour by portraying its MPs as 'Red Tories'. The same phrase was now deployed with vehemence and disgust against the leadership of the party and the majority of its parliamentarians. Subsequent polls between then and the end of the contest confirmed the findings of the private poll that had first revealed Corbyn's unanticipated advantage. As the date of the conference drew nearer, the evidence suggested that, contrary to all experience and logic, not only was Corbyn well ahead of his main rival – he looked set to win a four-way contest, held under the Alternative Vote (AV) system, on the first round.

July had also seen Corbyn's endorsement by Britain's biggest trade union, Unite, whose general secretary, Len McCluskey, had, in the early part of his career, been a supporter (but not a member) of Militant. In April 2014, during a speech to lobby journalists at the House of Commons, McCluskey had hinted strongly that he might support the creation of a new left-wing 'workers' party' if Labour lost the next year's general election. This was interpreted both as an expression of his personal frustration at Ed Miliband's reluctance to adopt a more blatantly left-wing platform to defeat austerity, and also as a shot across Miliband's bow in an attempt to pressure him to do so.

When Corbyn entered the leadership race, McCluskey, who understood better than most the possibilities that were opened up by the party's adoption of a new leadership election system, threw his and his union's weight behind him. Other major trade unions, including Unison, the Communication Workers' Union (CWU), the Transport Salaried Staffs' Association (TSSA) and the train drivers' union, Aslef, also rallied to Corbyn's banner, while the more moderate trade unions such as Usdaw, the shop workers' union, and the construction union, UCATT, supported Burnham. The steel workers' union, Community, opted to support Cooper.

In a previous era when Labour was stuck in opposition, the party leadership had come to rely on a generation of trade union leaders who were conservative in nature and fiercely loyal to the party. It was the trade unions that had provided the party's 'ballast', that maintained its vital links to the concerns and priorities of ordinary working people and helped defeat extreme leftist policies when they were proposed at annual conference.

No more. Unite was formed as a result of a merger between Amicus (formerly the moderate engineering union, the AEEU) and the Transport and General Workers' Union (TGWU). With McCluskey in charge, Labour's 'ballast' was steering the party in a definite leftwards trajectory. And a new captain was about to assume command.

CHAPTER ELEVEN

'STRONG MESSAGE HERE'

It was all over weeks before the announcement on Saturday 12 September. As the audience of party members, journalists and MPs gathered to hear the result at the Queen Elizabeth II Conference Centre, a stone's throw from the Palace of Westminster, news filtered through that Corbyn had won on the first round with 60 per cent of the vote. Standing at the back of the room, or engaged in some of the many and sometimes petty tasks expected of them, party staff members maintained sullen expressions. Many of them wore black – ties, dresses, suits – partly in ironic jest about the wake today's announcement would presage for the party, and partly as a genuine act of mourning. While the party's general secretary Iain McNicol had been appointed under the leadership of Ed Miliband and could not be described as a Blairite, most of the rest of the senior staff were exactly that – professionals who had dedicated their lives to serving a Labour government. Many of them had been appointed under either Blair or Brown. And they viewed the day's unfolding events with an undisguised mixture of horror and disgust.

Attention turned briefly to the results of the deputy leadership contest, which was announced first, and in which Tom Watson, he of the 'Curry House Coup' against Blair in 2006 and a union fixer in his own right, prevailed in a five-way contest after three rounds of voting.

Watson, although resented by many on the Blairite wing of the party, had nonetheless benefited from their support. Sensing the way the main contest was going, there were plenty of members and MPs willing to swallow any reservations they had about Watson's penchant for political manoeuvring, in fact to make the most of it. By putting Watson in the No. 2 spot in the party, Corbyn's opponents hoped to have helped undermine him even before he was formally announced as winner. This consideration, it should be pointed out, played only a very minor role in Watson's victory: the West Bromwich East MP had built up a broad base of support from across the party, thanks to his various high-profile campaigns, including against the left's traditional pantomime villain, Rupert Murdoch, and in support of press regulation following the *News of the World* hacking scandal in 2011, and his vocal support for the party's link with the trade unions (he was a former political officer with the AEEU, one of the predecessor organisations to Unite; he was also a friend and former flatmate of McCluskey's).

At noon, the results in the leadership ballot were announced. Corbyn had secured 251,417 votes (59.5 per cent), Burnham 80,462 (19 per cent), Cooper 71,928 (17 per cent) and Kendall 18,857 (4.5 per cent).

The former 100–1 outsider took to the stage to give the speech he never imagined he would have to make. In rambling but nonetheless heartfelt comments, Corbyn told conference that people were 'fed up with the injustice and the inequality' that prevailed in the country. 'The media … simply didn't understand the views of young people in our country. They were turned off by the way politics was being conducted. We have to and must change that.'

In fact, despite his reputation as a zealous leftist, the speech scared few horses; bland truisms about poverty were interspersed with the occasional criticism of the government's latest trade union curb, the importance of combatting poverty and offering shelter to refugees. Perhaps this meant the new leader would be prepared to curb his more radical instincts, aware that giving them full vent would seriously damage his efforts to form a coherent frontbench team drawn from across the parliamentary party.

The challenge that constructing such a coalition would pose was demonstrated in the first few seconds of Corbyn's leadership. As he started to speak, the BBC News's ticker tape announced to TV audiences that Jamie Reed, the Copeland MP and shadow Health Minister, had resigned from the front bench, citing Corbyn's 'poorly informed and fundamentally wrong' anti-nuclear views (the Sellafield reprocessing plant was the largest single employer in Reed's constituency and throughout Corbyn's career, his opposition to all things nuclear extended not just to weaponry but to civil energy production). This was followed by announcements that a string of serving shadow Cabinet ministers would refuse to serve in the new regime. Defeated leadership candidates Liz Kendall and Yvette Cooper, shadow Chancellor Chris Leslie, shadow Education Secretary Tristram Hunt, shadow Work and Pensions Secretary Rachel Reeves, shadow Minister for Housing Emma Reynolds and shadow Business Secretary Chuka Umunna all declared they would return to the back benches.

It's important at this stage to understand the mentality of the vast majority of Labour MPs and a significant minority of Labour Party members (including the majority of activists). Corbyn's election as leader had revealed the sharpest ideological divide in the party's history. Those MPs and members who had fought and organised against the hard left at a constituency level were in a state of shock that someone so closely identified with that same sectarianism should have been elevated to the top of the party. 'This wasn't a leadership election, it was a hostile takeover,' said one former frontbencher.

In the early 1980s, Labour had approached the brink, its divisions harshly and dangerously exposed by the challenge by Tony Benn to the incumbent deputy leader, Denis Healey. The ensuing contest between left and right, fraught with bitterness and cries of betrayal from both sides, and the desertion from the party's ranks of those parliamentarians and activists who joined the new SDP, could have destroyed the party entirely. Thanks to the solid support of a trade union movement that understood political realities and a membership that still yearned for electability, the final curtain didn't descend at the time. But thirty years before Corbyn's election as leader, the hard left had only come close to winning the deputy leadership of the party – within 1 per cent of the total vote, in fact. Michael Foot, whatever his drawbacks as a leader, was never of the 'hard' left as generally defined, despite his enthusiasm for unilateral nuclear disarmament. And he was a brilliant parliamentarian, well-read and intellectual, and a fine orator. Corbyn was none of these things but, unlike Foot, he was certainly of the 'hard' left. And now he was the leader – an achievement the left only dreamed about in the 1980s.

For that majority of MPs, outraged and desolate in equal measure by this turn of events, the burning question now was not 'Will a Corbyn leadership work?' but rather 'How long can a Corbyn leadership last?'

* * *

Why did Corbyn win?

Five years earlier, the Campaign Group nominee in the party's leadership contest, Diane Abbott, won less than 3 per cent of members' first preference votes, and barely 4 per cent of trade union and affiliated supporters' support. Yet her personal views were, at the time and since, known to be identical to Corbyn's in most areas. It might be argued that in 2010, before the abolition of the electoral college and the third of the weighted vote wielded by MPs and MEPs, members voted for a candidate whose policies were less to their liking but which were nevertheless more left-wing than what they had been used to in a leader. Yet it was the Blairite David, not the self-described leftist Ed, who ended the final round of voting with the most grassroots support. Perhaps, aware of the influence exercised by their parliamentarians under the electoral college, members saw little point in supporting a more left-wing candidate who they recognised could not win.

The fact is that in those five years of opposition, and particularly in the short three months after nominations for the leadership in the 2015 contest closed, Labour's membership changed.

The centre of gravity among Labour's members was, historically, always to the left of the parliamentary party and, indeed, of Labour voters. Those who join a party and who are prepared to give up their free time to deliver leaflets and knock on doors to proselytise on behalf of that party will inevitably care more about certain issues and consider themselves better informed about policies than the average voter. A greater commitment to a cause is demanded from someone willing to pay money to, and work for, a party than from those invited merely to place a cross in a box every few years. The great crisis points of Labour's modern history, from Hugh Gaitskell's fight to ditch unilateral nuclear disarmament in the 1950s to the internecine warfare that almost engulfed Michael Foot's leadership in the early 1980s, were played out in a context of left v right, with the majority of activists in the former camp. It is a paradox that helped shape the Labour Party (and not always in a healthy way) that the left were much more numerous and influential at constituency level than they ever were in the parliamentary party.

Still, after years of being told by successive leaders – Kinnock, Smith and Blair – that the party needed to reflect the priorities of the voters (and not just its own voters, but beyond the core), the membership seemed to get the message. In the only two meaningful leadership elections before 2015 – 1994 and 2010 – party members revealed themselves as pragmatic rather than ideological.

An analysis by YouGov shortly after the 2015 leadership contest ended revealed that 70,000 of the 423,000 who took part in the election had not voted Labour at the previous general election. Of these, 40,000 had voted for the Green Party, and 92 per cent of these voters had then backed Corbyn for Labour leader. But even among the 350,000 who had voted Labour in May, Corbyn won a plurality of the vote: 54 per cent. However, among longer-standing members – i.e., those who had joined the party before Ed Miliband became leader – Corbyn's support was 44 per cent. Among affiliated members – those who were members by virtue of their membership of an eligible trade union – and among those who paid £3 to become 'supporting members', Corbyn enjoyed high levels of support. Nearly 100,000 had signed up to become full members of the party since the general election: 60 per cent of these supported Corbyn.

While there had been a degree of infiltration of the mischievous Toby Young-type Conservative (see Chapter Ten), Corbyn's support came overwhelmingly from bona fide Labour Party members and supporters.

There is little doubt that Corbyn's entry to the race transformed it, and left the three 'mainstream' candidates flailing. Their messages of having to accept the hard realities of government – and harsh economic measures to balance the nation's books – would have been accepted with a tired resignation by the majority of members, had the same members not been offered an unexpected choice and a different message. It is notable that Corbyn's baggage on, for example, the IRA and his opposition to NATO was no deterrent to those members who embraced his campaign message of total opposition to all government cuts. His offer of radical socialism as a solution to the country's ills may not even have been accepted in its entirety, even by those willing to give him a chance, but it contrasted dramatically with the downbeat realism coming from the Burnham, Cooper and Kendall camps. After thirteen years in government and five years as a 'responsible' opposition (in the eyes of members, if not voters), the grassroots were seduced by the prospect of no longer having to compromise their beliefs. Why settle for half a loaf when they might, after all, seize the whole one?

Why not? What had 'responsible' opposition delivered, after all, other than another five years out of government?

*   *   *

The new leader's first job was to appoint a shadow Cabinet.

Having benefited directly from the reforms to the electoral system used for the leadership implemented by his predecessor, Ed Miliband, Corbyn now suddenly found himself strengthened by another of Miliband's reforms. In 2011, Miliband had asked for, and received, authority from his MPs to abolish the system whereby the PLP elected the shadow Cabinet. Party rules dictated that whoever was serving in the shadow Cabinet at the point where Labour moved into government must be included in the new Prime Minister's first actual Cabinet, after which point he had the authority conferred on him by the UK constitution to appoint whoever he liked. The shadow Cabinet elections of 2010, therefore, were the first since 1996 and, after the leader got his way, would be the last.

This seemed at the time a sensible reform; even those opposed to it did not consider that an unpopular (among MPs) far-left leader might benefit in future from this 'reform'. One of those who had opposed the abolition of elections was, ironically, Jeremy Corbyn, who described it as 'the wrong direction of travel. I do not see the need for this change, it increases the power of patronage, it reduces the accountability of the leader to Labour MPs.'

By 2015, however, Corbyn had come round to the principle that the shadow Cabinet should be entirely appointed by the leader.

John McDonnell, the MP for Hayes and Harlington, had been chair of the finance committee in the Greater London Council in the 1980s, and had been in the vanguard of far-left demands that local authorities which had been targeted by the Thatcher government for 'rate capping' – whereby the government set limits on how much local councillors could raise – should defy the law and refuse to set a budget. McDonnell's militant approach was too much even for Ken Livingstone, the council leader, and McDonnell was dismissed from his post. Before and since his election to the Commons in 1997, McDonnell had been an abrasive and enthusiastic supporter of the IRA's 'armed struggle'. He was known to support punitive rates of tax, the nationalisation of private companies without compensation and had frequently been criticised for publicly encouraging civil unrest and even, on one occasion, the practice of employees spitting in their bosses' tea in revenge for their not accepting striking workers' demands. He was also reported to have defended the actions of a student who was jailed for throwing a fire extinguisher from the top of a London building, which almost hit a police officer below, during a student demonstration in November 2010 (see Chapter Five). A founder member – and current chair – of the hard-left Labour Representation Committee (LRC), McDonnell could not be described as a divisive figure, as most MPs were united in their negative views of him.

By the evening of the Sunday following the leadership announcement, rumours that the new leader would defy many in the PLP and appoint McDonnell to the most senior job on Labour's front bench after Corbyn himself – that of shadow Chancellor of the Exchequer – were confirmed. This was seen as an act of courageous defiance by Corbyn; McDonnell was not a popular figure among his colleagues, rarely attending meetings of the PLP or seen in the tearoom where most political gossip and socialising took place. It was also known that every newspaper in the country held large files on McDonnell's past statements and campaigns that would inevitably be used to embarrass the party in the event of his ever being appointed to a position of influence. At the top of this list was McDonnell's remarks in May 2003, when he told an audience at a meeting held to honour the memory of the IRA hunger striker Bobby Sands: 'It's about time we started honouring those people involved in the armed struggle.' (See Chapter Nine.) Four days after Corbyn's victory and three days after his appointment as shadow Chancellor had been confirmed, McDonnell appeared on BBC's *Question Time*, where he was challenged on his remarks. He responded by claiming that at the time, the Northern Ireland Assembly was suspended and 'it looked like we were going to lose the peace process'. Close observers of McDonnell's political record could have been forgiven a degree of confusion at this point: in an interview with the IRA's official newspaper during the original peace negotiations in 1998, McDonnell said: 'An assembly is not what people have laid down their lives for over thirty years ... the settlement must be for a united Ireland.' By 2015, however, it seemed McDonnell was such an enthusiastic supporter of the assembly he had initially opposed that he felt the need to praise the bravery of those IRA gunmen and bombers who had, in some unspecified way, helped to establish it.

He told the *Question Time* audience on 17 September:

I accept it was a mistake to use those words, but if it contributed to saving one life or preventing someone else being maimed, it was worth doing because we did hold on to the peace process. If I gave offence, and I clearly have, from the bottom of my heart, I apologise. I apologise.

No authoritative research exists regarding evidence that McDonnell's comments led directly or indirectly to the saving of any lives or to the prevention of anyone being maimed (indeed, he once joked at a public meeting in London about the IRA practice of kneecapping people). But his 'apology' was skilfully made, in that it allowed him to claim he had apologised for what he'd said, while doing no such thing; he merely justified his behaviour, and then apologised for any offence caused. He pointedly did not accept that what he had said, the views he had held, were in themselves wrong or offensive.

MPs who had been in the Commons for the same length of time as McDonnell, and even some who had served for longer, reported that whereas in the previous eighteen years they had rarely exchanged a word and never a smile with him, now things had changed. McDonnell had changed. He was, for the first time since being sacked as chair of finance at the GLC, in a position of influence in the Labour Party, if not in the country. Colleagues now saw a great deal more of both him and his smile. The shadow Chancellor was more gregarious, charming and funny, in a way that none of his colleagues felt was remotely familiar and which many found initially disconcerting rather than disarming.

On the Monday, Corbyn set to work piecing the rest of his front bench together, with another shadow Cabinet post, that of shadow International Development Secretary, going to Diane Abbott, Corbyn's long-time friend and ally and another Campaign Group member. The rest of the positions represented an attempt to reach out to all wings of the PLP: Hilary Benn remained in the post of shadow Foreign Secretary, which he had inherited when his predecessor, Douglas Alexander, had been defeated at the general election. Andy Burnham, the (now twice) defeated leadership candidate, and the only one from the contest willing to serve under Corbyn, became shadow Home Secretary (replacing Cooper), meaning that the four people shadowing the so-called great offices of state – No. 10, Treasury, Foreign Office and Home Office – were uniformly male. In fact, despite the consequent criticism of this, fifteen of the twenty-eight appointees eligible to attend shadow Cabinet meetings (including Corbyn himself) were filled by women. Obsession with the 'four great offices of state', he told journalists, was dated and failed to comprehend the importance of other departments such as health or education.

Inquisitive lobby journalists loitering outside the leader's office in the Norman Shaw South building on the parliamentary estate were able to glean some colourful details about the machinations surrounding the reshuffle during the day, including a panicked response to criticisms on social media about the alleged gender imbalance at the top of the shadow Cabinet. Corbyn's chief of staff Simon Fletcher was reported to have been overheard saying: 'We are taking a fair amount of shit out there about women. We need to do a Mandelson. Let's make Angela [Eagle, one of the defeated deputy leadership candidates] shadow First Minister of State, like Mandelson was. She can cover PMQs. Tom [Watson] knows about this. Do the Angela bit now.' Eagle was duly announced as shadow Business Secretary and shadow First Secretary of State.

Yet Corbyn assumed a defensive and petulant demeanour when questioned about the composition of his new shadow Cabinet while he walked home from the Commons that evening. The Labour leader, accompanied by one (silent) member of staff, strode purposefully onwards, barely acknowledging the presence of Darren McCaffrey of Sky News who asked his retreating back whether there was any validity in the criticism of there not being enough women in senior positions in the shadow Cabinet. Viewers at home and on the internet were treated to the sight of Corbyn refusing to answer. 'Why are you not talking to the media, Jeremy?' persevered McCaffrey. 'Is it true that you've pulled out of the [BBC Radio 4] *Today* programme tomorrow morning?' The excruciating film ends with Corbyn apparently hailing a passing police officer, telling him that 'these people are bothering me'.

It was a grim start to Labour's new era, with Corbyn demonstrating no grasp of how to deal with the media, surely one of the most important qualifications for any leader in the modern world. The MP himself looked uncomfortable and embarrassed throughout the ordeal, almost as if the media attention he was receiving was somehow unexpected, something for which he had not prepared.

Corbyn needed a team around him, people he could trust, who had the knowledge and expertise to take the leader's message beyond the party and into the country, a team that would go with him into Downing Street after the next election.

An unapologetic Marxist commentator, Seumas Milne was still associate editor of *The Guardian* when it was announced that he would be joining Corbyn's staff as Executive Director of Strategy and Communications. An apologist for the former Soviet Union, he unashamedly blamed the West and NATO, not President Putin, for Russia's annexation of Crimea in 2014. Inevitably he was also a harsh critic of the Iraq War, of Tony Blair's role in it, and of Israel; he was, politically, a soulmate of the Labour leader's, though without the broad media experience that others who had filled the role under previous leaders – most notably Alastair Campbell, Tony Blair's Director of Communications – necessarily possessed.

To the centre-ground and moderate MPs who made up the majority of the PLP, Milne's appointment, coming so soon after McDonnell's appointment as shadow Chancellor, was another two-fingered salute by Corbyn to his MPs. Lord Mandelson, who had filled the role in the 1980s, described Milne as 'completely unsuited', given how far his views were from Britain's political mainstream. John Woodcock, the MP for Barrow and Furness, said that the appointment was an own goal by Corbyn, coming as it did when the government was under pressure from its own backbenchers on the subject of cuts to tax credits: 'We finally have Tory MPs squirming over the vote on tax credit cuts and we unleash more process barminess to divert attention. So fed up. This is not some middle-class columnista parlour game, it is people's lives who are being wrecked by the Tories. They deserve better.'

The Rochdale MP, Simon Danczuk, told *The Sun*: 'This is a totally bizarre appointment of a man more likely to become the story rather than control our party's message.'

Much criticism from within the PLP and in the media focused on Milne's published view that the savage murder of Fusilier Lee Rigby in 2013 by Islamists 'wasn't terrorism in the normal sense'. If Labour wanted to be seen as the party most likely to give the country's enemies the benefit of the doubt, Milne's appointment was a first-class move.

Another addition to Corbyn's office, however, was to prove even more damaging and brought the new leader's loyalty to the party itself into question.

Labour rules prevented any member from publicly supporting anyone who stood against an official Labour candidate. Breaking such a rule resulted in automatic expulsion. While an appeal usually formed part of the process, there was rarely need for an inquiry by the party machinery in such cases, especially where there was prima facie evidence of guilt.

Andrew Fisher was appointed as Corbyn's head of policy shortly after his election as leader. Fisher was well known in far-left circles and had played a prominent role in McDonnell's Labour Representation Committee (LRC) during the last Labour government. In August 2014 he tweeted: 'FFS ... If you live in Croydon South, vote with dignity, vote @campaignbeard'. @campaignbeard was Jon Biggar, the Croydon South parliamentary candidate of the anarchist Class War organisation. The official Labour candidate was Emily Benn, granddaughter of Corbyn's mentor, Tony.

The tweet would normally have been interpreted as, in effect, a resignation letter from the Labour Party. It unequivocally endorsed one of Labour's opponents in a contest with a Labour candidate months before a general election. At a meeting of the PLP in October, Caroline Flint and Chuka Umunna echoed Benn's anger that a supporter of Labour's opponents should be working for the party's leader, and in a senior position. McDonnell rushed to dismiss concerns and to defend Fisher. The tweet, McDonnell was reported to have said, was 'an innocent satire about the idea of anarchists standing for election'. Fisher himself claimed his tweet had been 'misinterpreted'; perhaps, in far-left circles, 'vote' has an entirely different connotation from the accepted meaning of the word. But he was obviously aware of the seriousness of his offence. In a grovelling letter to Iain McNicol, the party general secretary, Fisher wrote:

> I accept that the tweet has been misinterpreted and has caused embarrassment and understandable upset among party members, which I regret. I wish to completely and unreservedly apologise for this tweet. I have now closed my social media accounts and assure you there will be no repetition of such activity in the future.

Normally, the response to such a transgression would have been a formal letter from the general secretary to the offender stating the fact of their expulsion from the party for a minimum term of five years. But these were not normal times. Fisher was not expelled, instead he was suspended, pending an investigation by the party and a subsequent report to the NEC – not a process to which other, previous transgressors had been subjected. Corbyn himself made it clear that rules that had been followed for decades could no longer apply; at least, not to his own staff members and supporters. In a statement issued by his office, he said he had 'full confidence in Andrew Fisher and his work. I respect the integrity of the general secretary's office and trust that this matter will be settled as quickly as possible.'

There was little doubt about the outcome of the 'investigation'. Fisher's suspension was, in due course, lifted and he returned to his duties in the leader's office. It left a sour taste in the mouths of many MPs who had feared from the start that far-left activists' influence – and even presence – would be felt again in the party.

The drama of the reshuffle was one cause of mounting criticism against the new leader. But on the Tuesday of the following week, controversy over an event at St Paul's Cathedral risked defining Corbyn in an entirely negative way. At a service to commemorate the anniversary of the Battle of Britain, the congregation was invited to stand to sing the national anthem. Photos of the Labour leader, his tie drooping untidily below his unfastened collar, ostentatiously refusing to sing the words of 'God Save the Queen', dominated the following day's newspapers and that day's broadcast news.

A spokesman for Downing Street was eager to present a contrast with the 'enthusiastic' singing of the anthem by David Cameron, but beyond that, there was surprisingly little criticism from the Conservative Party, and what little there was, was muted.

Immediately speculation turned to Remembrance Sunday, a day when the Leader of the Opposition lays a wreath at the Cenotaph in Whitehall. Would Corbyn emulate the disastrous faux pas of one of his predecessors (and the one with whom commentators compared him most frequently), Michael Foot? If Corbyn refused to wear a traditional red poppy – eschewed by many in the peace movement as a celebration of militarism – the party might face another 'donkey jacket' moment, turning voters' memories back to 1981 when the then Labour leader, Michael Foot, was accused of disrespect after he wore a scruffy heavy coat to the Cenotaph service. In the event, Corbyn conceded the need to wear a red poppy.

There also emerged, in that first week, another controversy, initially over whether or not Corbyn would 'bow the knee' to the Queen when she made him a Privy Counsellor. As a committed republican, who had frequently spoken of his support for removing the hereditary monarch, could he subject himself to the humiliation of the ceremony that would give him the right to be addressed as 'The Right Honourable Jeremy Corbyn'? He declined to attend Buckingham Palace in October, when he had been originally expected to. Staff told the media that he had some 'long-standing private engagements' which couldn't be altered. These turned out to include a walking holiday in Scotland's Highlands and a fish tea in a hotel in Fort William, according to *The Independent*. Whatever his reservations about the ancient ceremony or the appropriateness of a council of advisers whose role in a democracy was rather less relevant than in the days when the monarch ruled supreme, Corbyn was finally welcomed as a member of the Privy Council in November, in a ceremony at which he did not, reportedly, bend the knee. A Buckingham Palace spokesman said that no new Privy Counsellor was forced to do anything that would make them feel uncomfortable, whatever tradition dictated.

And then, in that first week, there was Prime Minister's Questions. The centrepiece of the parliamentary week, the adversarial nature of PMQs had made it a popular institution for TV audiences throughout the world. It had been the making and the breaking of a series of high-profile politicians and aspiring leaders. There was nothing quite like the pressure a backbencher experienced in anticipation of being called to ask a question of the serving Prime Minister. Although Corbyn was an experienced backbencher, Wednesday 16 September 2015 was the first occasion he had ever spoken from the front bench: every Leader of the Opposition who preceded him had spent at least some time on the front bench in one capacity or another.

MPs of all parties held their breath as Corbyn was called by the Speaker, John Bercow, to fire his first sally at the government.

The Labour leader began by paying a self-serving tribute to those Labour Party members who had supported him in the recent contest, and encouraged the wider country to be 'very proud of the numbers of people who engaged and took part in all those debates'.

Now that, after thirty-two years on the back benches, Corbyn had finally arrived on the front bench, it was about time the Commons reformed itself, he told the House. And in an attempt to allow the voices of ordinary people to be heard in the chamber, he revealed that he had sent out a mass email asking supporters for suggestions as to what questions he should ask the Prime Minister. This tactic was to be used repeatedly by Corbyn, although with decreasing frequency, during his tenure as leader. Quoting a question (one of 40,000 received, he told an amused House) from someone he identified simply as 'Marie', Corbyn then asked Cameron about the shortage of affordable housing. His subsequent questions were relayed from Steven (asking about job losses in the housing association for which he worked), Paul (who asked about cuts to tax credits), Claire (who also asked about tax credits), Gail (mental health services) and Angela (another question about provision of services to mental health patients).

Welcoming his new opposite number to the front bench, Cameron also praised his new approach. If the new tactic was suited to Corbyn's style, it was even more useful to Cameron, who sailed through all six questions with obvious ease. The calmer, more methodical approach gave the Prime Minister plenty of latitude to give generalised answers and he clearly felt under no pressure. Additionally, Corbyn's scattergun approach to the topics he had chosen let Cameron off the hook by flitting from one question to the next without picking up on an earlier answer or attempting to exploit anything Cameron had said. Corbyn had his questions, they were prepared, and he was going to use them without deviation.

So his first outing at the despatch box was not the complete disaster his friends had feared and his critics had hoped for; but neither did it suggest that the government was going to face any serious opposition in the years ahead.

Two weeks after Corbyn's election as leader, the party's annual conference kicked off in Brighton. To some extent, this proved to be part of the 'phoney war': Corbyn-supporting members had not yet had time to organise in the constituencies and delegates, on the whole, represented the defeated moderate wing of the party. Furthermore, there were few decisive votes on which the new leader's authority could be tested. But there was one.

The reforms to conference since the early 1990s had been led by the leadership and only opposed to a lacklustre degree by a retreating and defeated left. They much preferred the heady days of 'full and frank' debate on the floor of conference and yearned for the days when the Chancellor of the Exchequer would be allowed a mere five minutes to explain his economic policy to the outside world as he suffered the heckles and jeers of his fellow party members. Knife-edge votes, very often accompanied by protests and aggressive demonstrations, would be witnessed by TV audiences, as would the intervention by trade union barons, wielding their 'card votes' worth millions of votes, in contrast to the constituency delegates' mere thousands. It was a very Labour mess and was cherished for exactly that reason. To gain control of the party and its rule book, the left had to organise in the constituencies and in the trade unions so that they could win crucial votes on the floor of conference, whatever the cost to the party in terms of the lost support of moderate voters.

The new regime, introduced by John Smith in 1993, involved policy forums meeting on a two-year rotational basis, with constant policy reviews presented to conference for approval; such reports were rarely able to be amended and could be either accepted or rejected in their entirety. Such was the status of the *Britain in the World* document submitted to the party's 2015 conference. It included a paragraph committing Labour to supporting a continuous-at-sea deterrent, which would mean the replacement of all four Trident submarines. Its contents were approved by conference without debate or even a vote. Two weeks after electing an uncompromising unilateralist and CND supporter as leader, Labour had recommitted itself to supporting Britain's independent nuclear deterrent. And, unless conference rules were changed, the policy would not be reviewed again for at least two years.

This presented a challenge to Corbyn, naturally. It would be unprecedented for a Labour leader to oppose the party's defence policy in a vote in the House of Commons; when Neil Kinnock had recognised the need to change his own views and that of his party on the subject in the late 1980s, he had done so by organisation and persuasion. Corbyn now found himself entirely at odds, not only with his MPs, which he had expected, but with his party's settled policy.

In the meantime, he had his first conference speech to deliver as leader. And he would use it deliberately to ignore the conference decision and to repeat the phrases and slogans he had used so often in the past, to so much acclaim from like-minded individuals. 'I don't believe that £100 billion spent on a new generation of nuclear weapons, taking up a quarter of our defence budget, is the right way forward,' he declared. And, as on previous occasions when he had stated his views, he received enthusiastic applause from some sections of the hall. The fact that the costs of Trident were estimated to be between £25 and £40 billion (not £100 billion) and would consume 6 per cent (not a quarter) of the defence budget was not dwelt upon by the media, which simply noted the comments as a signal that plenty more confrontation between the leader and his party lay ahead.

As with PMQs two weeks earlier, there were plenty of observers who feared – and hoped – that this vitally important set-piece event would go disastrously wrong. But as with PMQs, Corbyn managed to get to the end without a major catastrophe. There was one minor embarrassment, however. His unfamiliarity with the autocue (he had learned the lessons of Miliband's previous experiences) and his staff's inexperience of operating at the top level of politics resulted in this peculiar line: 'We need to be investing in skills, investing in our young people, and – strong message here – not cutting student numbers.' Whoever had been tasked with actually writing the requested 'strong message' had obviously not got round to it before the speech had been loaded onto the teleprompter.

Corbyn had consistently claimed he wanted to lead a reformation of 'politics as usual', that Labour under his leadership would be about a 'new kind of politics'. As the controversy over his refusal to sing the national anthem at the Battle of Britain memorial service had shown, he intended to follow these pledges with action. And before conference season was over, he intended to stick two fingers – in the nicest, politest way possible, of course – at another political convention, namely the convention that political parties are allowed to hold their own conferences without interference from their rivals' leaders. Gordon Brown had, ill-advisedly, ignored this convention when, during the Conservative Party conference in 2007, he had attempted to upstage David Cameron by paying a visit to British troops serving in Iraq (see Chapter One), and had taken a hit in the public opinion polls as a result. Corbyn, however, was reinventing the rules of politics.

On Sunday 4 October 2015, as delegates gathered in Manchester for the Conservatives' first post-general election conference, they walked a gauntlet of louder and angrier protesters than usual. An anti-austerity march through the city centre attracted an estimated 60,000 and, although it was largely peaceful, journalists as well as delegates found themselves the target of more aggressive protesters shouting 'scum!' One young Tory delegate was pelted with eggs as he entered the conference area. One man was arrested on suspicion of assault after a journalist was spat at.

And the next day, the new leader of the Labour Party travelled to Manchester to deliver a platform speech for the protesters. 'We've challenged the idea that the only show in town is austerity. And because we've challenged that and had a huge mandate in challenging that suddenly people are talking. People are excited.' His audience were indeed excited. Here was a Labour leader who actually seemed to be one of them, someone who at last understood the importance of rallies and protests. This was where Corbyn felt most welcome, felt most at ease, where no one challenged him and everyone agreed with each other.

Attending the anti-austerity rally, endorsing it, irrespective of the headline-catching bad behaviour by some, was unusual behaviour for a man who aspired to be Prime Minister one day. It was certainly an innovative approach.

Two and a half hectic weeks had passed since Jeremy Corbyn had been elected leader of his party. While he had survived the early tests and cleared the earliest hurdles, he had not done so unscathed. His antipathy towards the media, footage of his petulant refusal to talk to journalists, his misjudgement in refusing to sing the national anthem – none of these was a resigning matter. But all of them presaged the fact that a turbulent time lay ahead for both Corbyn and his party.

CHAPTER TWELVE

VIPERS' NEST

A fundamental and inescapable instinct of the British left is to found ad hoc committees or campaigning organisations that will do whatever the organisers believe the Labour Party should be doing, or is doing ineffectively. So Stop the War was set up partly as a response to Labour's support for US military action against Afghanistan in the wake of 9/11; UK Uncut, another left-wing umbrella organisation, sought to encourage a more militant opposition to the 2010 coalition government's austerity measures; and the People's Assembly Against Austerity was founded with much the same aim and out of the same frustration that Labour, having promised large cuts to public spending in the run-up to the 2010 general election, could hardly (with any credibility, at least) oppose the same cuts simply because they were being enacted by a government of a different political complexion.

The People's Assembly Against Austerity was launched with an open letter published in *The Guardian* in February 2013, signed by Unite's general secretary Len McCluskey, former Labour MP Tony Benn and Jeremy Corbyn. With funding from its affiliated trade unions, the Assembly had organised events throughout the country and built up an impressive network in the run-up to the 2015 general election.

But in October 2015, a new leader and a new direction for the Labour Party demanded an altogether new grassroots campaigning organisation, one that would be created with the sole purpose of supporting not the Labour Party, but Jeremy Corbyn.

A month after Corbyn was elected to the leadership, Jon Lansman founded Momentum. Lansman was well known to veterans of previous civil wars in the Labour Party. A supporter of the Campaign for Labour Party Democracy, he worked for Tony Benn during his bid to replace Denis Healey as deputy leader of the party in 1981. He also ran Benn's disastrous leadership campaign against incumbent Neil Kinnock in 1988. Since 2010 he had been working for left-wing MP Michael Meacher and in 2015 eagerly volunteered to help Corbyn's campaign.

But Lansman's reputation as a fixer and a class warrior didn't always prove helpful to Corbyn; he embarrassed the Islington MP by posting a spoof campaign poster for one of Corbyn's rivals, Liz Kendall, depicting her as a Conservative candidate to Twitter. This tactic was immediately disowned by Corbyn and his official campaign. However, there is little doubt that Lansman saw anyone to the right of himself, including Labour MPs, as Tories – a message that resonated with Corbyn's more enthusiastic supporters who regularly took to Twitter to fire off accusations of 'Red Tory' at Corbyn's opponents and their supporters.

Following Corbyn's victory, Lansman quickly realised that a separate campaigning organisation would be needed if the new leader's position was to be secured. He was well aware of how isolated the far left were in Parliament, even after the leadership election, and knew that his internal opponents in the party would seek to remove Corbyn, if they were able to, at the earliest opportunity. Momentum would fill the role of Corbyn's Praetorian Guard; it would harness the energy and commitment of the leadership campaign itself and direct it towards securing not only Corbyn's leadership, but the hard left's grip on the party and its institutions.

Labour MPs, now feeling increasingly frustrated and under siege, smelled a rat. Or, more accurately, a Trot. Many of the 2010 and 2015 intake of Labour MPs had had no experience of the long, arduous battles between the party and Militant in the 1970s and '80s. The entryist group had gone on to form the Socialist Party after it was finally removed from Labour's ranks. But many MPs retained the scars from those battles and were ever watchful lest a Trotskyist revival threaten the party's electability again. In Momentum – largely because of the involvement of its leader, Lansman – they saw the ghost of civil wars past. Coupled with these concerns over Momentum was a fear that many of those who had been successfully expelled in the past would now view a Corbyn-led Labour Party once more as a welcoming and tempting vehicle for their activities.

Momentum itself insisted that its own rules prevented any member of a party other than Labour from being able to vote on matters affecting the Labour Party. But members of rival parties could attend Momentum's public meetings and take part in debates on other campaigning topics.

In the early, less disciplined, days of Momentum, its long-term aims and the methods by which it sought to secure the dominance of the hard left within the Labour Party were occasionally and clumsily revealed. One such occasion was at the PLP meeting of Monday 16 November 2015, when MPs challenged Corbyn on his equivocal response to both the killing of Islamist terrorist

Mohammed Emwazi in Syria and the terrorist attacks, a day later in Paris, which claimed 130 lives (see Chapter Thirteen). Moderate, Blairite MP Ann Coffey, who had represented Stockport in the Commons since 1992, criticised Corbyn for his response to the Paris attacks. But reports of her comments were leaked from the ostensibly (but rarely) private meeting, and a tweet was soon posted by the Momentum group in Coffey's own area, warning her: 'You continue to disappoint and let down the people of #Stockport. Get behind the leader or kindly go'. The message was swiftly deleted, but a spokesman for the group said it had been posted 'in frustration' at the 'perceived disloyalty' displayed by Coffey. 'We are not campaigning for deselection nationally, nor was it a threat from the local group for deselection,' he added.

Coffey, meanwhile, had responded to the original tweet in her own robust style: 'So you say something nasty, get a kickback, and then pretend it wasn't a threat.'

Stella Creasy had been elected to the London seat of Walthamstow in 2010. She immediately made a name for herself by leading an effective and high-profile campaign against payday lenders, inspiring envious looks from older, more experienced colleagues. She had a long track record in supporting women's rights and campaigning to support women who had been the victims of violence. And in recognition of her campaigning and communication skills, she had come second in the contest for Labour's deputy leadership in September 2015, ahead of more experienced rivals Caroline Flint, Angela Eagle and Ben Bradshaw. On the evening of the Chancellor's Autumn Statement on Wednesday 25 November 2015, Creasy attended a fundraising event at a women's refuge in her constituency and expressed fears that this community resource would suffer as a result of proposed cuts in public spending announced earlier that day.

As Creasy met residents at the refuge and discussed their experiences, the shadow Chancellor John McDonnell was also fulfilling a speaking engagement, and in the same constituency – Creasy's. The event was organised by McDonnell's Labour Representation Committee (LRC) and was ostensibly held to discuss whether or not the LRC should affiliate to Lansman's Momentum. The identities of the speakers with whom the shadow Chancellor shared a platform were notable: Matt Wrack, the general secretary of the Fire Brigades' Union (FBU), had been, for many years, a supporter and funder of the Trade Union and Socialist Coalition (TUSC), which had regularly stood against official Labour candidates; Steve White, a Labour Party member and strong critic of Creasy, was another speaker.

Quite why it was deemed necessary to launch a new campaigning effort in Walthamstow was unclear: Creasy had a majority of more than 23,000 in 2015 and Labour held all twenty-seven seats on the local council already.

In the two months since Corbyn's victory, local Labour officials had reported an influx of up to 1,200 new members. MPs might, in ordinary circumstances, welcome an influx of new talent and resources, but the agenda of the leftist organisations that attached themselves to Corbyn's cause in the aftermath of his victory was not aimed at delivering leaflets or organising street stalls.

Automatic reselection of MPs was a consistent demand of the hard left throughout the '80s (see Chapter Nine). Corbyn's victory and the formation of Momentum provided two vital elements in a new push to replace moderate and centre-right Labour MPs. An added concern of MPs was the forthcoming review of constituency boundaries.

In 2009, in the wake of the MPs' expenses scandal (see Chapter

Two), the then Leader of the Opposition, David Cameron, in a blatant appeal to anti-politics sentiment, had promised to deliver an arbitrary reduction in the size of the House of Commons from 650 to 600. The figure was settled upon for no other reason than its roundness. This reduction would be coupled with a new rule that every constituency must be broadly the same size in terms of the number of voters on the electoral register; Labour, because it represented many more inner-city seats than the Conservatives, was seen as having an inbuilt electoral advantage because many of these seats had significantly fewer voters living there and therefore, theoretically, could return more MPs on fewer votes than Tory MPs in larger constituencies required.

Unfortunately for Cameron – and fortunately for most sitting MPs – the new boundaries fell foul of parliamentary procedure after the Conservatives' coalition partners, the Liberal Democrats, having initially agreed to support the plan, reneged on the agreement in revenge for Cameron's lack of resolve in pushing through reform of the House of Lords. So the new boundaries were kicked into the long grass until after the 2015 general election. And now that Cameron enjoyed an overall majority, the Boundary Commission was back at work. And this time, there would be a majority in favour of implementing the new electoral map.

Boundary reviews, understandably, make sitting MPs nervous. Normally such a review would be carried out every three parliaments and would make changes where necessary to account for a long-term population shift. Only once before had a deliberate decision been taken to reduce the number of seats, rather than redraw them to account for population shifts. That had been in Scotland in the run-up to the 2005 general election, when the number of Westminster seats (the number of seats returning Members of the Scottish Parliament remained unaltered) was deliberately reduced from seventy-two to fifty-nine in recognition of the new role to be played by the devolved parliament in Edinburgh. A very Scottish bun fight ensued and a number of sitting MPs – mostly Labour, since it was at the time the dominant party – found themselves without a seat.

And now the exercise was to be repeated across the whole of the United Kingdom, in all four nations. Since reselection (or 'deselection', as most on the hard left preferred to call it privately) was considered a central tenet of democratic socialism, the impending boundary review presented an ideal opportunity to cleanse the PLP of Corbyn's sceptics.

McDonnell's visit to Walthamstow in the company of Labour's opponents was part of a speaking tour of similar London seats. The night before he had welcomed Momentum activists into the party at a meeting in Bethnal Green and Bow, the constituency represented by Rushanara Ali, another moderate Labour MP. He had done so without observing the strict parliamentary convention of informing the local MP before making a public visit to her constituency. And on 4 December, McDonnell had been a speaker at Lambeth Academy, where activists of the Socialist Party (formerly Militant) gathered signatures on a petition criticising local MP Chuka Umunna for voting with the government in favour of military action against Islamic State (ISIS) in Syria.

According to one of the speakers on the panel that evening, this area was the 'vipers' nest for Progress', the hated Blairite think tank. Marlene Ellis, who was representing Momentum's Lambeth branch on the panel, spent some time criticising, not the Conservative government, but local Labour councillors, some of whom, she revealed, were even members of Progress. 'I want to suggest to you that there is a conflict of interest between serving Progress and serving our communities in Lambeth as a councillor,' she declared, to applause.

Observers reported the twin messages as 'Join the Labour Party and help influence its direction' and 'Hold MPs to account'. Momentum was on the march, with the full support of the party leadership.

The LRC, the Socialist Party, TUSC, the Socialist Workers' Party – they now all had some role in shaping the direction of the Labour Party, either as attendees at Momentum meetings or affiliates to it, or as co-ordinators and founders of Corbyn's favourite campaigning organisation, Stop the War. And now Ken Loach entered the fray. The esteemed British film director had once been a member of the Labour Party but had left when Tony Blair became leader. Since then Loach had supported Respect, the political party George Galloway helped to launch after his expulsion from Labour, and TUSC. In 2013 Loach even created his own party, ironically named Left Unity. A long-term critic of Israel and a supporter of the campaign to boycott and disinvest in the Middle East's only liberal democracy, he was also a strong opponent of the Iraq War. Inevitably, he was also a strong supporter of Jeremy Corbyn and, in 2016, produced a one-hour documentary, *In Conversation with Jeremy Corbyn*, as part of his efforts to boost Corbyn's second leadership campaign (see Chapter Fourteen).

The fundamental motivation for Momentum and all its hard-left allies and fellow travellers was a determination to force Labour off the centre ground and to the left. Labour, in 2010 and again in 2015, had failed to offer a valid alternative to the Conservatives, leading directly to Cameron's victories. A properly radical, socialist manifesto would convince voters to support Labour at the next election, so the argument went.

There was one fatal flaw in this line of reasoning: it held that people voted Conservative because the Labour Party was not left wing enough. The same argument had been deployed in the 1980s (apart from in the aftermath of the 1983 general election, when the manifesto had been deemed left wing enough, but traitors on the right of the party had undermined unity). If only Neil Kinnock had offered a more avowedly left-wing platform, then the country would have turned to him instead of Margaret Thatcher, the left claimed.

It was a brave and challenging premise. Every election since the advent of the universal franchise had been decided on a single factor: the degree to which those who had voted for the government at the previous election now switched their support to the main opposition party: the famous 'two-party swing'. The only three Labour Prime Ministers to win majorities at a general election – Attlee, Wilson and Blair – had done so by persuading enough Tory voters at the previous election to switch to Labour. It worked the opposite way round, too: Heath, Thatcher, Major and Cameron won elections because they presented an attractive offer to those who had voted Labour at the previous election.

But this sort of thing was not for Corbyn or his supporters. The very notion that Labour should compromise with the electorate or try to woo Conservative voters was anathema, a betrayal of the working classes. The next Labour government would win office, not by parroting the Conservatives, but by appealing to two previously untapped resources: voters who generally supported left-wing or 'progressive' parties (the Greens, the Scottish National Party and various hard-left outfits) and non-voters. The idea of a 'progressive alliance' on the left was one that had been mooted on a number of occasions in the past, particularly when Labour was going through one of its many extended periods in opposition. Such a strategy depended on persuading a high percentage of Lib Dem voters, as well as every Green Party supporter, to switch to Labour at a general election. Bold indeed.

As for non-voters, Corbyn's supporters had apparently paid little attention to the first syllable of the phrase. Anyway, surveys of those who chose not to take part in elections revealed that they split pretty much along the same dividing lines as those who did actually vote, so their participation would make very little difference to the result.

The disagreement between Labour's mainstream MPs and its hard-left contingent had always been present, indeed was an inevitable part of the party's character. But since Corbyn's election as leader and the establishment of Momentum as a campaigning force, since the creation of new relationships between factions of the Trotskyist left and the party itself, the disagreement had become a chasm. Labour had once been dubbed a party of comrades, but it had never quite lived up to the name. It had now become a party of enemies, a name that suited it perfectly.

The identification of Corbyn's enemies and allies was a task that few observers found a difficult one; battle lines had been drawn and few were unaware of who was 'one of us' and who was not. The last thing the party and its leadership needed was a formal, written document that outlined in exact terms who was onside, who was not and – more damagingly – to what degree Corbyn's detractors opposed him. This being Corbyn's Labour Party, however, that is exactly what they got.

A document leaked to *The Times* on 23 March 2016, and claiming to have been produced by the leader's office, listed every Labour MP and categorised them according to whether they were seen as 'core group', 'core group plus', 'neutral but not hostile', 'core group hostile' and 'hostile group'. The leader's office vehemently denied it had come from them and there was some speculation that it had in fact been produced by Damian McBride, Gordon Brown's former hatchet man, now back as an adviser to the shadow Defence Secretary, Emily Thornberry. McBride denied this categorically.

Inevitably, the Prime Minister, David Cameron, had some fun at the despatch box during the next Prime Minister's Questions: 'I don't know why the shadow Leader of the House [Chris Bryant] is shouting at me,' he said.

> We've got a very interesting document today; we've got the spreadsheet of which Labour MP is on which side. You are shouting, but it says here you are 'neutral but not hostile'. The Chief Whip [Rosie Winterton] on the other hand, the Chief Whip is being a bit quiet ... because she's in 'hostile'!

Tory and Labour MPs alike (most of the latter, at least) enjoyed a laugh at the expense of whichever apparatchik of ill-judgement had produced the list which, of course, turned out to be a major embarrassment to Corbyn, whatever denials were made by his office as to its origins. Labour MPs were now being defined politically, not just by their own views, but by how they were seen by Corbyn and his supporters. That divergence spoke to a more profound split, between those who saw winning elections as the party's overriding priority, and those who refused to compromise their ideals in the grubby pursuit of power.

This was the crux of the conflict that was tearing the party apart. A large majority of MPs understood the political truism that elections are won from the centre, and that telling voters they were wrong in their choice of priorities held out the prospect of limited electoral success. But the leadership and its grassroots supporters not only believed that elections could be won from the far left, they also seemed not too concerned about the prospect of such a strategy losing anyway. Lansman, in a heated exchange on Twitter with former Blair aide John McTernan in July 2016, described 'winning' as 'the small bit that matters to political elites who want to keep power to themselves'.

That tweet was sent on 10 July. Two days later, as Theresa May prepared to assume the office of Prime Minister, an ICM poll gave the Conservatives an eight-point lead in general election voting intentions, with Labour on 30 per cent – below what it had won in 2015. 'Winning' didn't seem to be something Labour needed to worry about.

All hard-left organisations split: some get on with it relatively early, others wait for a few years before the inevitable fallout occurs. Ideological purity can tolerate little deviation from the centrally agreed philosophy, and the joke in Monty Python's *Life of Brian* – the People's Front of Judea versus the Judean People's Front – hit home because of its accuracy. In Momentum, the inevitable started to happen – publicly, at least – at the end of October 2016, when Lansman found himself accused, by an organisation calling itself 'Labour Party Marxists', of trying to orchestrate an anti-democratic coup which was 'worse than anything Tony Blair managed to foist on the Labour Party'. Lansman's 'crime' was to introduce a one member, one vote (OMOV) system of policy making for Momentum, rather than a delegate-based system where entryist groups might find it easier to wield power. Despite repeated claims by Momentum that it was a 'mainstream, Labour Party' organisation, members of the Trotskyite Alliance for Workers' Liberty (AWL) had achieved influential positions on Momentum's steering committee, and now Labour Party activists feared a takeover. As far as the AWL was concerned, even Momentum could not be trusted to represent working-class priorities and was, according to an AWL leaflet published in October, 'politically conservative'.

Lansman's 'coup' succeeded, in that he moved the group's decision-making processes online and established a new constitution that insisted all new members of Momentum must also be members of the Labour Party. As Momentum's new steering group arranged to meet in Birmingham for the first time on 11 March 2017, a new rival organisation, formed by unhappy comrades who felt they had been betrayed by Lansman, announced that the inaugural conference of Momentum Grassroots would be held on the same date and in the same city.

CHAPTER THIRTEEN

THE PROBLEM WITH
THE JEWS

In the second half of 2015, the British public became more familiar than they would have liked with the terms Islamic State, Daesh, ISIS and ISIL: different names for the same brutal and fascistic Islamist military force then gaining ground in its incursions into Syria and Iraq, raping, torturing and slaughtering on a biblical scale as it went, evoking memories of, and comparisons with, the depraved Cambodian Khmer Rouge in the 1970s. In 2013, Labour had effectively vetoed UK participation in military action against the Assad regime in Syria after prima facie evidence had emerged of chemical weapons attacks on civilians by government forces (see Chapter Eight). Now, in November 2015, the enemy was different – Assad was one of the many enemies of the ISIL fanatics – but the cause was the same: the protection of blameless civilians against a ruthless and pitiless enemy. But such action meant the UK would be on the same side as the United States, already involved in bombing raids in Syria against the Islamists. Jeremy Corbyn had consistently denied he was a pacifist (and his remarkable tolerance for military action by other nations and organisations usually hostile to the UK and its NATO allies would seem to confirm this position) but it was never remotely likely that he would find himself voting for military action – in any circumstances – that would be supported by the United States.

Until 2003, UK Prime Ministers exercised prerogative powers to order the military into action in most circumstances, only seeking parliamentary approval retrospectively, or specifically for an extension or continuation of the action in question. But Iraq changed such practice, as it changed so many things in British politics. When Tony Blair sought specific authorisation from the Commons before committing the UK to join with US troops against the forces of Saddam Hussein in March 2003, he was, probably knowingly, creating a new precedent that would restrict and limit future holders of the office. Since then, no major military intervention had been given the go-ahead without a specific vote in the Commons.

On the evening of Monday 2 November 2015, Catherine West, the newly elected Labour MP for Hornsey and Wood Green and now a member of Hilary Benn's shadow Foreign Office team, told an event organised by the Stop the War coalition (chaired by Jeremy Corbyn until six weeks earlier) that Labour would consult the organisation about Syria before deciding its policy on military intervention there – a position subsequently confirmed by an official party statement.

Stop the War was set up in response to the Islamist attacks on the US on 11 September 2001, in order to campaign, initially, against international intervention in Afghanistan, where the mastermind of the Twin Towers attacks, Osama bin Laden, was thought to be a guest of the Taliban, then in control of much of the country. But the definite article, 'the', in the organisation's title quickly lost some of its meaning: Stop the War wasn't just opposed to one specific war – it opposed all wars fought by the imperialist West (in later years it would go to great lengths to understand the provocation by NATO that forced the Russians to invade and annex Crimea). Stop the War was set up and run by leading elements of the Trotskyist Socialist Workers' Party (SWP) and naturally Corbyn was pleased to take a leading role from the start. He had stepped aside from his position of chair within days of assuming the Labour Party leadership, but only after praising the organisation as representing 'the very best in British political campaigning'. As a backbencher, Corbyn's involvement with Stop the War was, where his parliamentary colleagues were aware of it, tolerated and indulged. Now that he was Labour leader, even if he was no longer Stop the War's chair, the notion that party policy could be subjected to influence by the group was greeted with revulsion by Labour MPs. For many, the fight against Islamist fascism was no different from the fight against any other form of fascism. This was not a view taken by Corbyn or by Stop the War, who saw all military intervention by the West – even intervention that could save the lives of civilians from death, or worse – as morally wrong. For the far left, fascism was very specifically defined, and it was Caucasian and Christian, not Arabic or Muslim. Instead of condemning outright and without qualification the barbarism of ISIL, most of the far left instead spent much of the latter half of 2015 trying to convince the world and themselves that ISIL itself had been created (inevitably) by the West and by its ill-considered intervention in Iraq.

On Thursday 12 November 2015, Mohammed Emwazi – better known to the British press as 'Jihadi John' – a British-born Islamist terrorist who had joined ISIL forces in Syria and had appeared in videos personally executing a number of the militant group's prisoners, was killed by an allied drone strike in northern Syria. Corbyn responded with a statement:

We await identification of the person targeted in last night's US air attack in Syria. It appears Mohammed Emwazi has been held to account for his callous and brutal crimes. However, it would have been far better for us all if he had been held to account in a court of law.

It became an inevitable pattern of Corbyn's statements as Leader of the Opposition that condemnation of Britain's enemies was followed by a 'however' or 'but'. His lukewarm welcome of Emwazi's death was scorned by his own MPs. Ian Austin first tweeted his own robust response to the news of Emwazi's death: 'Well done to UK & USA military & security personnel who've made sure barbaric murderer Mohammed Emwazi can't slaughter anyone else.' This was quickly followed by a passive aggressive mockery of his leader's response: 'Look, why couldn't the police just go and arrest Emwazi? It's not as if it's a really dangerous war zone & I'm sure he'd have come quietly.'

The row was an echo of the controversy that had erupted the previous month when comments Corbyn had made in 2011 on a discussion programme broadcast on the Iranian state-sponsored station Press TV – to which, as a backbencher, Corbyn had been a regular, paid contributor – were used by David Cameron four years later in his speech to his party's conference to attack Corbyn as a terrorist sympathiser. Cameron wrongly claimed that during the show, Corbyn had described the death of Osama bin Laden as 'a tragedy'. In fact, the Islington MP had described the failure to bring bin Laden to trial as such, and Cameron's cynical and inaccurate representation of Corbyn's words was leapt upon by Corbyn supporters. But the interview in question revealed much about Corbyn's approach to Islamist terrorism, equating the 9/11 attacks, in which nearly 3,000 innocent people died, with the failure to put bin Laden on trial: both were 'a tragedy', according to Corbyn. He used the same occasion to speculate, without challenge from his co-panellists, that the US had been involved in some form of conspiracy over the attack on bin Laden's compound in Pakistan: 'Why the burial at sea – if indeed there was a burial at sea – and indeed if it was bin Laden?'

A day after Emwazi's death, Islamist terrorists carried out a sequence of co-ordinated attacks in Paris which claimed the lives of 130 people. The following day, Stop the War published a statement on its website headlined: 'Paris reaps the whirlwind of western support for extremist violence in Middle East'. Although the post was subsequently taken down, it echoed its former chair's initial reaction to the news of the massacre. In an interview with the BBC, the Labour leader had said that the 'immediate fault' of the deaths lay with the terrorists, and then added: 'We have created a situation where some of these forces have grown.' In the same interview, he was asked if, as Prime Minister, he would support a 'shoot-to-kill policy' to combat terrorists. Corbyn replied:

> I'm not happy with the shoot-to-kill policy in general. I think that is quite dangerous and I think can often be counterproductive. I think you have to have security that prevents people firing off weapons where you can. There are various degrees for doing things as we know. But the idea you end up with a war on the streets is not a good thing.

The outrage felt by his own MPs at such even-handedness in the face of terror boiled over on Tuesday 17 November, when Cameron made a statement to the House on the recent G20 summit he had attended and on the Paris attacks. Labour backbenchers used their own contributions to launch thinly veiled attacks on their leader and on Stop the War. Emma Reynolds (Wolverhampton North East) was to the forefront of the criticism: 'Does the Prime Minister agree that full responsibility for the attacks in Paris lies solely with the terrorists and that any attempt by any organisation to somehow blame the West or France's military intervention in Syria is not only wrong and disgraceful, but also should be condemned?'

She was followed by another Wolverhampton MP, Pat McFadden, a former adviser to Tony Blair:

May I ask the Prime Minister to reject the view that sees terrorist acts as always being a response or a reaction to what we in the West do? Does he agree that such an approach risks infantilising the terrorists and treating them like children, when the truth is that they are adults who are entirely responsible for what they do? No one forces them to kill innocent people in Paris or Beirut. Unless we are clear about that, we will fail even to understand the threat we face, let alone confront it and ultimately overcome it.

And again, Ian Austin did not mince his words:

Does [the Prime Minister] agree with me that those who say that Paris is reaping the whirlwind of western policy or that Britain's foreign policy has increased not diminished the threats to our national security not only absolve the terrorists of responsibility, but risk fuelling the sense of grievance and resentment that can develop into extremism and terrorism?

Although Corbyn issued a statement welcoming the decision of Stop the War to delete the post that had caused such offence to his backbenchers and large swathes of the country, he never criticised it. More importantly, he insisted he would go ahead with fulfilling a commitment he had made earlier in the year to be the guest of honour at Stop the War's fundraising Christmas dinner the following month.

On 26 November, four days before a debate in the shadow Cabinet that would decide the party's whipping arrangements over the forthcoming vote on Syria, Corbyn appealed in writing to his MPs, setting out his (and presumably Stop the War's) arguments against the government's case for military intervention. This was an unusual tactic and hinted at the weakness of his position: a clear majority of his shadow Cabinet, led by Benn, were in support of the government.

But Corbyn went beyond his parliamentary party; his mandate, after all, came from ordinary party members, not from his MPs, and he would appeal directly to them. On the Friday evening (27 November), he emailed thousands of (though crucially, not all) Labour Party members, reportedly to seek their views on how Labour should proceed. In fact, since there was never any chance of the leader changing his position to one of support for military intervention, the email was actually a coded appeal to members to support his view and to put pressure on their own local MPs to follow his lead.

The tactic was condemned in brusque terms by veteran right-winger and former senior minister John Spellar, who called for Corbyn to resign over the issue. 'How does Jeremy Corbyn and his small group of tiny Trots in the bunker think they've got the unique view on it all?' he told the BBC's Radio 5 live. The correct place for the leader to set out his views was at the following Monday's shadow Cabinet meeting, not in a letter stating his position, a move that would make it impossible for him to accept a contrary, collective view if that was what the shadow Cabinet decided. Spellar added that the shadow Cabinet 'thought they were going away [over the weekend] to resume that discussion on Monday. He's now trying to pre-empt that and whip up a storm inside the party. It is, as I say, unacceptable.' When asked if shadow Cabinet members who took a different view from their leader should resign, Spellar said: 'If anyone should resign after this incident, it should be Jeremy Corbyn.'

Corbyn did not get his own way. He had wanted a three-line whip supporting his own position, but he had to settle for an agreement that Labour MPs would be given a free vote on the issue – the first time in living memory when the main opposition party had expressed no official view on the wisdom of sending British military forces into action. And another unfortunate precedent was created: since the Prime Minister would be stating the case for military action at the start of the debate, held on Wednesday 2 December, Corbyn would be expected to lead for the opposition. But as shadow Foreign Secretary, Benn would wind up the debate for the opposition, even though he had a diametrically opposite view on the issue from his leader.

Corbyn's speech received only lukewarm support from his own benches and none from anywhere else in the House (except from the massed ranks of the SNP). He recycled most of his well-beloved clichés and slogans in opposition to UK involvement in Syria, praying in aid of his arguments the spectre of Iraq and its aftermath.

Cameron's reported comments the previous day to the 1922 backbench committee of Conservative MPs, when he had allegedly said: 'You should not be walking through the lobbies with Jeremy Corbyn and a bunch of terrorist sympathisers' had provoked anger on Labour's back benches and caused several MPs – including Blairites Caroline Flint and John Woodcock – to defend their leader with interventions that attempted to put Cameron on the back foot by demanding an apology. Cameron deftly sidestepped the attacks, but was visibly uncomfortable at having to do so.

Given the special circumstances of the debate, the House had agreed that all other business be removed from the order paper and the entire day be given over to the debate on Syria, which lasted from 11.33 a.m. (after prayers, naturally) and ended when the final vote was declared at 10.33 p.m. Benn rose to make his own contribution at 9.30 p.m., beginning with a forceful rebuke of Cameron for his comments the previous day and a robust defence of his own leader.

> Although my Right Honourable Friend, the Leader of the Op-
> position, and I will walk into different division lobbies tonight,
> I am proud to speak from the same despatch box as him. He is
> not a terrorist sympathiser. He is an honest, principled, decent
> and good man, and I think the Prime Minister must now regret
> what he said yesterday and his failure to do what he should have
> done today, which is simply to say, 'I am sorry.'

Having won the sympathy of his own side and of very many others across the chamber, Benn then went on to deliver a tour de force that was lauded by countless MPs and media outlets in the hours and days afterwards. As Corbyn sat on the front bench, glaring balefully from Benn's right-hand side, the shadow Foreign Secretary destroyed the arguments of the pacifists and anti-war lobbies,

particularly those who regularly made much of their alleged ab-
horrence of fascism.

No one in the debate doubts the deadly serious threat that we
face from Daesh and what it does, although we sometimes find
it hard to live with the reality. In June, four gay men were thrown
off the fifth storey of a building in the Syrian city of Deir ez-
Zor. In August, the 82-year-old guardian of the antiquities of
Palmyra, Professor Khaled al-Asaad, was beheaded, and his
headless body was hung from a traffic light. In recent weeks,
mass graves in Sinjar have been discovered, one said to contain
the bodies of older Yazidi women murdered by Daesh because
they were judged too old to be sold for sex.

Benn knew that in highlighting the barbaric nature of the Islamists, and the similarity in their behaviour to the worst excesses
of Nazism in the 1930s and '40s, he was presenting a direct and
unambiguous challenge to those in his party who were reluctant
to draw such a comparison. The hard left had long argued that Is-
lamism itself was a product of Western imperialism – an argument
that was nothing more than a desperate attempt to avoid having
to side with the hated West against an enemy which was, they
needed to claim, more of a victim than an oppressor.

But having started with an expression of solidarity with his
leader, Benn was now pulling no punches.

As a party we have always been defined by our internationalism.
We believe we have a responsibility one to another. We never
have and we never should walk by on the other side of the road.
We are faced by fascists – not just their calculated brutality, but

their belief that they are superior to every single one of us in this chamber tonight and all the people we represent. They hold us in contempt. They hold our values in contempt. They hold our belief in tolerance and decency in contempt. They hold our democracy – the means by which we will make our decision tonight – in contempt.

What we know about fascists is that they need to be defeated. It is why, as we have heard tonight, socialists, trade unionists and others joined the International Brigade in the 1930s to fight against Franco. It is why this entire House stood up against Hitler and Mussolini. It is why our party has always stood up against the denial of human rights and for justice. My view is that we must now confront this evil. It is now time for us to do our bit in Syria. That is why I ask my colleagues to vote for the motion tonight.

Applause is rarely heard in the House of Commons and never officially approved by the Speaker. But as Benn sat down it would have been impossible to halt the wall of applause from all sides that greeted his comments. Corbyn did not join in.

Responding to Benn, the Foreign Secretary Philip Hammond called his remarks 'one of the truly great speeches in parliamentary history'. Sixty-six Labour MPs, including eleven frontbenchers, voted with the government, giving it a 174-seat majority for UK military involvement in Syria. Almost immediately, the backlash from Corbyn's grassroots supporters began. Benn and the other Labour MPs who had spoken and voted in favour of the government motion were once again branded 'Red Tories' and 'traitors' on social media and various websites.

* * *

The Middle East had long been a flashpoint for the clash of phi-
losophies on the left of British politics. Long before the debates on
weapons of mass destruction, Iraq and 9/11, there was Israel.

It would be wrong to suggest that Israel's occupation of territory on the West Bank, as a consequence of the ill-fated Six Day
War launched by neighbouring Arab states in 1967, sparked the
beginning of anti-Jewish sentiment on the left; as in many other
parts of society, and in many political parties, a mindless, latent
anti-Semitism, and oft-unspoken suspicion of the Jewish community, was present throughout history, even into the twentieth
and twenty-first centuries. But the Six Day War helped justify and
mask some of that prejudice.

While the far right, in the form of Britain's National Front, had
warmly embraced the cause of the Palestinian people's right to a
homeland of their own (particularly if that meant the removal of
Israel), the hard left found itself playing host to similarly extreme
individuals whose hatred for Jewry was camouflaged by a publicly
expressed objection to 'Zionism' rather than to Israel itself. Historically, Zionism was the movement that supported the creation of
a Jewish state in the area where the historical Israel existed until
the early Christian era. In modern terms, Zionism is the philosophy which supports and protects the state that was established by
United Nations resolution in 1948. Yet the repeated use of 'Zionist'
by the hard left to decry the actions of the Israeli government in
its dealings with its Palestinian neighbours assumed a pejorative
meaning. 'Zionist' became, in the language of Marxists and their
fellow travellers, an insult. Even to tolerate the continued existence of Israel was now seen as objectionable. This approach met
with the full-throated, enthusiastic support of organisations such
as Hamas, whose governance of the area around Gaza since 2007

had resulted not only in regular missile attacks into Israeli civilian areas but a gradual and sometimes violent subjugation of the Palestinian population's own civil liberties. Hamas's charter obliged it to campaign for the complete removal of Israel from the map and its replacement by an Islamist government under Sharia law.

But to the hard left, 'Zionist' as a term of abuse meant something else. It meant 'Jew'.

Jeremy Corbyn's hostility to Israel was well known when he became leader. If he ever had any intention of smoothing off the rough edges of his antipathy, the resolve failed him at the first hurdle: the party leader traditionally attends and speaks at the annual reception at conference of Labour Friends of Israel. The organisers of such events were used to dealing with protesters – usually young students who somehow blagged their way into whichever venue the event was being held in, in order to regale the audience with pro-Palestinian slogans until someone thought to switch the microphone off. In 2015, no such protest was required. In fact, Corbyn's speech was not inflammatory. But neither did it mention, at any point, the word 'Israel'. Although an admittedly minor offence, this was nevertheless interpreted as just that – an offence.

In February 2016, Alex Chalmers resigned from his post as chairman of the Oxford University Labour Club. In a statement posted on his Facebook page, he said that members of the club's executive committee had been 'throwing around the term "Zio" with casual abandon' and that senior members of the club had been 'expressing their "solidarity" with Hamas and explicitly defending their tactics of indiscriminately murdering civilians'. Chalmers concluded that 'a large proportion of both OULC and the student left in Oxford more generally have some kind of problem with Jews'.

Chalmers later explained to *Prospect* magazine:

I do not believe that the majority of Labour Party members and supporters are anti-Semitic. Instead, there is a tendency among some in the party to turn a blind eye to anti-Semitism. In discussions about the Israel–Palestine conflict, people too often frame their arguments in unacceptable language, whether it be use of the old trope that sinister Jewish influence controls government policy, or claims [by] former Liberal Democrat MP David Ward, that Jewish people should have learnt some kind of lesson from the Holocaust.

Within days, an inquiry into Chalmers' allegations was launched by the Labour Party's national student organisation, Labour Students. However, when the report was submitted to the party's National Executive Committee, it was decided that it would not be published. Instead, a second inquiry was ordered, this time led by Baroness Jan Royall. Immediately allegations circulated that the report had not been published because Corbyn's supporters on the NEC were eager to protect two of the students criticised in the report – one was a member of the Young Labour national committee and a second was a candidate for election to the NEC. Both were strong supporters of Jeremy Corbyn.

Royall's own report was also not instantly made available to the public after it was submitted to the NEC in early summer 2016, but the *Jewish Chronicle* obtained a copy and published it online at the beginning of August 2016. The report concluded that while 'some incidents' of anti-Semitic behaviour had indeed occurred at meetings of the Labour Club, and that 'behaviour and language that would once have been intolerable is now tolerated', it found no evidence that the club itself was 'institutionally anti-Semitic'. However, two student activists who were members of the OULC and who were identified in the report as being anti-Semitic were subsequently cleared of all wrongdoing by the party's disputes committee. Chalmers said at the time that the decision was 'entirely in line with the indifference, lack of transparency and bad faith that has characterised the response of certain parts of the Labour leadership to claims of anti-Semitism'.

Given the solidarity felt by adherents of Islam across the world, it should be no surprise that British Muslims have traditionally felt a large degree of sympathy for their co-religionists living in the Palestinian territories. If Naz Shah had known in 2014 that she would be a Labour MP a year later, or that her social media activities would become the source of a national political scandal, she might have chosen to exercise a little more judgement. Shah had won the Bradford West seat from incumbent MP George Galloway, a regular and consistent thorn in the side of his former party, who had gained the seat in a spectacular by-election victory in 2012.

In April 2016, it emerged that two years earlier Shah had shared a graphic on Facebook that showed a map of Israel superimposed on a map of America, suggesting that the solution to the Middle East crisis was to relocate the entire population of Israel to the United States. For good effect, Shah had added her own comment – 'problem solved' – before sharing it with her Facebook friends. When, in 2016, news of this was reported, Shah immediately resigned as parliamentary private secretary (PPS) to the shadow Chancellor John McDonnell, and apologised. The next day, Corbyn tried to draw a line under the matter and hoped that Shah's suspension from the party could be avoided. However, it was announced that afternoon that she would indeed be suspended, pending an investigation into her conduct. David Abrahams, who had been a major donor to the party under Blair and Brown, announced that he was withdrawing his support, telling the *Jewish News* that he was 'appalled by the growth of anti-Semitism in the party'.

In an effort to be helpful, Ken Livingstone, the former London mayor, appeared the next morning on local London radio to defend Shah and, to the bewilderment of most listeners, suggested that Adolf Hitler had been a supporter of Zionism 'before he went mad and ended up killing six million Jews'.

As MPs lined up to demand that Shah's suspension be followed by Livingstone's, he was given an opportunity the following day to apologise for his remarks. He replied: 'How can the truth be an offence? If I had lied that would be offensive.' Livingstone had got into hot water on this issue earlier in his career, when, in 2005, the then London mayor compared a Jewish newspaper reporter to a concentration camp guard. Now, in 2016, an unrepentant Livingstone was suspended from the party. He would face a disciplinary panel of the party's National Constitutional Committee (NCC) the following March (see Chapter Sixteen).

A week later, it was announced that Shami Chakrabarti, the former head of the civil rights campaigning body Liberty, had been invited by Corbyn to lead a formal inquiry into all aspects of racism in the party, including anti-Semitism and Islamophobia. The leader himself, however, saw little need for such an inquiry and told reporters:

Labour is an anti-racist party to its core and has a long and proud history of standing against racism, including anti-Semitism.

I have campaigned against racism all my life and the Jewish community has been at the heart of the Labour Party and progressive politics in Britain for more than 100 years.

A little over two weeks later, Chakrabarti, who had been a constant critic of the previous Labour government over its civil rights and security policies, announced she had joined the party but that this would have no bearing on her objectivity in leading the inquiry.

On 30 June, the Labour Party formally announced the conclusions of the Chakrabarti report, which included recommendations on disciplinary procedure but which concluded, helpfully, that the party was not 'over-run by anti-Semitism' (a claim that no one had actually made in the first place).

Regardless of how helpful Corbyn's office had hoped the report would be to the party, the launch event itself became a flash point, a perfect example of the leader's moral ambivalence towards anti-Semitism. Ruth Smeeth, who had been elected as MP for Stoke-on-Trent North in 2015, was present at the event and became the unexpected target for a bizarre attack by a Corbyn-supporting activist. Before the invited audience of journalists and MPs, Marc Wadsworth of Momentum Black Connexions, who had previously handed out copies of a press release urging the deselection of Labour MPs who wanted Corbyn to resign, was invited to ask Chakrabarti a question on the report. He used the opportunity to accuse Smeeth – who was Jewish – of working 'hand in hand' with the *Daily Telegraph*. The use of language echoed a traditional anti-Semitic trope of media conspiracies headed by shady Jewish paymasters. Smeeth, embarrassed and enraged, shouted: 'How dare you!' before leaving the room, managing to control her emotions until she was outside the venue, at which point she burst into tears.

Corbyn observed the drama silently but did nothing to defend his MP. In fact, he was seen chatting amiably with Wadsworth as the crowd exited when the event came to an end.

The reaction from Labour MPs, not least from Smeeth herself, was brutal. In a statement released later that day, she explicitly called for Corbyn's resignation. 'It is beyond belief that someone could come to the launch of a report on anti-Semitism in the Labour Party and espouse such vile conspiracy theories about Jewish people, which were ironically highlighted as such in Ms Chakrabarti's report, while the leader of my own party stood by and did absolutely nothing.' She added: 'No one from the leader's office has contacted me since the event, which is itself a catastrophic failure of leadership. I call on Jeremy Corbyn to resign immediately and make way for someone with the backbone to confront racism and anti-Semitism in our party and in the country.'

Smeeth's colleagues were just as incensed. Ilford North MP Wes Streeting tweeted to Corbyn: 'You sat there and watched our colleague Ruth Smeeth abused at a Labour event this morning. Your words are hollow.' And Stella Creasy, the MP for Walthamstow, said: 'Very angry at way Ruth Smeeth treated today – no place for such vile views in Labour movement or modern Britain.'

The Smeeth affair was not the only controversy of the day. During his prepared comments on the report, Corbyn said: 'Our Jewish friends are no more responsible for the actions of Israel or the Netanyahu government than our Muslim friends are for those of various self-styled Islamic states or organisations.' This seemed to be an argument that Israel was no more legitimate a state than Daesh/ISIL, although Corbyn subsequently denied this was the intended meaning.

Concerns over anti-Semitism – in the Labour Party and beyond it – were then taken up by the House of Commons Home Affairs Select Committee, which launched an inquiry entitled 'Anti-Semitism in the UK', to which the Labour leader agreed to give evidence as a witness. In October the committee's report concluded that under Corbyn's leadership, Labour had not done enough to tackle the issue. It also revealed that following the launch of the Chakrabarti report, at which Ruth Smeeth was abused by Wadsworth, the MP had reported more than 25,000 instances of abuse, mainly on social media. And it revealed that in a three-day period in 2014, Jewish Labour MP Luciana Berger had received 2,500 abusive tweets. The inquiry found that police-recorded anti-Semitic hate crime in England and some parts of Wales had increased by 29 per cent between 2010 and 2015, compared with a 9 per cent increase across all other hate-crime categories, and that one-fifth of British Jewish people responding to an Institute for Jewish Policy Research study had experienced at least one anti-Semitic harassment incident during the previous year, with two-thirds of the incidents taking place online.

Jeremy Corbyn dismissed the report as having a 'disproportionate' emphasis on Labour.

Also in line for criticism in the MPs' report was Malia Bouattia who, the previous April, had been elected president of the National Union of Students (NUS), despite – or perhaps because of – her record of controversial outbursts. As a member of the union's executive committee, she had managed to block a motion condemning ISIL, calling the motion 'Islamophobic'. She had dismissed the threat of 'so-called terrorism' in the UK and claimed that the government's anti-terrorism policy was influenced by the 'Zionist' lobby. She was also reported to have described Birmingham University as 'a Zionist outpost'. Bouattia was not a member of the Labour Party, but nevertheless would declare herself a strong supporter of Corbyn's when his leadership was challenged in June 2016 (see Chapter Fourteen).

Throughout the year, various examples of Labour Party members distributing or repeating anti-Semitic comments online were highlighted by the media, each one cited by Corbyn's detractors as evidence of the party's extremism under his leadership, and dismissed as rare exceptions by his supporters. Naz Shah was subsequently readmitted to the party, following her suspension and the internal inquiry, having delivered what was widely seen as a generous and sincere apology for her behaviour.

In September 2016, the Campaign Against Anti-Semitism (CAA) had claimed that Labour's anti-Semitism problem had 'deepened' under Corbyn's leadership, and produced polling that concluded that nine out of ten British Jews believed the party was soft on those who used anti-Semitic terms of abuse. Earlier in the year, in May, a poll for the *Jewish Chronicle* found support for Labour in the Jewish community had fallen to 8.5 per cent.

There was an odd postscript to the Chakrabarti inquiry.

According to an ally of Corbyn's, during the 2015 Labour leadership contest Corbyn had restated his long-held opposition to the unelected House of Lords and insisted he would never, as leader, appoint anyone to this undemocratic institution. After becoming leader, however, Corbyn immediately came under pressure to reverse his position; the upper House had won encouraging victories against the government but its continued success – Labour's continued success – would be put at risk if Labour refused to exercise its nomination rights.

Under pressure, allegedly, from a senior backbench ally, Corbyn finally agreed to consider appointing new Labour peers, provided they were female and had a BAME (black, Asian and ethnic minority) background. This was at least a step in the right direction as far as his ally was concerned; perhaps Corbyn could be prevailed upon to widen his selection criteria in the future. In the meantime, a list of six candidates was drawn up by the leader's office at the behest of Downing Street, which needed to submit the names for approval to the House of Lords Appointments Commission. Among the six names was none other than that of Shami Chakrabarti, who had joined the party just two weeks after agreeing to head the anti-Semitism inquiry.

Due to the leader's office's well-deserved reputation for efficiency, the list was not transmitted in time to Downing Street, prompting the Prime Minister himself (Cameron had announced his departure from Downing Street but was still in post) to call Corbyn personally, demanding one final time to know who he was nominating. The only name Corbyn could remember off the top of his head was that of Chakrabarti, who was duly added to the list of new peers – the only Labour nomination in 2016.

CHAPTER FOURTEEN

'SEVEN AND A HALF
OUT OF TEN'

Results in the May 2016 local elections and in elections to the Scottish and Welsh devolved bodies were widely expected to be poor for Labour and its leader. The *Daily Mail*, on 5 April, gleefully predicted the party could suffer losses of up to 150 seats, partly due to the fact that the same seats had last been contested in 2012, when Labour had secured a share of the vote seven percentage points greater than that won by the Tories. Opinion polls suggested a major fall in Labour's vote this time around.

But while the results in Scotland were every bit as bad as predicted – Scottish Labour suffered the humiliation of relegation to third place behind the Conservatives who assumed the role of official opposition to the re-elected SNP government at Holyrood – Labour, by the end of the night, had lost only eighteen seats in England. Corbyn supporters took to social media to boast of an electoral triumph. Even more importantly, they claimed (as did the party), that the result represented a major advance on the general election outcome of a year earlier, because a deficit of six percentage points to the Conservatives in 2015 had been turned into a one-point lead. The uncomfortable fact, however, was that the results in 2016 were ominously poor. Even after leading the Conservatives by a clear seven points four years earlier, Miliband had been unable to convert that triumph into support at a general election. And now the lead was only a single percentage point. The performance was particularly poor when compared to the record of previous party leaders at their first local elections. In 1995, less than a year after Tony Blair had become Labour's leader, the party gained 1,807 seats; in 2006, David Cameron's first nationwide electoral test as Tory leader, his party gained 316 seats.

Whatever unease felt by Labour's parliamentarians was quickly swallowed, however; a far more important electoral test was about to challenge all the parties.

The first time Jeremy Corbyn stated unequivocal support for the UK's continuing membership of the European Union was in the days immediately following his election as Labour leader in September 2015. Shadow Cabinet colleagues – as well as pro-EU Conservative government ministers – were anxious that the new Leader of the Opposition didn't offer comfort to those gearing up to fight for Britain's departure from the continental trading bloc. Their fears were amply justified. At the 1975 referendum on Britain's continued membership of the European Economic Community (EEC) or 'Common Market', Corbyn had voted No. That referendum had been called by the Labour Prime Minister, Harold Wilson, in an effort to heal (or hide) the fractures in his own party on the issue. Creating a new precedent, Wilson allowed serving ministers to campaign on either side of the argument without the threat of being sacked.

Having taken the country into the EEC on 1 January 1973, the Conservatives, now in opposition, managed to maintain a broadly united front in support of a Yes vote, led by the new Leader of the

Opposition, Margaret Thatcher. In the years following the decisive 2:1 vote in favour of Britain's EEC membership, both parties
experienced disagreements within their ranks to varying degrees
on the subject. The Conservatives, perhaps by virtue of having
spent the longest time in government in the four decades before
2016, suffered the most from ideological disagreements over the
constitutional and legal implications of EEC (and subsequently
EU) membership. While Europe was a passion of former Tory
leader and Prime Minister Edward Heath, it proved the down-
fall of his successor and usurper, Thatcher. In a convoluted way,
it led to the earlier, second greatest crisis of Thatcher's premiership – the Westland affair in 1986 – which claimed the careers of
two Cabinet ministers, Michael Heseltine and Leon Brittan. It
also led to the resignation of former Thatcher friend and ally, Sir
Geoffrey Howe, as Leader of the House, which itself led directly
to Heseltine's attempt to replace her as party leader in November 1990. It was the EU and the prospect of Britain joining the
European single currency – subsequently named the euro – that
created headline after headline and acres of dramatic copy for the
newspapers during John Major's benighted second term of office
following his 1992 general election victory. Almost as soon as that
campaign was out of the way, the government descended into ac-
rimony and chaos over the terms of the Maastricht Treaty which
Major had negotiated the previous winter, a treaty that guaranteed Britain's opt-out from membership of the euro for as long
as it wished. But that wasn't enough for the Tory rebels, nine of
whom were deprived of the Tory whip for refusing to support the
government during the ratification process in the Commons. Ill-
judged, off-camera comments by Major about 'Cabinet bastards'
made the headlines, exposing the fault lines in the government

to even more glaring and damaging daylight. When speculation about a challenge to Major's leadership threatened to overwhelm the party in the summer of 1995, Major issued a 'put up or shut up' challenge to his detractors. The Cabinet minister who did exactly that was John Redwood, a devoted Eurosceptic, who was beaten in the subsequent contest, but not by a large enough margin to allow Major to claim he led a united party or government.

Even in opposition, following the 1997 general election, the Conservatives never quite managed to reconcile their pro- and anti-EU wings. All their leaders during the opposition years – William Hague, Iain Duncan Smith (one of the nine whipless rebels from Maastricht days), Michael Howard and David Cameron – expressed Euroscepticism to one degree or another, usually as a reaction to the Labour government's generally consistent pro-EU approach. But back in government from 2010, albeit with the requirement of support from their coalition partners, the Liberal Democrats, Prime Minister Cameron was clearly comfortable in his seat at the top table of the EU. Nevertheless, the perceived emerging threat of Nigel Farage's UK Independence Party (UKIP) and rumours of imminent defections from his own parliamentary party persuaded Cameron that a gesture must be made. A commitment to including an In/Out referendum in the next Conservative election manifesto would be nothing more than that – a gesture. After all, no psephological expert or opinion poll suggested Cameron could win an overall majority. Forced into another coalition post-2015, or even into minority government, the referendum promise could be quietly ditched.

On Saturday 20 February 2016, having secured a modest package of reforms from his EU partners, Cameron fired the starting gun on the In/Out referendum, naming Thursday 23 June as polling day.

When Cameron called the referendum, Jeremy Corbyn had been leader of the Labour Party for five months. There was no question that Corbyn would lead the official Remain campaign – that was a role given to former Labour Home Secretary, Alan Johnson, a passionate and committed pro-European, a likeable and respected figurehead who could motivate cross-party support. Nevertheless, the success of the campaign – particularly in the face of opposition from the outgoing Mayor of London, Boris Johnson, and the Justice Secretary (and one of Cameron's closest friends), Michael Gove, who had both declared that they would back the Leave campaign – depended on unambiguous support from the leaders of the country's two biggest parties. There would be no room for equivocation or qualification; this was a fight for the future of the country; the stakes were too high to allow personal reservations to overshadow the central campaign message.

Later, following the defeat of the Remain campaign, Corbyn's supporters would claim that he had delivered an impressive 122 speeches in thirty-three days, the equivalent of 3.7 speeches per day, an effort which Angela Eagle later described as 'an itinerary that would make a 25-year-old tired'. It transpired, however, that this claim was false. The '122 speeches' were not speeches at all, but were the total number of media appearances Corbyn had made during that time. Following media inquiries to the leader's office, a statement downgraded the '122 speeches' claim to 'dozens of meetings, events and rallies'.

One media appearance made, and which was almost certainly included in the '122' figure, was on Channel 4's Friday-night comedy show *The Last Leg* on 10 June, two weeks before polling. In fact, at any other, less politically crucial time, it could have been a helpful experience for Corbyn, showing as it did a sense of humour for which he was not universally renowned. He agreed to be filmed climbing out of a Bentley (registration plate: COR BLIMEY), wearing a tuxedo and an expensive-looking fur coat, then walking down a red carpet, a stunt that might well have endeared him to viewers who like to see politicians poking fun at themselves. The actual interview that followed, however, provided his many enemies within the Labour Party with useful ammunition in their battle to depict him as a liability, not only to the party but to the Remain campaign. He was initially asked why he refused to share a platform with Cameron as part of the campaign, and he responded with an extended and fairly dry explanation of the differences between his and Cameron's approach to the EU, Cameron's being based on free markets and exploitation of workers and Corbyn's on co-operation and workers' – particularly migrant workers' – rights. The presenter, Adam Hills, then asked: 'On a scale of one to ten, where one is "I really couldn't care less about the EU" and ten is jumping up and down on the couch like Tom Cruise on *Oprah*, how passionate are you about staying in the EU?'

Corbyn replied, languidly: 'Oh, I'd put myself in the upper half, from five to ten, so we're looking at seven, seven and a half...'

Having already declared, a few minutes earlier, that 'I'm not a huge fan of the European Union,' Corbyn's answer sent Remain campaign leaders into a state of frenzy. Although criticism of the Labour leader by his own side was necessarily muted for the duration of the campaign, by the morning of Friday 24 June the gloves were well and truly off. An unnamed Labour MP told the Huffington Post website:

The EU referendum simply shone a light on how utterly out of touch Corbyn and [John] McDonnell are with so many traditional Labour voters outside of London. Jeremy made the biggest issue of concern for traditional Labour voters thinking of voting Leave – i.e. the impact of freedom of movement – his almost sole reason why Britain should Remain. It was a sort of political suicide of genius proportions.

On that same Friday morning, Corbyn's own reaction to the shock result of the night before simply made the situation worse when, in a live TV interview, he seemed to demand that Article 50 – the clause in the EU treaties that allows a member state formally to trigger exit negotiations – 'has to be invoked now'.

To his many detractors who had long suspected that Corbyn's support for EU membership had been lukewarm at best and entirely false at worst, this was the final straw. Since before his election as leader, MPs had speculated on how long Corbyn would last in the post, and there had been uninterrupted speculation as to how he could be removed in the event that he would not resign voluntarily. A leadership challenge was considered by many to be inevitable; all that was needed was a trigger. On 24 June 2016, it arrived.

For years, and certainly since the 2015 general election delivered its ominous wake-up call to Labour MPs, Labour strategists had had serious misgivings about the loss of support in their so-called heartlands of the north of England and the West Midlands. An analysis of the EU referendum results carried out by University of East Anglia academic Chris Hanretty showed that a majority of voters in 70 per cent of Labour-held seats had voted Leave, despite the virtually united front the party had presented in support of the Remain campaign (although subsequent analysis of individual votes found that 30–35 per cent of Labour voters actually voted

Leave). With the loss of Scotland in 2015, a cataclysm that was a direct result of the party's stance in the 2014 independence referendum campaign (see Chapter Seven), Labour MPs feared that the turbulence resulting from the referendum result would engulf the party's English heartlands too.

And the polls were offering little comfort. On 17 March, YouGov reported a Labour lead over the Conservatives of one point in general election voting intentions. On 12 April and again two weeks later, the same polling company showed a Labour lead of three points. And those three slim opinion poll leads were very different from the polling average – assumed by pollsters and political scientists to be a much more accurate prediction of voting behaviour – for the same period. By the day of the EU referendum, forty-two different polls had been published since the start of the year. One, on 13 March, had shown a dead heat between the two main parties and three had reported the results as noted above. But the remaining polls – thirty-eight of them – showed a clear Conservative lead of up to fourteen points. According to the average polling figures for this period, Labour was never ahead of the Conservatives. This was worrying given that opposition leaders in the past – even those who had subsequently been heavily defeated at general elections (Foot, Kinnock, Miliband) – had first led their parties to significant poll leads over the government. And now, in the weekend following the EU referendum, Labour was behind in the polls, had suffered a major reversal in the local elections and discovered that it was at odds with a significant proportion of its own voters on the key issue of the EU.

On the Saturday evening following the referendum, *The Observer* published an exclusive story revealing that the shadow Foreign Secretary, Hilary Benn, had been contacting individual members of the shadow Cabinet in order to gauge support for a move against the leader. The newspaper reported that Benn would ask Corbyn to stand down if enough colleagues agreed on that course of action. That same evening, after Benn had received a text message from Corbyn requesting that Benn phone him, the two had a calm and polite conversation, during which Benn told Corbyn he should resign as leader and that if he remained in post, Benn could no longer serve under him. Corbyn sacked Benn there and then. In a statement he issued afterwards, Benn said: 'It has now become clear that there is widespread concern among Labour MPs and in the shadow Cabinet about Jeremy Corbyn's leadership of our party. In particular, there is no confidence in our ability to win the next election, which may come much sooner than expected, if Jeremy continues as leader.'

On Sunday morning, Heidi Alexander, the shadow Health Secretary, resigned, telling Corbyn in a letter: 'As much as I respect you as a man of principle, I do not believe you have the capacity to shape the answers our country is demanding and I do believe that if we are to form the next government, a change of leadership is essential.'

Alexander was quickly followed by Gloria De Piero, shadow minister for Young People, Chris Bryant, the shadow Leader of the House, Angela Eagle, the shadow First Secretary of State and shadow Business Secretary, Ian Murray, the shadow Scottish Secretary, Lilian Greenwood (Transport), Kerry McCarthy (Environment), Lucy Powell (Education), Seema Malhotra (shadow Chief Secretary to the Treasury), Vernon Coaker (Northern Ireland), Lord Falconer (Justice) and Karl Turner (shadow Attorney General). Andy Burnham, the former leadership candidate and now shadow Home Secretary, who had already made known his interest in leaving Parliament to stand as Labour's candidate for the Greater Manchester mayoralty, tweeted: 'I have never taken part in a coup against any Leader of the Labour Party and I am not going to start now.'

Early on Monday morning, Corbyn announced a new line-up of frontbenchers to replace those who had resigned, moving supporter Emily Thornberry from Defence to Foreign Affairs and promoting Clive Lewis to the shadow Cabinet to take Thornberry's old job at Defence. However, a Westminster farce ensued when Lewis didn't arrive back in London early enough to appear at Defence Questions in the Commons at 2.30 p.m. (he had spent the weekend at the Glastonbury music festival) and Thornberry was forced temporarily to return to her old job for an hour.

Also on his way back from the muddy fields of Glastonbury was the party's deputy leader, Tom Watson, whom many Corbyn opponents saw as vital to negotiating a settlement with Corbyn that might preserve the party as a functional entity.

A key meeting on Monday morning gave a hint of the role John McDonnell was playing – and would play for some time to come – in Corbyn's leadership. Five shadow ministers, considered to be on the 'soft left' of the party – Owen Smith, John Healey, Lisa Nandy, Nia Griffith and Kate Green – had requested a meeting with the leader, not to offer their resignations but to seek reassurances from him about his future. But as the conversation progressed, the meeting was reportedly interrupted by a furious McDonnell, who promised that those who had already resigned would be punished for their disloyalty rather than brought back into the fold. The five shadow ministers were appalled by McDonnell's behaviour and the bunker mentality it betrayed. 'They got a lecture from John McDonnell with Corbyn doing his best woodwork teacher impression,' a Labour source told the *Daily Telegraph*. All five quit.

Corbyn still had to appear at the despatch box in the Commons that afternoon to reply on behalf of the opposition to the Prime Minister's statement on the EU referendum. Cameron had announced, early on the previous Friday morning, that following the victory of the Leave campaign, he intended to resign, sparking a leadership battle in the Conservative Party. But by the following Monday it was Labour, not the Tories, who were in crisis.

Cameron, perhaps more relaxed in the job now that he had decided to give it up, couldn't resist taunting Corbyn. Welcoming the arrival in the chamber of Rosena Allin-Khan (who had been elected to represent Tooting in the by-election caused by the resignation of Sadiq Khan, the new London mayor), the Prime Minister warned her: 'I'd advise her to keep her mobile phone on, she might be in the shadow Cabinet by the end of the day.' McDonnell and many Labour MPs laughed. Corbyn did not.

'And I thought I was having a bad day,' Cameron continued, to more laughter.

As Corbyn struggled through his preprepared statement on the EU referendum result, his own backbenchers shouted: 'Resign!' Only Dennis Skinner, the veteran left-winger and staunch Corbyn ally, came to his defence by sticking two fingers up towards the jeering Corbyn critics sitting behind him, much to the delight of reporters and non-Labour MPs.

The resignations, from both shadow Cabinet and more junior frontbench positions, continued during the day. And in the evening, the weekly meeting of the Parliamentary Labour Party (PLP) took place.

Corbyn had never been a regular attendee at such events. As

leader he was now expected to go, if not every week, then certainly at times of great importance. Now was such a time. He sat impassively as speaker after speaker in the crowded room (his Director of Communications and Strategy, Seumas Milne, was reportedly refused entry by security guards because the room – the largest of Westminster's committee rooms – was already filled to capacity) regaled him with the reasons why he must resign for the good of the party. Alan Johnson, the deflated and disappointed leader of the Remain campaign, told Corbyn angrily: 'I'll take my responsibility, you need to take yours!'

In response, after those who had wanted to speak had had their chance, Corbyn reiterated his intention to win a general election. This cut no ice with his frustrated, angry MPs. At the end of the meeting's formal business, Ann Coffey and Margaret Hodge submitted a motion of no confidence in the leader in the hope that a large enough majority supporting it would persuade Corbyn to go (although the motion itself would serve no formal purpose within party rules). Voting would take place the following day, with the results to be announced at 4.00 p.m.

Exhausted from the day's drama, Corbyn just wanted the meeting to end so that he could do what he enjoyed most: join a rally of Momentum supporters in Parliament Square across from the Commons. The rally had been organised at short notice as the resignations mounted. This was where Corbyn felt most at home, not in the claustrophobic corridors of Westminster, where most people he met disagreed with him and wanted him gone. Here, in the open air, faced by young, eager, idealistic activists waiting for him to tell them exactly what they wanted to hear – this was where he belonged, where he felt welcome, this was where he would be reinvigorated.

By the end of play on Monday 27 June, forty-seven Labour MPs had resigned their front-bench responsibilities. That evening, the *Daily Mirror*, Labour's only consistent and reliable supporter in what used to be called Fleet Street, revealed its front page for the next day. It, too, had had enough of Corbyn's leadership. In a full front-page splash, illustrated by a picture of the Labour leader looking older and more beleaguered than usual, an editorial declared: 'Britain is in crisis and now, more than ever, we need a strong & united Labour Party. So today we send this heartfelt message to Jeremy Corbyn. You are a decent man. But for the sake of your party ... and for the sake of your country ... GO NOW!'

Such a brutal dismissal of a Labour leader, by the *Daily Mirror* of all newspapers, was unprecedented. It was unthinkable that Corbyn could try to remain in post now.

* * *

As MPs filed into the PLP offices in the cloisters of the Palace of Westminster, Angela Eagle was preparing her challenge. No one expected the result of the day's ballot to be anything other than an overwhelming rejection of Corbyn's leadership, yet few thought it would persuade him to stand down. That being the case, an open challenge, under party rules, was the logical next step. Eagle, whose occasional outings at the despatch box, substituting for Corbyn at Prime Minister's Questions, had won her good reviews, and whose performance as shadow Leader of the House under Ed Miliband had earned her the admiration of those who had previously suspected she did not possess a sense of humour, was fired up and ready to go.

Under party rules, a challenge to an incumbent leader required the nominations of 20 per cent of Labour's MPs and MEPs: fifty. In the circumstances, this would be an easy hurdle for Eagle to clear; what was less clear was Corbyn's own status. The party rulebook was ambiguous on whether an incumbent leader also required nominations to appear on the ballot paper. If he did, then the contest would be transformed. Corbyn would find it a challenge to receive even the thirty-six nominations he had been given in 2015, when the nominating threshold had been only 15 per cent (the threshold was lower in the case of a vacancy than when there was an incumbent leader). He would have no hope whatever of gaining fifty nominations. In which case, it was assumed that the contest would be reopened to new nominations and members would be offered a choice of mainstream candidates.

That procedural decision would be taken by the NEC at a later date, after a challenger had formally declared and nominations had been received. In the meantime, MPs awaited the inevitable result of the no-confidence motion and Corbyn's less certain response. When the numbers were declared they were unequivocally damning: 216 of 229 Labour MPs took part; 172 supported the motion that 'this PLP has no confidence in Jeremy Corbyn as Leader of the Parliamentary Labour Party', with forty voting against. On a turnout of 95 per cent, 80 per cent of Corbyn's MPs had declared their opposition.

In modern parliamentary politics, it would be unthinkable for any leader to continue with the opposition of four out of every five of his MPs. But Labour's new system of electing its leaders had created a democratic paradox, a circle that simply could not be squared: MPs had no confidence in Corbyn, but the members still, apparently, wanted him to continue. The members saw the MPs as the problem, and the feeling was mutual.

Corbyn's response was robust and unequivocal:

I was democratically elected leader of our party for a new kind of politics by 60 per cent of Labour members and supporters, and I will not betray them by resigning. Today's vote by MPs has no constitutional legitimacy. We are a democratic party, with a clear constitution. Our people need Labour Party members, trade unionists and MPs to unite behind my leadership at a critical time for our country.

A challenge now seemed the only way to resolve the impasse. But it was a high-stakes gamble. There were few indications that the members who had so enthusiastically flocked to Corbyn's campaign rallies a year earlier were any less enthusiastic now; yes, the party was unpopular and not making the headway that was needed if it were to make a serious challenge at the next general election. But many of those who had voted for Corbyn in the first place were, like Corbyn himself, committed opponents of the previous Labour government, and for them electoral success was not the be-all and end-all that MPs seemed to think it was. In fact (and this was a common perception on the British hard left) wasn't electoral popularity an indication that you had sold out your principles for power? Corbyn certainly had not done that.

Any challenger risked humiliation. But what alternatives were there? It was unthinkable to consider going into a general election with Corbyn as leader, given the ammunition he had provided the party's opponents over the years as a supporter of unwise and unpopular causes. Even without such baggage, he was one of the least gifted political communicators in the country. He would have to go. And if not by defeat in an internal election, then how?

Tom Watson was not trusted by Corbyn or his team. As a minister in both the Blair and Brown governments, the deputy leader made no pretence of being on the party's left wing; his strength was his background as a union fixer, a pragmatist, a gregarious member of the PLP and a networker. Watson was, above all else, a deal maker. And in the week following the vote of no confidence, he tried to do a deal with Corbyn.

Watson was known to be a fan of *The Godfather* movies; could he make his leader an offer Corbyn couldn't refuse?

Reports about the discussions between Watson and Corbyn are conflicting; that Watson asked Corbyn to resign, and that Corbyn refused, is not disputed. Neither is it denied that at one point, a request from Watson for a private one-on-one with his leader was rejected because Corbyn's staff feared Watson might end up 'bullying' Corbyn into doing something Corbyn might later regret. Nevertheless, a reliable source close to Watson insists that the leader did, in fact, seriously consider stepping aside at Watson's request: 'He only changed his mind because Angela Eagle announced she was standing against him and that decided it for him. If she'd just waited until Tom had done his job, he might have gone.'

Another, perhaps more likely, scenario was that Corbyn's brief moment of doubt about whether he should continue was brought to an abrupt end by the intervention of McDonnell. Watson told the BBC on 30 June: '[Corbyn] has obviously been told to stay by his close ally John McDonnell. They are a team and they have decided they are going to tough this out. So it looks like the Labour Party is heading for some kind of contested election.' McDonnell dismissed the claim as 'ludicrous', but there is one very good reason to suppose that Corbyn's continuation in post at that time was essential for the wider hard left. The nomination threshold for leadership candidates, even in the event of a vacancy, remained too high to guarantee the inclusion in any future ballot of a member of the Campaign Group of MPs. Were Corbyn to go now, he would inevitably be replaced by someone from the right or centre of the party, and the left's one great opportunity to control the Labour Party would be lost, probably for ever. Until some way could be found to alter the nomination rules, Corbyn must remain in place.

On Monday 11 July 2016, Angela Eagle formally announced her candidacy for the leadership of the Labour Party. Unfortunately, and through no fault of her own, her launch event coincided with dramatic developments in a parallel political soap opera, as Andrea Leadsom announced that she was withdrawing from the Conservative Party leadership contest, effectively handing the crown to the Home Secretary, Theresa May, the only other candidate still in the race to succeed David Cameron. This meant that much of the coverage of Eagle's event was either minimal or reflected the David v Goliath news balance.

The following day, 12 July, the NEC met to decide on the procedure for the leadership contest, which was now official on the basis that Eagle had collected enough nominations. The central decision, however, was whether the leader would be forced to seek nominations too. The meeting dragged on for hours into the early evening. On the terrace of the House of Commons, Labour MPs and their guests nervously checked and rechecked their mobile phones, hoping for news on the decision. Rumours circulated about which faction's supporters had been able to attend, who was late, who was absent, and who was willing to change their minds. This was not a decision that would be taken on a cool appraisal of the facts and the wording of the rulebook; this would be decided on the basis of whether Team Corbyn or Team Everyone Else had the votes.

Just before 8.00 p.m., a ripple of excitement coursed through the crowd of drinkers and news started to spread: after a heated and unpleasant discussion, the NEC had ruled that Corbyn would not need to seek nominations, his name would appear on the ballot paper by default of being the incumbent. MPs shook their heads resignedly and ordered more alcohol. It was going to be a long summer.

The following day, Owen Smith, the MP for Pontypridd and, until a fortnight earlier, the shadow Work and Pensions Secretary, announced that he, too, wished to be considered as a candidate in the forthcoming contest. An MP only since 2010, Smith had previously worked as a lobbyist for Pfizer, the pharmaceutical company, and as a special adviser for the then Northern Ireland Secretary, Paul Murphy. Ambitious and articulate, Smith considered himself of the soft left and more able to take on Corbyn than Eagle. Crucially, he had not been an MP during the 2003 vote on military intervention in Iraq, whereas Eagle had and had supported Blair at the time. This could prove decisive in a contest in which mostly anti-war, or at least anti-Iraq War, members would take part.

The two candidates agreed that only one of them could appear on the ballot paper, and it was decided that whoever managed to secure the highest number of nominations by the deadline imposed by the NEC would stand and be supported by the other. There was some unhappiness that Smith had declared relatively late in the day and only after Eagle had put her head above the parapet and suffered a significant amount of abuse from Corbyn supporters for doing so. Further, there was a degree of frustration that a woman might not be chosen to lead the fight against Corbyn. Nevertheless, a week later, Smith, having managed to secure about twenty more nominations than his rival, was declared the PLP's champion and Eagle gracefully withdrew her nomination.

The NEC had decided that the contest would last until shortly before Labour's annual conference in Manchester began on 24 September. A series of hustings was organised throughout the country and Corbyn embarked on a carbon copy of the campaign that had secured his victory a year earlier, addressing rallies attended by hundreds of enthusiastic supporters. Smith performed well in the debates, regularly scoring points off Corbyn, who retreated into his well-worn and comfortable slogans that he knew were guaranteed to provoke applause from his supporters in the audience. These supporters were angry at MPs – MPs like Smith – who had sparked a 'coup' just as (Corbyn supporters claimed) Labour was edging ahead in the polls. Smith's background as a former Pfizer employee was used viciously by Corbyn supporters who regarded the private sector and anyone who had ever worked in it with suspicion. Smith's background even prompted Corbyn to announce a new party policy, telling one meeting in July that 'medical research shouldn't be farmed out to big pharmaceutical companies like Pfizer and others but should be funded through the Medical Research Council.' The MRC at the time spent £506 million a year on research, compared with £4.8 billion by Pfizer alone. Appearing on the BBC's *The Andrew Marr Show* three days later, John McDonnell said his friend had been misinterpreted and proceeded to row back on the bizarre announcement.

The centrepiece of Smith's campaign was a commitment to holding a second referendum on Britain's EU membership following Brexit negotiations. This was a courageous move, given the unease felt by many of his moderate parliamentary colleagues about the potential loss of Labour support to UKIP, particularly in the north of England and even in Wales, Smith's home ground. But Smith had calculated that this could be a defining issue on which the contest might yet turn: while a majority of Labour members – even those who had joined following the 2015 general election in order to support Corbyn's first leadership campaign – considered themselves further left than Smith himself, they were also, according to various surveys, overwhelmingly positive about the EU and shared Smith's bitterness at Britain's impending departure from it. But would their support for the European project trump their support for Jeremy Corbyn when the ballot papers were issued?

Smith's parallel strategy was, optimistically, to depict himself as every bit as left wing, and just as radical, as his opponent; it was Corbyn's inability to communicate the wisdom of his socialist message, not the unattractiveness of the message, that demanded his replacement, Smith maintained at hustings, to considerable derision from Corbyn supporters in the audience. The tactic was understandable, given where the centre of gravity of Labour members was located. But Smith never came close to establishing the genuine nature of his offer.

Railway renationalisation had long been a favoured aim across the left ever since the industry's privatisation by John Major's government in 1996. Although passenger numbers had massively increased in the intervening period, more weekday services had been introduced, most of the actual carriages had been replaced with new rolling stock and the industry's safety record had – eventually – improved, public ownership was still seen as an iconic policy. Commuter unhappiness about cancellations and disruptions caused by strikes and, most importantly, the perception that fares were too high and were helping to line the pockets of private sector executives, were all used by Labour, under both Miliband and Corbyn, for political advantage. But while a Miliband government would have committed to ensuring that a public sector company could compete with private transport companies for the right to run rail franchises, under Corbyn, one of the earliest policy changes was to support full-blooded renationalisation. This was an example of Corbyn's, and the left's, prejudice towards the private sector, believing that whatever the specific challenges in any particular industry, public ownership was the answer.

So on Thursday 11 August, en route to a leadership hustings event in York, the Labour leader could not resist the opportunity to put his case. A video later released by his office showed him sitting on the floor of a Virgin train and Corbyn then explaining why he was not using a seat: 'This is a problem that many passengers face every day, commuters and long-distance travellers. Today this train is completely ram-packed. The staff are absolutely brilliant, working really hard to help everybody. The reality is there are not enough trains, we need more of them – and they're also incredibly expensive.'

What the film did not show was Corbyn then moving to a seat in a near-empty carriage where he spent the rest of the journey in comfort. Incensed by the criticism it received following the release of Corbyn's video, Virgin Trains East Coast took the unusual step of releasing part of its own CCTV footage from the journey which showed Corbyn and his staff walking past scores of empty seats on their way to a vestibule where the film would be shot. An angry and unseemly to and fro then began about the facts of the event, with Corbyn supporters insisting no deception was involved and his critics insisting he had been caught out playing a very cynical game. It was only after the Virgin CCTV footage was released that a spokesman for Corbyn said:

When Jeremy boarded the train he was unable to find unreserved seats, so he sat with other passengers in the corridor who were also unable to find a seat. Later in the journey, seats became available after a family were upgraded to first class, and Jeremy and the team he was travelling with were offered the seats by a very helpful member of staff.

This shed no light on why Corbyn had been seen walking past empty seats before he recorded his video message. Labour MPs were not reluctant to get involved in the controversy. Chris Bryant told the PoliticsHome website: 'This makes Corbyn seem like a charlatan, pretending to be one thing when he is really quite another.' Another unnamed MP said: 'There's as much chance of a Virgin Trains' sandwich becoming Prime Minister as Jeremy Corbyn.'

Unfortunately for Corbyn's opponent, Owen Smith, the controversy did little damage to the Labour leader's own campaign for re-election. A YouGov poll of members, released at the end of August, predicted Corbyn would not only win, but would secure a larger margin of victory than in 2015. Corbyn was heading for 62 per cent of the vote compared to Smith's 38 per cent.

The poll turned out to be extraordinarily accurate. When the result was announced in Manchester on Saturday 24 September, Corbyn was re-elected with 61.8 per cent of the vote compared to Smith's 38.2 per cent. Against a single candidate, the leader had triumphed with a bigger share of the vote and a bigger majority than when he had faced three candidates the previous year.

Affecting a conciliatory tone, Corbyn told delegates that in the Labour Party, 'we have much more in common than that which divides us. As far as I'm concerned the slate is wiped clean from today.' Corbyn later expressed the belief that 'lots of MPs' who had resigned would now be willing to support him as he took the fight to the Tories.

A summer of mass resignations, an unprecedented vote of no confidence and a full-frontal challenge to Corbyn's leadership had ended with Corbyn renewing, even strengthening, his mandate. And hopes (fears?) that at least some of the refuseniks whose resignations had sparked the leadership challenge might return to duty were swiftly confirmed. One Corbyn critic (revealed as 'hostile' in the infamous memorandum – see Chapter Twelve) was the Opposition Chief Whip, Rosie Winterton, Ed Miliband's choice for the role, whose appointment had spelled the end of her predecessor, Nick Brown's reign (see Chapter Five). Armed with his new mandate, Corbyn dismissed Winterton – whose loyalty he and his supporters had always suspected was less than skin-deep – and replaced her with Brown. An experienced and apparently loyal enforcer, it was the third time Brown had been appointed to the role, including two separate occasions while Labour was in government. If Corbyn's detractors had hoped to undermine the leader through the whips' office, that hope had now been snatched away after an unexpectedly clever move by the leader.

CHAPTER FIFTEEN

POSTCARDS FROM SWITZERLAND

After Corbyn's re-election, few moderate MPs could suggest a way forward that attracted the support of the majority. Some had argued that an annual challenge to Corbyn would eventually wear down his support as well as the man himself, but this was opposed by many MPs who feared it might have the opposite effect, and encourage those who had only joined the party in order to support Corbyn to renew their annual memberships where they might otherwise have allowed them to lapse. Also, the tactic risked making the party's defeat at the next election even larger; few voters will support an extreme party, or one led by an extreme leader, but even fewer will support an extreme party that is openly divided over its extreme leader.

Instead, the PLP (or the large majority of it) chose to learn a lesson from Labour's unhappy history.

In the run-up to the 1983 general election, the Labour MP John Golding, a ferocious opponent of Militant and its fellow travellers such as Tony Benn and Eric Heffer, was scornful of the party's various policy documents that had been published in recent years, their heavy emphasis on left-wing policies illustrating the dominance of the Bennite left within the party. Convinced that Michael Foot, the party's hapless leader, was taking Labour to certain and cataclysmic defeat at the next election, Golding decided he would make sure the left took responsibility for it.

The joint meeting of the shadow Cabinet and the party's National Executive Committee (NEC) that decided the content of Labour's general election manifesto was known as the 'Clause V meeting', since that was the clause in the party's rulebook that stipulated the membership and authority of such a meeting. During the Clause V meeting in advance of the 1983 general election, Golding made a generous and apparently conciliatory offer: instead of fighting over which policies should be chosen to go in the manifesto on which Labour's candidates would seek election, why not simply aggregate all the previous policy documents into a single volume and call it a manifesto?

The left fell for it. The manifesto was not dubbed 'the longest suicide note in history' by the late Gerald Kaufman for no reason; it was both electorally suicidal and very, very long indeed. And after polling day on 9 June, when Tony Benn had lost his own Bristol seat (and his chance to contest the leadership vacancy soon to be created by Foot) and Labour had sunk to a paltry 28 per cent of the vote – barely 2 per cent ahead of the SDP/Liberal Alliance – no one doubted at whose door the blame for the rout should be placed.

While claims by Corbyn supporters that Labour had been making progress in the polls up until the point when the 'coup' had been launched in June could be dismissed with a glance at polling data, it was nevertheless agreed that Corbyn must be deprived of an opportunity to blame anyone else for his failure. A decree of *omerta*, silence, was issued. Perhaps, if Labour MPs were seen to be, if not loyal, then at least not obviously critical, Corbyn and his team might yet have to face reality and choose to quit the battlefield rather than lead the party to disaster. At the very least, if Corbyn insisted on the Labour ship going down with its captain, then, just like Golding's gambit three decades earlier, this new tactic would ensure everyone knew who to blame when the general election arrived and the iceberg hoved into view.

On 21 June 2005, Jamie Reed had addressed the House of Commons for the first time. He used his maiden speech to out himself as a Jedi, before adopting a more conventional and traditional approach to the occasion, offering his audience a colourful tour of his Copeland constituency.

A decade later, the number of parallels offered by George Lucas's *Star Wars* saga were probably too many to count, but the unexpected elevation of the anonymous and ineffectual Senator Palpatine to the job of Chancellor of the Galactic Senate probably rang a few bells for him. At one point his Twitter profile included the phrase 'Red Leader, Rebel Alliance'. Reed, famously, had become the first frontbencher to resign after Corbyn's election (see Chapter Eleven). During his time as a Member of Parliament, Reed had gained a reputation for being capable, intelligent and hard-working. He was fiercely loyal to the area where he had been born and raised and a strong supporter of the nuclear industry which was the area's main source of employment. He was also a member of the first generation of Labour MPs to miss out on ministerial preferment. More fortunate, better-connected, colleagues of the 2005 intake had found themselves installed in ministerial cars almost immediately after making the transition from spad to MP. But Reed and most others from the intake had had to wait, pay their dues and do the legwork needed in minor, unpaid roles. Had Labour remained in office in 2010, there is little doubt that

Reed would have become a minister. A similar fate befell another, earlier generation of capable Labour MPs, elected in 1979, who found themselves shut out of office, Labour returning to government only after many of these MPs had retired or been defeated.

Reed's home and constituency in England's far north-west meant a challenging six-hour commute, twice a week, for a man whose day job was in Westminster. Increasingly frustrated with the direction of Labour under Ed Miliband and, with Corbyn's election, seeing the party becoming as remote from its voters as his home town of Whitehaven was from London, Reed had been unhappy as an MP for some time. His safety valve, an unremitting stream of humorous, self-deprecating and sometimes bizarre tweets about his party and its leader, made life in Westminster only barely more tolerable. By late 2016, Reed had already told his closest friends that he planned to quit. On 21 December, as the Commons geared up for the start of the Christmas recess, Reed announced that he had accepted a job with the nuclear processing facility in Sellafield, based in his constituency, and would resign his seat at the end of the following month.

The tribal nature of British political life has resulted in many of each party's supporters adopting a 'party comes first' mentality, a mentality that hardly resonates with ordinary voters, who would view such loyalty to – of all things – a political party as odd. Only in the Labour Party would a relatively young man or woman with abilities that could be deployed in another industry for greater reward and closer to home, who had no prospect of ministerial office and therefore no opportunity to make decisions that would benefit his constituents or anyone else in the country, be considered a traitor for taking another job. Yet in the strange, febrile culture of Labour in the twenty-first century, representatives of the party were expected – at least by some – to sacrifice their careers and even the happiness of their own families, rather than choose a better, more satisfying life.

Reed's colleague, Ian Austin, the MP for Dudley North, regretted his friend's decision but understood it. It was 'terrible somebody of his talent, commitment and hard work doesn't see his future in the Labour Party in Parliament', Austin told *The Guardian*. But the Corbyn-supporting Skwawkbox website took a more critical view of Reed's behaviour, branding him 'one of Labour's worst and most embarrassing MPs'. Undoubtedly echoing the more excitable part of left-wing activism, Skwawkbox added:

> The Progress member, who once accused leader Jeremy Corbyn of creating a 'toxic' environment in the Labour Party, apparently sees no irony in going off to work in the nuclear industry, although it will presumably come as a relief to him to no longer be the most poisonous element in his vicinity.

On Friday 13 January 2017, Reed was joined in the escape tunnel by Tristram Hunt, who announced he was giving up his parliamentary seat in Stoke Central to become director of the prestigious Victoria and Albert Museum in London.

Hunt, first elected to the Commons in 2010 and once seen as a potential party leader (he had tried to stand in 2015 but fallen short of the nominations required to enter the race), had been a successful academic and historian with a broadcasting career before entering Parliament. Like Reed, he was known to be unhappy in Parliament now that Corbyn was his party's leader and Labour's prospects of returning to power had all but disappeared. And, like Reed, Hunt had also been a vocal critic of Corbyn.

Neither man took the opportunity provided by their resignations to publicly criticise Corbyn; they were both adherents to the PLP's new strategy of allowing him to fail on his own terms. While the reaction of many parliamentary colleagues to Reed's and Hunt's announcements was envy – rumours of further resignations abounded – not all of Corbyn's critics were happy the two men were leaving Parliament. Every by-election afforded Corbyn an opportunity to get one of his own supporters elected to Parliament, which would potentially diminish the ranks of moderates. Hunt subsequently reported, philosophically, the anger of some of the PLP's more militant anti-Corbynites to his announcement, and understood why they felt this way. Nevertheless, both he and Reed were more often described as 'lucky bastards' than 'traitors' by those left behind. Hunt recalls that one particularly enthusiastic critic of Corbyn's told him: 'When you write to us from your new job, it'll be like those men in Colditz getting postcards from their mates who've escaped and made it to Switzerland.'

Once both men had formally resigned from the Commons, the party moved quickly to set the date for when elections for Reed's and Hunt's replacements would take place: Thursday 23 February.

It was Labour's record in by-elections since Corbyn had assumed the leadership that gave his supporters at least some encouragement. In Oldham West and Royton, which Corbyn's ally, Michael Meacher, had held until his death in October 2015, the Labour candidate, Jim McMahon, had held on with an increased majority and a 7 per cent increase in the share of the vote since the general election. In the contest in Sheffield Brightside and Hillsborough, brought on by the death of newly elected MP Harry Harpham, and which was won by his widow, Gill Furniss, Labour's vote again represented a significant increase on the general election result. And in the Tooting by-election on 16 June 2016, caused by the resignation of Sadiq Khan on his election as London mayor, Labour's Rosena Allin-Khan increased her party's share of the vote by almost 9 per cent.

But Copeland and Stoke both threatened to be different.

First, Labour's fall in the national opinion polls in the second half of 2015 had been steep and steady. By the start of 2017, under Theresa May's leadership the Conservatives were regularly scoring more than 40 per cent, while Labour was struggling to hit 30 per cent. Second, unlike Oldham, Sheffield and Tooting, neither of the contests scheduled for February were in what could be regarded as 'safe' Labour seats. Reed had won Copeland in 2015 with a majority of only 2,500 and just over 42 per cent of the vote, with the Conservatives in second place. In Stoke, Hunt had won just 39 per cent of the vote and a majority of 5,179, on a turnout that had been the lowest in the country.

Third, and most ominous for Labour, which had campaigned unequivocally for Remain in the EU referendum just six months earlier, voters in both seats had voted overwhelmingly for Leave – an estimated 62 per cent in Copeland and as much as 69 per cent in Stoke-on-Trent Central, making it potentially the highest winning margin for Leave in the UK (precise figures for parliamentary constituencies were unavailable because the referendum results were compiled and announced by local authority areas).

The bookmakers immediately installed the Conservatives as favourites to win Copeland and – initially at least – banked on UKIP to take Stoke.

A Conservative victory in Copeland seemed at once both likely and unlikely. It was viewed as likely because the Conservatives had only lost the seat at the general election by 2,500 votes, making it a marginal in most senses of the word. On the other hand, a Tory victory could also be considered as extremely unlikely, because in UK by-elections government parties simply did not gain seats from the opposition. It had happened in the past, but only in peculiar and unusual circumstances: in 1982, during the Falklands' crisis and at a time of national patriotic fervour, the Labour MP Bruce Douglas-Mann, having defected to the Social Democratic Party, chose to give his constituents the chance to re-elect him under his new party colours. They chose instead to elect a Conservative MP. Beyond these unusual and unique circumstances, to find a precedent for the main opposition party losing a by-election to the governing party you had to go back to 1960, when the Conservative Party had narrowly won the Brighouse and Spenborough seat from Labour.

In Stoke, meanwhile, Labour faced a challenge from the new leader of UKIP, Paul Nuttall, who, at least initially, threatened to run a strong campaign in a seat the tabloid newspapers had started to call 'Brexit Central'.

Nuttall's campaign missteps – particularly his admission that a claim on his website that he had lost personal friends in the Hillsborough disaster in 1989 was untrue – were a godsend to Labour's candidate, Gareth Snell, a Corbyn critic whose own campaign had been unsettled by revelations that he had previously tweeted ill-advised comments that could have been considered misogynist and offensive.

In the event, despite a swing to UKIP of just over 2 per cent, Snell managed to beat off Nuttall's challenge. But Labour's winning majority, of 2,620 votes, was almost 50 per cent less than that which had been achieved by Tristram Hunt, who had held the seat at the 2015 general election.

Meanwhile, Copeland's voters returned the first Conservative to represent the seat since 1931. Trudy Harrison beat Labour's Gillian Troughton with a majority of 2,147 and a swing from Labour to the Conservatives of 6.7 per cent.

The loss was particularly sharply felt because Labour had chosen to make local NHS provision the centrepiece of its campaign. Surely no Labour voter would back the Conservatives when the future of local hospital facilities was at stake? The tactic was, at least in part, an attempt to divert attention from the various hostile remarks Corbyn had made in the past about nuclear power: the Sellafield nuclear reprocessing facility was Copeland's largest employer and the government planned to build a new nuclear plant, Moorside, in the same vicinity, providing a major boost to the local economy. The Conservatives, scenting blood at the very start of the campaign, had done all they could to exploit Corbyn's anti-nuclear comments in the past, issuing a leaflet offering voters a direct quote from the Labour leader: 'I say NO nuclear power, decommission the stations we've got.' The voters' final judgement suggested they trusted the Conservatives more, not only with their local jobs, but with their local hospital too.

While cooler observers judged the result to be at least of significance, if not a political earthquake, and a herald of dark times indeed for the Labour Party, Labour itself, more ambitiously, attempted to spin the result. Cat Smith, the MP for Lancaster and Fleetwood, in a courageous act of loyalty to her party leader, told ITV News: 'At a point where we're fifteen to eighteen points behind in the polls, to push the Conservatives within 2,000 votes I think is an incredible achievement here in Copeland.'

The general secretary of the public sector Unison trade union, Dave Prentis, previously a Corbyn supporter, chose to take a different line from Smith, and told reporters that while the party leader was not entirely to blame for the defeat, 'he must take responsibility for what happens next'. It was the most explicit, though coded, warning to Corbyn yet made by a trade union leader.

On the Friday morning, according to the *Daily Telegraph*, when Corbyn was asked by reporters whether he had 'looked in the mirror and asked yourself the question: "Could the problem actually be me?" Corbyn replied simply: "No." Asked why not, he said: "Thank you for your question."'

A projection by the Electoral Calculus website suggested that if the Copeland result were to be replicated throughout the country in a general election, the Conservatives would win a majority of 108–130. Such projections are rarely accurate, and even by 2015, the notion of a 'uniform swing' that affected every seat to the same degree had long disappeared. Nevertheless, there was no way to interpret the results of 23 February as anything other than disastrous for Labour.

The left-wing journalist and *Guardian* columnist, Owen Jones, who had supported Corbyn's first leadership campaign in 2015, told his readers: 'There is no pussyfooting around Labour's Copeland rout. Opposition parties simply do not lose by-elections to governing parties. Yes, Labour's support has been in decline in the constituency since 1997; and we know that working-class disillusionment kicked in under New Labour. But wasn't the whole point of the Jeremy Corbyn project to reverse that trend, not have a further dramatic drop of support just two years after the last general election? And while Labour activists in Stoke should beam with pride for routing UKIP, there, too, there was a swing to the Tories.'

Jones concluded: 'I understand the dilemma torturing so many who supported Corbyn. Lifelong commitment to a good and noble cause; fear that if Corbyn falls the cause will fall with him; yet fear that his project is failing badly and risks destroying the cause in any case.'

CHAPTER SIXTEEN

A SPECIAL TYPE OF IDIOCY

The decision by UK voters, on 23 June 2016, to leave the EU, had ended the career of the Prime Minister, David Cameron. It had also provided the excuse rebel Labour MPs had been seeking to launch an ultimately doomed challenge against Jeremy Corbyn's leadership. And it triggered renewed nationalist demands for the break-up of the United Kingdom.

In the frenetic last few months of 2016, two court decisions – by the High Court and then confirmed by the Supreme Court – obliged Cameron's replacement, Theresa May, to seek the authority of Parliament, in the form of an Act, to trigger Article 50 of the Lisbon Treaty and formally begin the countdown to Britain's departure from the EU.

Having, perhaps overexcitedly, called for Article 50 to be triggered 'now' in the first hours following the unexpected and dramatic referendum result in June, Jeremy Corbyn was not trusted by many of his pro-EU MPs to hold the government to account on the details of the new legislation. In fact, the government made it clear from the outset that the Bill should contain no details of Britain's negotiating position and that it should simply authorise the Prime Minister to trigger Article 50; May's own priorities had been set out in a speech at Lancaster House, London, on 17 January 2017, and she had no intention of tying her government's hands by establishing any of those aims in a statute before negotiations began.

Corbyn let it be known that he would impose a whip on his MPs to vote in favour of the Bill at Second Reading – the first vote that takes place on a Bill, before any amendments are moved and debated. Worse still (as far as his large minority of diehard Remain-supporting MPs were concerned), he announced that Labour would support the Bill in principle during its passage through Parliament, even if all of the amendments his party planned to table were defeated. In fact, Corbyn enjoyed the support of a majority of his MPs for this tactic; nervous about the still live threat from UKIP as well as from a resurgent Conservative Party (even the Liberal Democrats were enjoying something of a revival, if the results of local council by-elections were to be believed), Labour feared that being seen to oppose the will of the majority of voters would deal a severe blow to its electoral fortunes. While up to 70 per cent of Labour voters had voted Remain, the government's dramatic U-turn, from opposing leaving the EU under Cameron to supporting it under May, had so far not done the Conservative Party any harm in the polls.

Nevertheless, there were enough Labour MPs in Corbyn's ranks, and on his front bench, who maintained a devotion to the Remain cause, to prevent the Labour leader from presenting a united front to the country. It also meant that splits in the party grabbed the headlines in the run-up to the introduction into Parliament of the European Union (Notification of Withdrawal) Bill.

On Thursday 26 January Corbyn was reported as having decided to impose a three-line whip in favour of supporting the Bill's

Second Reading, but briefings on his behalf suggested that front-benchers who defied the whip might not have to resign their posts. Later the same day, the MP for Hampstead and Kilburn, Tulip Siddiq, the shadow Education minister, resigned from the front bench after just four months in the job. She was followed the next day by Jo Stevens, the shadow Welsh Secretary. Both women were committed to voting against Article 50. Now Corbyn seemed to take a harder line on discipline. During an interview with Robert Peston on ITV the following Sunday, the Labour leader said: 'It's obviously impossible to carry on being in the shadow Cabinet if you vote against a decision made after a very frank and long discussion of the shadow Cabinet earlier this week.'

By Sunday 5 February, this line seemed to have changed again. Corbyn told BBC Radio 4's *The World This Weekend*, when asked whether frontbenchers who defied the whip could retain their jobs: 'You are asking me a very hypothetical question here. I will be making an announcement during the week. I am a very lenient person.'

During the debate on the floor of the House of Commons, another two Labour frontbench MPs who opposed Article 50 resigned – Dawn Butler, the shadow minister for Diverse Communities, and Rachael Maskell, the shadow Environment Secretary. There was also speculation that Clive Lewis, the shadow Business Secretary and one of Corbyn's most high-profile supporters, was considering his position, having spoken out publicly on a number of occasions against leaving the EU.

After a two-day debate (which presaged a three-day debate the following week, with the House sitting as 'a committee'), the Bill was approved by a margin of 494 in favour and 122 (including forty-seven Labour MPs) against. However, one prominent name was absent from the list of Labour MPs supporting their leader's policy. Whatever the personal views of the shadow Home Secretary, Diane Abbott, regarding Article 50, she was under no illusions that a large majority of voters in her Hackney constituency had supported Remain. When her absence from the Commons at the point of the crucial vote was explained, Abbott came under some very unfriendly 'friendly fire' from her own colleagues. Abbott had let it be known that she had missed the vote in order to nurse a migraine at home. However, at least one MP, Ronnie Campbell, had travelled to the Commons to vote for the Bill, despite being officially on sick leave while undergoing treatment for cancer.

The Bassetlaw MP, John Mann, told the BBC News channel: 'We have some very, very ill people who turned up to Parliament to vote yesterday who are so sick they cannot carry on with their work as MPs. They voted and she gave herself a sick note at 5.00 p.m. We all know what is going on here. She bottled the vote. It is cowardice. You don't abstain on the big votes. It is embarrassing to see that. She ought to give an apology to the Labour Party for doing so. That is not leadership, that's cowardice.'

Former shadow Cabinet member Caroline Flint adopted a more light-hearted approach. 'We used to have man flu, we now have Brexit flu that Diane has created,' she told Robert Peston the following Sunday, in advance of the committee stage of the Bill.

The following week, the Bill returned to the House where MPs were given the opportunity to propose and vote on amendments. Despite valiant attempts to secure concessions from the government over the rights of EU nationals living in Britain after its departure from the EU, and to secure a meaningful vote in Parliament on whether or not to accept the government's final deal, the Conservative whipping arrangements held, and the Bill was approved, unamended, at the Third Reading debate on Wednesday 8 February. One of those voting against the Bill, and against the Labour whip, was Clive Lewis, who joined fifty-one Labour colleagues in opposing Article 50 and his own leader. Explaining his decision to rebel and to step down from the shadow Cabinet, Lewis said: 'When I became the MP for Norwich South, I promised my constituents I would be Norwich's voice in Westminster, not Westminster's voice in Norwich. I therefore cannot, in all good conscience, vote for something I believe will ultimately harm the city I have the honour to represent, love and call home. It is therefore with a heavy heart that I have decided to resign from the shadow Cabinet.'

Speculation about Lewis's leadership ambitions were immediately ratcheted upwards. Corbyn's spokesman issued a warm response, thanking Lewis for his work on the front bench. In fact, Lewis had endured a difficult relationship with the leader's office, if not the leader himself, since the previous year's annual conference, at which Lewis, then shadow Defence Secretary, had been expected to deliver a keynote speech. Seconds before he began speaking, Lewis had been ordered – not by Corbyn but by Seumas Milne – to drop a line in the speech conceding that he would not attempt to change conference's pro-Trident policy. Lewis reportedly vented his anger by punching a nearby wall.

As government MPs congratulated the Prime Minister for getting a 'clean' Bill through the Commons, Corbyn, having made it clear from the beginning that Labour would support the Bill, amended or not, ill-advisedly took to social media.

'Real fight starts now. Over next two years Labour will use every opportunity to ensure Brexit protects jobs, living standards & the economy,' he tweeted.

He was inevitably and mercilessly mocked, with more than one Twitter user comparing Corbyn's challenge to that of the Black Knight in *Monty Python and the Holy Grail*, whose four limbs are hacked off in a duel before he graciously calls it a draw.

With Labour still nursing the wounds it had suffered in the loss of Copeland to the Conservatives, and the EU Bill expected to pass through Parliament on Monday 13 March (assuming the Lords accepted that the Commons had the right to overturn two amendments it had made), the country's attention turned briefly to economic matters – Philip Hammond's first Budget statement was due on 8 March – before returning once more to Scotland.

That the most difficult job facing any Leader of the Opposition is responding to the Budget is a statement that has been made so often it has almost become a cliché. Nevertheless, it is true. With no prior briefing as to the contents of the Chancellor's famous red box, the leader has to deliver a first response, usually based only on snippets of information that have been previously leaked to the media, with perhaps one or two more contemporaneous observations about what the Chancellor has just said. By the time he stood up to respond, Corbyn seemed the only person in the country not to have realised that the Chancellor had just broken a Conservative Party manifesto promise made at the previous election, namely that the government would not increase national insurance (NI) contributions. Hammond had just announced an NI hike for the self-employed, and social media was buzzing with excitement as Corbyn cleared his throat at the despatch box. Afterwards, the *New Statesman*, the in-house journal of the Labour Party, was not encouraging. 'Philip Hammond's threadbare Budget broke a key Tory manifesto pledge and offered little substantive engagement with the biggest challenges facing the economy (neither the Chancellor nor the Treasury's Budget book mention Brexit *once*) – but the leader of the opposition still failed to land a decisive blow,' wrote Patrick Maguire. 'The critique that made up the bulk of his response … was, for the most part, a valid one. But, as ever, Jeremy Corbyn's response was shouty and diffuse and displayed little substantive engagement with the Budget itself.' Corbyn's only line on the NI increase – 'We have long argued to clamp down on bogus self-employment but today the Chancellor seems to have put the burden on self-employed workers instead' – was, said Maguire, 'oblique at best'.

A week later, following a wave of protest from government backbenchers, Hammond was forced into a humiliating climb-down. Half an hour before the weekly session of Prime Minister's Questions, a letter explaining the U-turn was published. It could have been a gift to Corbyn, but even now he could barely make a dent in Theresa May's composure. Instead of using all six of his allotted questions to try to embarrass the Prime Minister on having tried and failed to break a manifesto promise, he asked two, before moving to his chosen subject of the week, education. *The Guardian*'s Andrew Sparrow commented: 'A better leader would have taunted her with a series of questions about why she defended the policy last week, or at least produced an effective sound bite as the SNP's Angus Robertson did. Instead, even when Corbyn was commenting on NICs, he diverted into employers' abuse of self-employment – an important topic, but one where May has a case.'

In the preceding week, however, Scotland had exploded back on to the political agenda, and again Corbyn found his intervention less than welcome.

On 23 June 2016, while the whole of the UK voted, by a narrow but clear margin, to leave the EU, Scottish voters had opted by 62 to 38 per cent to support the Remain camp. This, claimed the SNP, might well be the 'material change of circumstance' required to justify a second independence referendum, notwithstanding assurances made by the party's leadership during the first campaign that the 2014 vote was a 'once in a generation opportunity'.

Now, as Westminster prepared to pass the European Union (Notification of Withdrawal) Bill into law, speculation mounted that Nicola Sturgeon, Scotland's First Minister, would tell her party's spring conference later that week that she intended to seek the Scottish Parliament's authorisation to request the power from Westminster to hold a second independence referendum. Assurances from Theresa May that the devolved institutions would be consulted in the run-up to the triggering of Article 50 had not been honoured, Sturgeon argued, and the SNP's own preference for special treatment for Scotland – in effect to be allowed to continue to be part of the EU single market even as the rest of the UK left – had been rejected.

Scottish Labour, along with the Conservatives and Liberal Democrats at Holyrood, had long opposed, in principle, a second independence referendum. During a campaign visit to Glasgow on 11 March, Corbyn was asked by the Press Association what he thought of the prospect of another independence referendum. He replied: 'If a referendum is held then it is absolutely fine, it should be held. I don't think it's the job of Westminster or the Labour Party to prevent people holding referenda.'

This was in direct contradiction of the position of his Scottish party, whose sole MP, Ian Murray, said via Twitter: 'Often asked why I resigned from shadow Cabinet. Ladies & Gentlemen I give u Jeremy Corbyn. He's destroying the party that [so] many need.'

Sturgeon herself tweeted: 'Always a pleasure to have @jeremycorbyn campaigning in Scotland.'

Abandoning any attempt to conceal his feelings about his leader, Ilford North MP Wes Streeting tweeted: 'When Tories are on ropes over budget, it takes a special type of idiocy to back an independence referendum. Slow clap @jeremycorbyn. Enough.'

It was not enough for Corbyn who, two days later, blamed the media for 'mischievous, misrepresenting reporting': 'But just to be absolutely clear, I do not think there should be another referendum.'

On 2 April, research by academics Colin Rallings and Michael Thrasher concluded that Labour was heading for a loss of up to fifty seats in the local elections due at the beginning of May 2017. A day later, Robert (Lord) Hayward, a polling expert, predicted Labour was in danger of losing up to 125 seats.

* * *

As Labour MPs and party members braced themselves for – at the very least – uncertain results in the local elections, and with both the Liberal Democrats and former Respect MP George Galloway claiming to be Labour's main challenger in the Manchester Gorton by-election caused by the death in March of the veteran Labour MP Gerald Kaufman, few chinks of light seemed visible for Labour. The opinion polls told a miserable story of double-digit leads for Theresa May's government while Corbyn's chief response was to attack and get angry at the media.

There was one chink of light, however.

Len McCluskey, the former Militant supporter whose hard-left views had barely mellowed since he took up the reins of the country's largest trade union, Unite, was Corbyn's most enthusiastic and powerful supporter, providing crucial political cover from the trade union wing of the movement. McCluskey's close friend, Karie Murphy, whose parliamentary ambitions had been thwarted by Ed Miliband in Falkirk (see Chapter Six), was now Corbyn's chief of staff. The Unite leader had won re-election as general secretary once before, in 2013, when he had beaten a single challenger by a margin of 64–36 per cent. But only 15 per cent of Unite members eligible to take part in the election had done so.

Although elected for a five-year term, McCluskey chose to trigger an early election by resigning at the end of 2016 and announcing he would stand again. A second re-election would give him extra time in office in the crucial run-up to an expected general election, whereas serving out his original term of office would have meant coming under pressure to retire in 2018. As expected, Gerard Coyne, the union's West Midlands regional secretary, and viewed by moderate Labour MPs as a centrist figure, announced his intention to run against McCluskey. Normally such contests would have little impact on the Labour Party, of which Unite is its biggest donor and most influential affiliate. However, shortly before Corbyn had been announced as winner of the 2016 leadership contest, McCluskey, via the BBC's *Panorama* programme, sent a not remotely veiled threat to disloyal Labour MPs: 'Some of the MPs have behaved despicably and disgracefully and they have shown no respect whatsoever to the leader and they should be held to account.' And no one doubted that 'held to account' meant deselection when the time came for the party to choose candidates for the next general election. McCluskey's defeat at the hands of Coyne would be a severe setback for Corbyn's leadership, depriving the Labour leader of an essential ally. As one Labour MP and

Unite member said: 'If Coyne loses, the fight against Corbyn goes on. If McCluskey loses, Corbyn's finished.'

The result would be crucial to moderates' hopes of defeating the party rule change proposed by Corbyn supporters at the 2017 conference, should it be debated there. The 'McDonnell amendment' – so-called by Richard Angell, the director of Progress – would reduce the required amount of MP or MEP nominations needed by any future leadership candidate from 15 to just 5 per cent of the total number of parliamentarians, meaning that in future contests, the hard left would be guaranteed a candidate on the ballot paper. Moderates recognised the change as pivotal, one that would, if passed, consign the party to perpetual control by the hard left and, therefore, unending opposition. Unite would play a key role in deciding the outcome of any vote on the issue at both the NEC and on the floor of the conference. McCluskey's defeat, therefore, was seen as vital to the future electoral recovery of the party.

In mid-March 2017, shortly before ballot papers were issued, an unexpected spat between Tom Watson and the founder of Momentum, John Lansman, promised (or threatened) to raise the profile of the Unite contest. An audio recording of Lansman addressing a meeting of Momentum supporters in Richmond at the start of that month revealed Lansman's hopes that following McCluskey's expected victory, 'Unite will affiliate to Momentum and will fully participate in Momentum, as will the CWU [the Communications Workers' Union].' Lansman also used his speech to encourage Momentum members to organise within the Labour Party in order to dominate the local constituency delegates' vote at the party's annual conference in the autumn in order to secure support for the McDonnell amendment.

Lansman was immediately taken to task by Watson, who told him via Twitter: 'You've revealed your plan. If you succeed you will destroy the Labour Party as an electoral force. So you have to be stopped.'

The exchange blew up into a full-scale sectarian battle, with Corbyn's (and McCluskey's) supporters countering accusations of a secret deal between Lansman and Unite to divert some of the union's resources towards an organisation that had always been regarded by Labour MPs as a 'party within a party'. Watson was himself accused of deliberately provoking a fight only in order to raise the profile of the Unite internal contest, and thus increase turnout among its members, increasing the chances of his former friend, McCluskey, being defeated.

Ballot papers were sent out to the union's 1.4 million members in late March and early April, with the winner scheduled to be announced later that month.

* * *

On 30 March 2017, former London mayor Ken Livingstone stopped to talk to reporters as he made his way to the first day of what would turn out to be a three-day disciplinary hearing before a panel of the party's National Constitutional Committee (NCC). Asked whether he regretted his previous comments about Hitler and Zionism, he said, cheerfully: '[Hitler] didn't just sign the deal. The SS set up training camps so that German Jews who were going to go there could be trained to cope with a very different sort of country when they got there. When the Zionist movement asked, would the Nazi government stop a Jewish rabbi doing their sermons in Yiddish and make them do it in Hebrew, he agreed to that. He passed a law saying the Zionist flag and the swastika were the only flags that could be flown in Germany. An awful lot. Of course, they started selling Mauser pistols to the underground Jewish army. So you had right up until the start of the Second World War real collaboration.'

The belligerent tone in which Livingstone repeated and embellished the claims that had landed him in hot water had already infuriated his critics. Nevertheless, after two full days, the disciplinary panel had still not reached a conclusion and announced that it would meet again on the following Tuesday (4 April).

Finally, in the early evening of the hearing's third day, Livingstone left the building with a smile on his face. He had been suspended – not expelled – from Labour, despite having been found guilty of three breaches of the party rules that meant he had brought it into disrepute.

The ruling seemed to give encouragement to Livingstone. He said afterwards: 'If I'd said Hitler was a Zionist, I would say sorry. You can't apologise for telling the truth. I apologise for the offence caused by those Labour MPs who lied.'

Condemnation was immediate and angry. Tom Watson issued a statement attacking the NCC's decision. 'I find it incomprehensible that our elected lay members on the disciplinary panel found Ken Livingstone guilty of such serious charges, and then concluded that he can remain a member of the Labour Party … My party is not living up to its commitment to have a zero-tolerance approach to anti-Semitism.'

Luciana Berger said the NCC's decision was 'a new low for my party … Why is anti-Semitism being treated differently from any other form of racism?'

Wes Streeting, appearing alongside Livingstone to discuss the day's events on the BBC's *Newsnight*, pointed out the existence of a website whose sole purpose was to monitor the number of times Livingstone mentioned Adolf Hitler.

The chorus of disapproval finally spurred Corbyn himself into action. The following day it was announced that Livingstone's further comments – those made since the original complaints had been made against him and which therefore had not been considered during the earlier hearing – would now be considered by the NEC. 'It is deeply disappointing that, despite his long record of standing up to racism, Ken has failed to acknowledge or apologise for the hurt he has caused,' said Corbyn.

*   *   *

At least some of the criticism Corbyn had faced since becoming leader was unfair. Journalists were quick to report whenever he failed to show up at the weekly Monday night meetings of the PLP, yet none of his predecessors had been expected to address their parliamentary colleagues more than two or three times a year, usually at the first meeting following the start of a new term, or after a particularly important set of election results. Corbyn's reluctance to attend at all was obvious and, to most observers, entirely justified. He was rarely extended a warm welcome or given much support; such events were a far cry from the comforting embrace of his compatriots on the hard left whose campaigning causes and political goals he shared.

On 20 March 2017, the leader was treated to a particularly hostile reception by MPs who vented their frustration at his failure either to lead a discussion on the party's disastrous result in Copeland or to offer any analysis of the result himself. Anger had also been heightened by briefings from Corbyn's office aimed at undermining Tom

Watson following the deputy leader's comments on Momentum and Unite. Dave Watts, a former chair of the PLP and now a member of the House of Lords, told Seumas Milne that he was 'a disgrace', while Ian Austin warned Corbyn that to discover the source of Labour's unpopularity, he had only to look at himself in the mirror.

Afterwards, Corbyn sloped off to the safety of his own office. And there, he decided he would address the party – the real party, the members, not the MPs or the Lords. The video of Corbyn appealing for calm and unity was posted online later that evening, with him telling his audience, as he apparently attempted to suppress a chuckle: 'Sometimes spirits in the Labour Party can run high. Today has been one of those days.'

'High spirits' is a phrase usually used to describe those of a jolly or cheerful disposition. Corbyn's use of it surprised and confused many, for few outside or inside the party in the first half of 2017 would have considered it an accurate description of Labour's mood at any level. But the point of posting the video was not lost on his critics: MPs and peers could shout and criticise all they liked. As Corbyn had shown repeatedly since first being elected, he was accountable to the wider party, to its membership, not to the PLP. And it was to the members he would address himself. The internet and social media allowed a leader in his position to bypass Parliament in a way that could never have been anticipated by any of his predecessors. Of course, none of his predecessors had ever needed to.

The video did not go down well with his MPs (nor was it intended to). Jess Phillips, the straight-talking Labour MP for Birmingham Yardley since 2015, detected a deliberate and unsubtle element of passive aggression in her leader's comments. 'He had a face like my husband's, when I'm recovering from a hangover and he deliberately hoovers around me to make a point.'

CHAPTER SEVENTEEN

'NOTHING HAS CHANGED'

Theresa May had repeatedly assured her country and her party that she would not call an early general election. Speculation about an early poll was always inevitable when a Prime Minister was replaced between elections. In fact, in July 2016, May had become the seventh British Prime Minister since the end of the Second World War to accede to office between elections, out of a total of fourteen to hold the office in that period, and only one of them – Anthony Eden – had held an immediate election in order to legitimise his leadership. The woman who, as shadow Leader of the Commons, after Gordon Brown performed his abrupt U-turn on a snap general election in October 2007, accused him of 'running scared' of a general election, seemed unambiguously committed to emulating her predecessor-but-one. Unlike Brown, however, May was careful not to allow speculation about an imminent poll to gather steam and to raise expectations: there would be no snap election and that was that.

And then, on Tuesday 18 April 2017, journalists were informed that the Prime Minister would be making a statement on the steps of Downing Street at 11.00 a.m., following a meeting of the Cabinet. This caught even the most assiduous political reporters off guard, and in the absence of any clues as to what such an announcement might be about, on-air speculation about an early general election became the inevitable focus of the excited journalists. When May, hair blowing wildly in the wind, duly arrived at the podium and announced that she would indeed be calling an election for Thursday 8 June, commentators were bewildered. May's repeated denials that she was planning an early poll sat uneasily with this volte-face; what had changed her mind?

Given subsequent events, it has become fashionable to claim that May's U-turn was ill-considered and politically incompetent. In fact, examining the decision without the benefit of hindsight, it made perfect political sense.

The previous week, YouGov had announced details of its latest poll of general election voting intentions. It gave the Conservatives a significant 21-point lead over Labour, with May's party on 44 per cent and Jeremy Corbyn's on 23. The YouGov opinion poll revealed that while 50 per cent of respondents believed May would make the best Prime Minister, the equivalent figure for Corbyn was 14 per cent – 22 per cent behind the proportion who ticked the 'Don't Know' box. Other polling organisations had produced similar results.

The Copeland by-election, while strengthening the hand of Corbyn's enemies and giving voice to criticism from previously loyal supporters, had also caused much angst in the government's ranks. Could the Prime Minister really fail to take advantage of such propitious circumstances? Under the terms of the Fixed Term Parliament Act (FTPA), the next general election would not be held until May 2020. Could the Tories' opinion poll lead – and May's popularity – last that long? Would she and the party be forgiven if they did not take advantage of current favourable circumstances, only to lose the initiative if and when Brexit negotiations failed to produce an electorally popular deal?

It was later briefed that May had changed her mind on whether or not to call an election while on a walking tour of Snowdonia in Wales during the Easter parliamentary recess. The snap election was necessary, she told sceptical reporters in Downing Street, 'because we have at this moment a one-off chance to get this done while the European Union agrees its negotiating position and before the detailed talks begin'.

She may have been keen to avoid the same mistakes as Brown, but May risked duplicating one specific one: just as Brown, after 5 October 2007, had sought to convince the media that his decision not to hold a snap election had had nothing whatsoever to do with opinion polls, so May tried to claim that her decision to go ahead with a snap poll was similarly not based on electoral calculations. Few believed her.

Before the advent of the FTPA, Prime Ministers had enjoyed the luxury of being able to analyse local election results at the beginning of May and then decide (parliamentary timetable permitting) whether or not to risk a general election a month later – the pattern followed by Margaret Thatcher in 1983 and 1987. However, since 2010, a Prime Minister's room for manoeuvre had been significantly reduced by the FTPA. If May was set on 8 June for polling day, then she could not afford to wait until the local elections in May were out of the way before calling the general election; the terms of the Act could have meant a long and complicated process that might have seen polling day being kicked further into the summer months, with May looking dangerously like the victim of events rather than in control of them.

The Act did not rule out an early election before the statutory five-year term had ended, but it did make that outcome more difficult to secure than in the days before the Act became a part of political life under the Conservative–Liberal Democrat coalition government. There were only three ways May could get her way: the first was to call for a vote in the Commons where two-thirds of MPs would have to support a motion for an early poll. Failing this, an early election might be held if a vote of no confidence in the government were carried by a simple majority. But this was not an attractive prospect for any incumbent Prime Minister hoping to earn the confidence of the electorate. The third option would be to amend the Act, a process which could be progressed in a relatively short period of time, provided the House of Lords agreed. The journalist John Rentoul of *The Independent* newspaper has revealed that this third option was the one that May considered to be most likely. Given the state of the opinion polls and the Copeland result, not to mention the continuing rebellion within the ranks of Labour MPs against Corbyn's leadership, she believed that the Labour leader, while claiming to welcome the prospect of an early election, would instruct his MPs to abstain on the crucial government motion, depriving May of the necessary 434 votes in favour.

Rentoul wrote: 'She expected Corbyn to say something like: "I'm happy to have an election, but May is doing this for her own purposes and it is her mess to fix. We can have a vote of no confidence if she thinks the government can't govern."'

May's Plan B, the amendment to the Act, would have taken some time to implement, which is why, Rentoul claims, she announced the 8 June general election date a full seven weeks in advance – an unusually long campaigning period in recent historical terms.

In fact, Corbyn surprised May and many others, in both his party and the media, by announcing within an hour of the Prime Minister's statement that he would instruct his MPs to support the motion. The following day, after a ninety-minute debate, the Commons voted by 522 to thirteen in favour of holding a general election on 8 June.

*   *   *

Labour had been claiming for some months that it was on an 'election footing', but like the media, it was wrong-footed by May's announcement, with not a single official parliamentary candidate in place. This was not unusual: the party had expected a drastic redrawing of constituency boundaries before the next election, and there would have been little point in selecting candidates based on the old boundaries. The party had fallen foul of this trap once before, in the run-up to the 1983 general election, when it had selected candidates based on the old electoral map, only to have to run many selections over again when new constituency boundaries were confirmed by Parliament. Now, in 2017, the task was to get every candidate in place before the 11 May deadline for nominations.

Meeting on the same day that the Commons voted for May's motion, Labour's NEC quickly agreed that, since there would be very little time to hold full selection contests, all sitting Labour MPs who wished to stand again should be allowed to do so. This was a blow to some of the leader's allies who had viewed the anticipated boundary changes as an opportunity to rid the parliamentary party of some of Corbyn's more persistent critics. Now, any of those critics who chose to stand would be on the ballot paper on 8 June. Pete Willsman, a left-wing supporter of Corbyn's on the NEC, tried to persuade fellow members to adopt his idea that no candidate should be endorsed by the party unless he or she signed a loyalty pledge to the leader. But the initiative was quickly dismissed by the NEC, which recognised that many MPs would simply refuse to sign, resulting in an unedifying stand-off that would further damage the party's electoral prospects by drawing unnecessary attention to splits in the PLP. All vacant seats, including those currently held by Labour MPs who intended to step down, would be filled by either the NEC or by local regional party committees.

Almost immediately, Labour MPs known to be unhappy with Corbyn's leadership and who had given up hope of returning to ministerial office during their lifetimes, announced they would be standing down. The most high profile of these was the Barnsley East MP, Michael Dugher, a close ally of Tom Watson's, who had been sacked as shadow Culture Secretary by Corbyn in 2016. Iain Wright, the Hartlepool MP and chair of the Commons Business and Enterprise Select Committee, had focused on his committee work during the civil war of the last two years but was known to be unhappy with Corbyn's leadership. Wright decided he would not contest the general election. Other MPs who opted to step down included Gisela Stuart, who had led the Vote Leave campaign in 2016, and former Home Secretary and inheritor of Denis Healey's title of 'Best Labour Prime Minister We Never Had', Alan Johnson. Tom Blenkinsop, who had arrived in the Commons in 2010 as MP for Middlesbrough South and East Cleveland, was another vocal critic of Corbyn's. A leading member of the moderate steelworkers' trade union, Community, Blenkinsop saw no future for himself on the green benches.

Some MPs, like Dugher and Blenkinsop, resigned in despair at the direction Corbyn was taking the party; others, like Rob Marris, who had returned to the Commons two years earlier after a five-year absence, representing his old seat of Wolverhampton South West, were simply convinced that they could not turn the tide of opinion back in the party's favour, and did not relish the prospect of another defeat.

From the very start, Labour's campaign was professional and enthusiastic, if falling short of the 'slick' label. 'June will mean the end of May,' Brent Central MP Dawn Butler told a busy Labour rally that had been hastily organised for London's Church House on Thursday 20 April. It was a confident, upbeat start to the party's campaign, and Corbyn himself told assembled supporters, staff and MPs that 'Labour in government will do what the Conservatives never could, and end this rigged system,' although he mysteriously failed to specify which system in particular was 'rigged' and in what way. Asked by a journalist if he believed the Labour brand had been tainted after a year and a half of internecine strife, the leader responded smoothly and unselfconsciously, responding that 'There are people in the audience who are wearing badges of Keir Hardie. He was vilified, vilified beyond belief when he was elected as the first Labour MP.'

Aside from effortless self-comparisons with one of the Labour movement's most iconic and revered figures, Corbyn, at least publicly, never allowed a trace of doubt about Labour's imminent victory to be detected in either his speech or countenance. Despite truly appalling polling numbers at the start of the campaign, and many predicting a historically low share of the vote for Labour and a calamitous slump to fewer than 200 parliamentary seats, Corbyn maintained an energy and calm that impressed many observers.

Replicating his two successful leadership campaigns, he addressed packed rallies across the country, both indoors and outdoors, enjoying a rapturous reception from mostly younger audiences. Meanwhile, Theresa May was revealing what must have been, to her staff and wider circle of colleagues, a disturbingly flat-footed and wooden approach to campaigning.

Almost as soon as the election was called, Labour enjoyed a modest strengthening of its support in the opinion polls. As John Rentoul observed: 'I assume this was a partisan reaction to an unexpected election. People who had been unenthusiastic about Jeremy Corbyn's leadership, telling pollsters they didn't know how they would vote in an election that was probably three years away, suddenly reverted to their Labour allegiance.' Nevertheless, most opinion polls still predicted an overwhelming three-figure Conservative majority. In the period from the announcement of the election on 18 April to voting day in the local elections on 4 May, twenty-six separate polls were published, only five of which measured Conservative support at less than 45 per cent. ComRes's figures for the *Sunday Mirror*, published on 23 April, suggested that May's party would receive a staggering 50 per cent share of the vote – exactly double the level of support enjoyed by Labour. On the eve of local election polling day, YouGov for *The Times* put support for the Conservatives at 48 per cent – a full 11 points higher than its level of support in 2015 – with Labour trailing on 29 per cent, the same percentage secured by Gordon Brown in 2010 and just 1 point up on Michael Foot's disastrous modern-day low watermark for the party in 1983.

The results of the GB-wide local elections held on 4 May brought little comfort to Labour. Thirty-five authorities in England, including six new directly elected combined authority mayors, plus all the councils in Scotland and Wales, were up for election. Not only did the Conservatives increase their equivalent share of the vote compared with the last time these councils had been elected (up 8 per cent to 38), Andy Street, the Conservative candidate and former managing director of John Lewis, won the West Midlands mayoralty – a devastating blow to Labour hopes in an electorally crucial area of the country. It was the best local government electoral performance for the Conservatives in ten years. The omens for an overwhelming Conservative victory on 8 June remained favourable.

Shortly after the May elections, it was announced – to the fury of Labour moderates – that Andrew Murray, a long-time Communist Party member, Stalin admirer and defender of the North Korean regime, had been seconded from Unite to head up Labour's general election campaign. This, predicted the leader's internal party critics, was further evidence of Corbyn's true political instincts.

The Prime Minister was not known for her warm and sparkling personality. In her various shadow Cabinet roles during the Conservatives' years in opposition, May had earned a reputation for a 'no nonsense' approach to politics. She eschewed the chummy camaraderie frequently indulged in by frontbench colleagues, and was never to be seen having a post-adjournment drink in the Strangers' Bar in the Commons. She seemed something of a throwback to the age of more serious politicians, an antidote to those weary of a more modern, sound-bite-heavy, celebrity-light form of politics. That is almost certainly what a majority of Conservative MPs who voted for her as leader in 2016 believed, and opinion polling in the months that followed reinforced her reputation as a straight-talking, practical leader, someone whom one might not necessarily wish to have a drink with in the local pub, but who could be relied upon to deliver on the government's promises. By the start of 2017, May's steely evocation of Margaret Thatcher seemed the perfect foil to Jeremy Corbyn's unpopular, divisive and unrealistic vision for Britain.

The historically high opinion poll lead enjoyed by the Conservatives created a sense of impregnability, which led to an almost fatal complacency. This was revealed in two different ways. First, May calculated that refusing to engage with Corbyn in a head-to-head televised debate with the Labour leader would have little effect on the standings of the parties. The media, naturally, were outraged that the institution they had created five years earlier, and which they desperately hoped would become part and parcel of every future general election campaign, was being so casually treated by the Prime Minister. It was a subject Corbyn sought to exploit on 19 April, in the second-last Prime Minister's Questions before Parliament was dissolved: 'She says that it is about leadership, yet she refuses to defend her record in television debates.'

May responded: 'I have been answering his questions and debating these matters every Wednesday that Parliament has been sitting since I became Prime Minister.' She intended to take her case to the country rather than repeat the weekly exercise with Corbyn in a television studio.

For a time, the issue remained important only to journalists, politicians and those inside the Westminster bubble. As the campaign continued, however, May's reluctance to debate Corbyn fed into a wider narrative, that she was, in fact, less confident of her arguments than she appeared, and – most damaging of all – that she was hiding from the electorate. Corbyn, meanwhile, with very little to lose, embraced the campaign with genuine enthusiasm and apparent confidence. If he was to play the underdog in this election, he would do it well and for all it was worth.

The second way in which May's and the Conservatives' complacency was revealed was in their manifesto, published exactly one month after May's surprise announcement of a snap election, on 18 May. Included in the party's plans for social care reform was a commitment to force elderly people to pay for the costs of their care from the value of their homes. A plan to impose a £72,000 cap on such costs in 2020 would be scrapped, but to offset this, those with assets worth up to £100,000 would be protected – an increase from the current £23,250 threshold. The value of a person's home would be taken into account when being means tested for the costs of care in their own home. This would mean a significant increase in the number of older people contributing to the costs of their care.

The policy was, counter-intuitively, more progressive and redistributive than Labour's. That did not stop the opposition party immediately coining the headline-friendly label 'dementia tax' in order to exploit the Conservatives' difficulties, and Labour went on the attack in defence of asset-rich pensioners who formed much of the Conservatives' electoral base. The issue of spiralling social care costs and how they could be met in the long term had been a major headache among policymakers of both parties for years; in biting the bullet and acknowledging that property assets might play a bigger part in the funding solution, May and her special adviser Nick Timothy, who wrote much of the manifesto, calculated that there might never be a better time to win a mandate for a socially necessary but politically unappetising policy. All that was necessary was for the leader and her Cabinet to hold their nerve against the attacks that would follow.

They didn't. Things started to fall apart almost immediately. The Health Secretary Jeremy Hunt spent the next day explaining the progressive nature of the policy and arguing that the alternative would be to benefit financially the better-off, asset-rich citizens. But by Sunday, the constant attacks on the 'dementia tax' had started to unnerve ministers. While Damian Green, the Work and Pensions Secretary, told Andrew Marr on BBC that there was no prospect of reviewing the policy, the Foreign Secretary Boris Johnson told Robert Peston of ITV that 'there will be a consultation on getting it right'.

The following day, at a campaign event in Wales, May publicly conceded that, contrary to what had been announced the previous week, there would, after all, be a limit (she refused to use the word 'cap') on the amount of social care costs to be met by any individual. But not only did she refuse to state a figure for such a limit, she adopted a visibly irritated tone as she told her audience: 'Nothing has changed; nothing has changed.'

But something had changed.

Writing in *The Independent*, John Rentoul acknowledged that May had attempted to make a bad system fairer and more sustainable. 'However, good government is not the same as good politics, especially if there is an election on … she has made a bad policy worse.'

The shambles that threatened to define the Conservatives' manifesto was in stark contrast to the launch of Labour's own programme. A draft version of the party's manifesto had been leaked on 10 May. By the time of the official launch in Bradford six days later, little of the final document had changed. The Ministry of Labour, scrapped by Harold Wilson's Labour government in 1968, would be reintroduced, giving the trade unions a central role in government once again. New taxes would be announced for those earning £80,000 or more; the railways, water, energy, Royal Mail and buses would all be renationalised. The party aimed to appeal both to disappointed Remain voters and also to Leave supporters by promising an end to EU freedom of movement rules as well as committing to maintaining the full benefits of single market membership (a promise dismissed by the Labour-supporting *New Statesman* as being in 'have your cake and eat it' mode). Surprisingly, the party maintained its commitment to the Trident nuclear deterrent, despite its leader's well-known support for unilateralism.

The uncritical, positive mood music that accompanied Labour's launch event was in sharp contrast to the defensiveness and subsequent blame game of their rivals that ensued once their manifesto went public.

On Sunday 21 May, three days after the Conservatives' manifesto launch and five days after Labour's, a YouGov opinion poll for the *Sunday Times* revealed the first single-digit lead for the Conservatives since the start of the election campaign, with the Conservatives on 44 per cent and Labour on 35 per cent.

Terror struck at the heart of British democracy on the evening of Monday 22 May, when a bomb was detonated as fans left a concert by American singer Ariana Grande at the Manchester Arena. The home-made device, built by Islamist terrorists working in the name of the ISIS militia in Syria and Iraq, claimed the lives of twenty-two people and injured 250 more. Twelve days later, a second violent Islamist terror attack unfolded in the capital when a van was deliberately crashed into pedestrians on London Bridge. Three terrorists then abandoned the vehicle and attacked nearby citizens using knives. Eight people were killed and forty-eight injured before police marksmen shot the attackers dead.

On the first occasion, in Manchester, a tense ceasefire between the political parties held for a short while; voters were known to take a dim view of politicians who sought to capitalise on such tragedies for their own ends. Nevertheless, it was inevitable that in the middle of a general election campaign, some political point-scoring would occur. Criticism was made of the Conservatives for their austerity-driven public sector cuts which, claimed Labour, reduced unnecessarily the number of police officers on the street and, therefore, increased the risks to the public. After the London Bridge incident, Corbyn wasted little time before going on the offensive. Speaking in Carlisle the following day, the Labour leader said, 'You cannot protect the public on the cheap.' Aware that any appearance of lack of resolve towards the assailants would deeply damage him and his party's electoral prospects, Corbyn sought to draw a line under the controversy of 2015, when, in the aftermath of the Paris terror attacks, he had opposed a 'shoot-to-kill' policy against terrorists (see Chapter Thirteen). Now, he told his audience: 'Our priority must be public safety and I will take whatever action is necessary and effective to protect the security of our people and our country that includes full authority for the police to use whatever force is necessary to protect and save life.'

For more than a year, Conservative strategists had assumed that Corbyn's record on the IRA and his sympathy towards Islamist 'hate preachers' would fatally wound any general election campaign he led. But now, following two brutal attacks on the public, carried out by people whose political philosophy was virtually identical to that of Corbyn's 'friends' in Hamas, it was the Conservatives, not Labour, who found themselves on the defensive over police funding.

It was a remarkable development. During the 2015 Labour

leadership election and in its immediate aftermath – and in a relatively constant drip-feed ever since – Labour's opponents had
done all they could to highlight Corbyn's past associations. The
tactic, according to the opinion polls and most electoral results,
had worked. But now, especially on social media, voters were being
targeted with an avalanche of pro-Corbyn propaganda, much of
it fabricated, promoting the (false) narrative, for example, that
Corbyn had played some role, however minor, in the Northern
Ireland peace process that had led to the Good Friday Agreement
of 1998. His many meetings with Sinn Féin while the IRA's terror
campaign was in full swing, and even his appearance in 1987 at
a ceremony in London to honour dead IRA gunmen, were now
reinterpreted by Corbyn's online army as 'working towards peace'.
Whether the constant attacks on Corbyn had simply lost their
impact through repetition, or whether younger voters in particular
no longer saw the relevance of a dispute that had ended two decades earlier – perhaps the 'alternative history' being perpetuated
by Momentum and others was taking hold and convincing people
– Corbyn's historic political judgement became less of a drag on
his and his party's popularity than many had assumed.

On 26 May, Corbyn was interviewed by veteran commentator
Andrew Neil in a BBC election special. Challenged about his past
associations with the IRA, Corbyn insisted he had never met with
the IRA, and that former prisoners with whom he had met had
told him they were no longer members of the terrorist organisation. In response to questioning on the 1987 Conway Hall event
(see Chapter Nine), organised by the Irish republican Wolfe Tone
organisation, the Labour leader insisted that he had attended in
order 'to honour all those who had died in Northern Ireland'.
Although it was unlikely that the occasion could have assumed

such an ecumenical intention, the opinion polls suggested that enough potential Labour voters were willing to be satisfied by the explanation.

Corbyn and May both faced hostile questions during a BBC *Question Time* special on Friday 2 June with each of them appearing separately in front of an invited audience and also fielding questions from David Dimbleby. May came under pressure on her social care policy, while Corbyn was challenged repeatedly over his refusal to say whether or not he, as Prime Minister, would ever use nuclear weapons. His biggest cheer from the audience, notably, was when he began by regretting that the Prime Minister had refused to take part in a face-to-face debate with him.

The opinion polls throughout the long campaign had shown a gradual narrowing of the Conservatives' lead; in the twenty-six published polls between May's announcement of the election and polling day in the local elections just over a fortnight later, the Conservatives had averaged 46 per cent support and Labour 27 per cent. In the next twenty-five polls that were published, that gap narrowed to fifteen points, with the Conservatives still on forty-six but with Labour rising to thirty-one. In the thirty-six polls published between the Manchester terror attack and voting day itself, Labour closed the gap to seven points, a 43–36 split in the Conservatives' favour. The most bullish member of Corbyn's team throughout the campaign had been the shadow Chancellor, John McDonnell. He had confidently predicted that Labour would not only close the gap with the Conservatives but would win the election outright. Few others in the party's team shared his optimism, although morale rose as the gap narrowed.

The polls varied widely. There had been much talk, earlier in the campaign, of Labour MPs in safe seats having given up hope, of refusing to mention Corbyn in their literature, or refusing to host campaign visits by him to their areas. But the narrowing of the opinion polls had confounded such rumours. Appalling (for Labour) polling in Wales at the start of the campaign had suggested an unprecedented victory there for May's party, but by the last fortnight before the election, the Tory opinion poll lead in Wales had been reversed.

At 10.00 p.m. on the night of the general election, no one knew for sure what was about to happen. The BBC/ITV/Sky News exit poll in 2017 was the most highly anticipated of the modern campaigning era. And as Big Ben chimed the closure of polling booths throughout the country, the truly shocking result was announced: the Conservatives would be the largest party in a hung parliament, twelve seats short of an overall majority. Theresa May's party (assuming the exit poll was correct) had lost seventeen seats. David Cameron's remarkable achievement of winning an overall majority when no one had anticipated it had been overturned by a successor whom almost everyone in the country had expected to harvest a large working majority. Labour, meanwhile, was predicted to have added thirty-four seats to its House of Commons total.

The final result was gratifyingly close to the exit poll numbers provided by the relieved polling organisations. The Conservatives won 317 seats (a loss of thirteen), Labour 262 (a gain of thirty) and the SNP thirty-five (a loss of twenty-one seats from two years earlier). The Liberal Democrats managed to increase their tally from the eight they had secured in 2015 to twelve, despite their leader Tim Farron spending large amounts of time on the campaign trail trying publicly to square his evangelical Christian beliefs with his party's, and the country's, more liberal outlook on sexuality.

With Northern Ireland's Democratic Unionist Party (DUP)

taking eight seats and Sinn Féin expected to continue its boycott of Westminster by not taking up the seven seats it had won, speculation immediately turned to Arlene Foster's party as the key to Theresa May's continued occupation of No. 10.

The two parties that had won the 2017 general election were the Conservatives and, in Scotland, the SNP. Paradoxically, the leaders who ended the campaign most seriously damaged were Theresa May and Nicola Sturgeon.

And the leader of the Labour Party, the party that had just lost a third successive general election, emerged stronger and, for the first time in his short tenure, unchallengeable.

CHAPTER EIGHTEEN

CAPITULATION

Labour had lost, again. And Corbyn had won. When the near fatally wounded Theresa May returned to Downing Street following her brief audience with the Queen, at which the monarch invited her to form a new government, the Prime Minister gave a brief factual statement to the assembled media, ignoring their questions about resignation and humiliation, and returned inside No. 10 without even an acknowledgement of the drama of the night before.

For Corbyn, the result was more of a cause for celebration than even his initial election as party leader had been nearly two years earlier. He had proved his critics wrong, he had not turned out to be the electoral liability they had warned of; rather, he had led the party to a historic increase in Labour's vote from 31 per cent in 2015 to 40 per cent now. A rise of five percentage points in the Conservative vote meant that the combined two-party vote had surged to 82 per cent, a significant increase on the 65–70 per cent range of recent elections. But the similarly historic rise in the Conservatives' share of the vote served to blunt Labour's electoral achievement by producing only a modest 2 per cent national swing in its favour. Nevertheless, when the exit poll was announced, moderates, awaiting their own results at town halls and community centres throughout the country, knew the game was up. Corbyn was now secure in his position as party leader for as long as he wanted to remain there. While few of the moderates actively wanted Labour to be wiped out, they believed an electoral catastrophe would at least have allowed them to regain control and begin the long march back to the top of the electoral mountain.

How should they respond? Whether or not the Conservatives' plans to reduce the number of seats in the Commons went ahead – nothing was guaranteed in a chamber where no party had a majority – the spectre of reselection still haunted Labour MPs. With the bit between their teeth, Corbyn's supporters in Momentum would seek revenge on his detractors. The moderates' only hope, surely, was to bend the knee?

And they did. On the day after polling, leading lights of the rebellion against Corbyn, including the man who had challenged him the year before, Owen Smith, battled for air space in order to pay homage to a leader they had previously held in such contempt. 'I was clearly wrong in feeling that Jeremy wouldn't be able to do this well. And I think he's proved me wrong and lots of people wrong and I take my hat off [to him],' Smith told reporters. 'I don't know what Jeremy's got but if we could bottle it and drink it we'd all be doing very well.'

The party's deputy leader Tom Watson was forced into an even more humiliating apology to the daughter of comedian and actor Steve Coogan. Clare Coogan-Cole had been working part-time for Watson on the campaign. As a Corbyn enthusiast, she had been dismayed by the level of contempt and hostility expressed by the deputy leader and his team towards the leader. Following the publication of the exit poll, Coogan-Cole's father later reported,

Watson offered a public apology to Clare. 'The best part of the whole campaign for her was that Tom Watson was just about to go off to do his speech at his own constituency count,' Coogan told newspapers weeks later. 'And in front of all the other campaigners, he turned and saw that Clare was smiling. He stopped. He made everyone listen and said: "Clare, I just want to say, you were right and everyone else was wrong".' Watson's final, definitive capitulation would not occur for some months yet, however, and when it happened it would be even more public, even more humiliating.

Chuka Umunna, the Streatham MP and one-time leadership candidate who had publicly announced his refusal to serve on Corbyn's front bench the moment Corbyn had been elected leader in September 2015, said Corbyn had had 'a brilliant campaign', stating: 'Jeremy has fought this campaign with enthusiasm, energy and verve.' And, speaking on behalf of both wings of the party, he added: 'Jeremy Corbyn remains leader of the Labour Party, quite rightly so, after this campaign.' And in a not remotely veiled hint that he would now be willing to serve on Corbyn's front bench, Umunna was reported as saying: 'I want to see Labour get into government and I'll do that in every and any way that I can.' At time of writing, Umunna's offer to serve had not been taken up by his leader.

Moderates disinclined to humiliate themselves publicly instead kept their own counsel. But there were some – a very few – who held on to their previously expressed views about the leader, though in more qualified, more careful tones. Chris Leslie, the former shadow Chancellor who had, like Umunna, refused to serve on the front bench after Corbyn became leader, complained that Labour had failed to score an 'open goal' against the Conservatives. He told BBC Radio 4:

We shouldn't pretend that this is a famous victory. It is good, as far as it's gone, but it's not going to be good enough. Five years of Conservative government – I just can't, I'm afraid, be a cheerleader for that particular outcome because this was an open goal for all of us. We should have been getting in there.

When asked about his previous criticism of Corbyn, he replied: 'I'm not going to pretend that I have suddenly changed my views about this. You know that I've got disagreements with Jeremy on particular issues, whether it's security, economy. I think we're past the period where we should be asking people to pretend they've got different views.'

In other words, large swathes of the new parliamentary party were smiling through gritted teeth when Corbyn arrived on the front bench of the Commons the following Tuesday to take part in the re-election of the Speaker, the first business of the House following a general election. By far the most significant aspect of the capitulation was the abandonment of opposition to Corbyn on ideological grounds; formerly recalcitrant MPs – as well as jubilant Corbynistas – were singing from the same hymn sheet: opponents had claimed Corbyn would prove to be electorally toxic, they had been proved wrong and therefore Corbyn deserved the loyalty he had, until June, been denied.

No one bothered disturbing the sleeping elephant in the room. What would be the point? Why continue to express public doubts about the leader's past associations with terrorists and his sympathy for their causes? Why raise continuing reservations about his political instinct to blame the West (particularly the US and Israel) for all the world's woes? What was the point in asking difficult questions about dismantling Britain's independent nuclear deterrent, or the UK's long-term commitment to NATO and its principles of collective self-defence, when Jeremy had, after all, improved Labour's share of the vote significantly? Corbyn's critics, particularly in the PLP, where there were colleagues who had worked with him closely, knew him best and who had therefore made their judgement as to his suitability for office many years earlier, now found themselves obliged to dispense with the real reasons why they had opposed him. Instead they said publicly that their only concern had been his electability, and now that he had exceeded expectations on that score, there was no need to oppose or challenge him.

After a difficult and dramatic twenty months as leader, Corbyn looked, for the first time, to be enjoying himself in the position. His instinctive reaction to the Grenfell Tower disaster in Kensington just days after the general election, when a devastating fire spread through a tower block in one of the wealthiest parts of London claiming seventy-one lives, became emblematic of the stylistic differences between him and the Prime Minister. When Theresa May visited the scene to talk with rescue services, she was heckled by local residents. Corbyn, in contrast, went out of his way to meet survivors and local people, hugging them and empathising in a way that May simply was unable to. Towards the end of the month, Corbyn was a major draw at the Pyramid Stage at the Glastonbury music festival, where his speech was greeted by the crowd's rendition of a new version of the White Stripes song, 'Seven Nation Army'. TV and radio bulletins, not to mention social media, were awash with the sound of the nation's younger generation serenading their hero to the rhythm of 'Oh, Jeremy Corbyn!'

An illustration of how far Corbyn's stock had risen since the

general election came in the immediate aftermath of his Glastonbury appearance. The festival's founder, Michael Eavis, who had
stood hand in hand with the Labour leader on stage, subsequently
revealed that in a private conversation with Corbyn, Eavis had
asked him when he was going to rid the country of the Trident
nuclear missile system. 'As soon as I can,' was the reported reply.
That this was in direct contradiction of Labour policy, and even
of statements Corbyn himself had made during the election campaign, would, a year earlier, have spelled another round of damaging criticism, internal strife and, no doubt, a new sequence of
frontbench resignations. Now, in June 2017, few in his own party
raised any objections – at least, not publicly. The party had won 40
per cent of the vote, after all – why rock the boat over Trident now?

While Corbyn's appearance at Glastonbury quickly became
part of political mythology, a young crowd chanting the Labour
leader's name in loud and enthusiastic tribute to the man who
they believed would be Prime Minister, it is worth noting that
once again, as he had done throughout his political career, Corbyn
regaled his audience, not with soaring oratory, but with tired,
meaningless clichés: 'Peace is possible and must be achieved!' And
in the certain knowledge that his antipathy towards President
Donald Trump was amply reflected in the festival: 'Build bridges,
not walls!'

In the long run-up to Labour's annual conference in Brighton in 2017, the Labour ship seemed uncharacteristically tranquil.
However, if the parliamentary party now seemed more compliant
than it had been before the election, members of Momentum
seemed determined to bring former and current rebels to heel in
the constituencies. At the beginning of August, *The Times* reported that all but one of the executive positions in Chris Leslie's local

constituency party in Nottingham East had been won by Momentum candidates: 'A letter seen by *The Times* and circulated among local Labour members by Momentum activists, urged them to back candidates "who will stand up to make sure that our MP is accountable to us",' the newspaper reported. 'Canvassers for Momentum are said to have flanked the entrance to the local party's AGM "like bouncers" and one local member involved in a dispute with a hard-left activist was allegedly warned: "This is going to get very difficult and dirty."'

Luciana Berger, the MP for Liverpool Wavertree, faced a similar challenge after the majority of positions went to Momentum. The local party's new trade union liaison officer, Roy Bentham, told the local newspaper: 'Luciana needs to get on board quite quickly now. She will now have to sit round the table with us the next time she wants to vote for bombing in Syria or to pass a no-confidence motion in the leader of the party – she will have to be answerable to us.'

Corbyn's spokesman continued to insist that the leader did not support mass deselections of sitting MPs, but nothing in Momentum's behaviour or strategy suggested its priority was supporting those who had, in the past or present, been critical of the leader. The announcement by the government during the summer months that the arbitrary reduction in the size of the Commons would not, after all, go ahead, should have offered crumbs of comfort to moderate MPs feeling under siege. But it did not. Under existing Labour Party rules, trigger ballots in seats that had not changed shape or size would still go ahead, and with the majority of affiliated trade unions firmly behind the Corbyn project, such ballots could easily be lost, leaving incumbent parliamentarians open to challenge by any new candidate with local support.

Attention then turned to the looming annual conference, at which it was expected the so-called McDonnell amendment would be introduced and debated. The name of the amendment had come from Richard Angell, director of the Blairite think tank Progress. It had long been the fear of moderates on the centre right and centre left of the party that the nomination threshold for leadership candidates in future would be reduced from the current 15 per cent of all parliamentarians (MPs plus MEPs) to just 5 per cent, making it inevitable that the far left would always succeed in getting a candidate on the ballot paper in future contests. Without the power to act as gatekeeper, MPs saw their relevance in such contests diminishing in indirect proportion to the increasing influence of the hard-left grassroots membership. Naming the rule change 'the McDonnell Amendment' was a deliberate act of propaganda to warn the party of the possible consequences of such a change and to identify a particular individual who might benefit directly from it. In August, not for the first time, McDonnell ruled out ever standing for the leadership himself, and suggested some form of compromise might be made.

At the end of August, moderates were dealt yet another blow, this time from an entirely unexpected direction. Kezia Dugdale, the leader of Scottish Labour, had fought an ultimately victorious battle with Corbyn a year earlier over whether two new seats on the party's National Executive Committee should be taken up by the leaders of Scottish and Welsh Labour (or their appointees) or whether the new representatives on the party's decision-making body should be elected by members. With a large and supportive membership behind him, Corbyn naturally preferred the second option, particularly since his opponents at that time enjoyed a vanishingly slim one-seat majority over his own supporters. But

Dugdale and the Welsh First Minister Carwyn Jones were steadfast in their insistence that they should be given the right to take the seats, a position subsequently endorsed by conference.

Just under a year later, at the end of August 2017, Dugdale unexpectedly announced her resignation as leader with immediate effect. Had she chosen to remain in post until her successor was chosen, she would have been able to use her crucial vote on the NEC in the run-up to conference. Instead, she gave way to her Corbynista deputy, Alex Rowley, who duly took up the vacancy.

Since the general election, most opinion polls had given Labour a modest lead of between two and five points, not a position from which any opposition party could confidently expect to win office in the event of an imminent election, yet a significant improvement on the position that had held sway during almost all of Corbyn's leadership so far.

On 19 September – a week before conference kicked off in Brighton – the NEC approved a raft of changes to the party's rules for conference to approve. These included the reduction of the nomination threshold in future leadership elections from 15 to 10 per cent (the compromise at which McDonnell had hinted the previous month) and three new constituency representatives for the NEC. But perhaps the most important decision was the setting up of a review, led by Corbyn's political secretary (and former MP) Katy Clark, of the party's democratic structures and procedures. Clark's review, expected to deliver an initial report within a year, would look at key aspects of the party's structure, including the election of the leader and the role of 'associate' and 'supporting' members in that process, the composition of the NEC, the structure of local constituency parties and – most worrying for moderates – 'developing democratic policymaking procedures'.

Internal party democracy had long been a euphemism used by far-left groups such as the Campaign for Labour Party Democracy (CLPD) going as far back as the 1970s. Clark, who as an MP was a member of the hard-left Campaign Group of MPs alongside Corbyn, McDonnell and Diane Abbott, could be relied upon to produce proposed reforms that satisfied the agenda of her leader and his various support networks, inside and outside of the party.

While more radical plans for party 'reform' were kicked into the middle distance, delegates met in Brighton to adore their leader. To the amusement of attending journalists, there was some debate as to the identity of the party that had won the general election three months earlier. Len McCluskey, the Unite general secretary and Corbyn's strongest supporter in the trade union movement, told delegates: 'Let me say this to those merchants of doom, the whingers and the whiners, who say we should have done better, we didn't win. I say we did win! We won the hearts and minds of millions of people, especially the young.'

When the NEC's proposed rule changes were put to conference, there wasn't even a vote; they were passed unanimously.

As if there was any doubt about the final capitulation of Corbyn's opponents who still represented a large majority of the PLP, it was left to Tom Watson, the deputy leader, to prostrate himself before his former foe. The man who had led the coup that had successfully deposed the party's most successful vote-winner, Tony Blair, in 2007, had been the last great hope of moderates who had at least some confidence that this legendary trade union fixer could do to Corbyn what he'd done to the last Labour leader to win an election. Watson had certainly tried. He had left the party and the country in little doubt of what he thought of his leader. In fact, Watson had come closer than anyone on the outside was aware to persuading Corbyn to step down during the heated, eventful days after the EU referendum in June 2016.

But he had failed: through no fault of his own, through no lack of effort or political will. But he had failed. He had aimed at the king and he had missed.

And now, during his deputy leader's speech, Watson completed the capitulation of the moderates with gruesome, cringing finality. Referencing the drama of the previous year, when he had been at Glastonbury as the shadow Cabinet coup against Corbyn kicked off, Watson said: 'One of the most surreal moments of my political life happened to me late at night, in a field, surrounded by people much younger and far more stylish than me. I realised something as the crowd at Glastonbury's silent disco began to sing: "Oh, Jeremy Corbyn…"'

And at this point, Watson himself began to croon, encouraging his audience to join him. After a lacklustre echo in some parts of the hall, he continued: 'And as they sang, I realised it's actually better to be loved than to be feared. And Jeremy has shown us that it's possible. Thank you, Jeremy.' The few moderate MPs still in the hall for the speech stared at their feet and muttered curses under their breath.

EULOGY

On the morning of 7 April 2017, Britain awoke to the news that President Donald Trump had ordered a missile attack against the Shayrat air base in central Syria, in retaliation for a chemical weapons attack on civilians earlier that week. The forty-fifth President of the United States, a billionaire businessman and reality-show star, was a hate figure across the political spectrum; his absurd populist prejudices and impossible promises had won him the presidency the previous November, but not the popular vote. And one of his first acts of office, an executive order preventing access to the United States for those travelling from six Muslim countries in the Middle East, had solidified and united progressive opinion against his administration.

Now Trump had done what many on the moderate left had been demanding of the West for the last four years, and had struck a blow against the murderous tyrant, President Assad. How would Labour respond? Would it welcome a tough but proportionate response from Britain's allies? Or would it criticise the action as potentially inflaming an already complicated situation?

The answer was yes.

Tom Watson, the deputy leader, in response to a query by his local

Birmingham newspaper, spoke for many moderate and centre-left MPs: 'Indiscriminate chemical weapons' attacks on civilians can never be tolerated and must have consequences.' And he described the American action as 'a direct and proportionate response'.

But what of his leader? Why did it take three and a half hours of intense debate in Jeremy Corbyn's office before an opinion was offered? No one doubted what his view of the military intervention was, or that it would be precisely mirrored by that of his Director of Strategy and Communications, Seumas Milne. Both men had made their views on exactly this sort of scenario known over many years. Was the inordinate length of time being taken to write a response an indication that a sea change was in prospect? Was Jeremy Corbyn, the former chair of the Stop the War Coalition, about to depart from his lifelong hostility to the United States and its military adventures?

No.

There was no explanation for the delay, but when the statement was finally issued, it could have been written at almost any point in the last two decades:

> The US missile attack on a Syrian government air base risks escalating the war in Syria still further. Tuesday's horrific chemical attack was a war crime which requires urgent independent UN investigation and those responsible must be held to account. But unilateral military action without legal authorisation or independent verification risks intensifying a multisided conflict that has already killed hundreds of thousands of people. What is needed instead is to urgently reconvene the Geneva peace talks and unrelenting international pressure for a negotiated settlement of the conflict.

An irritated Corbyn spokesman later complained to the press that Watson had not consulted his leader before issuing his own earlier statement welcoming Trump's actions.

The two opposing wings of the Labour Party were once again exposed, as were their conflicting views of the world. Corbyn's political instincts were again with the Stop the War Coalition (which immediately announced an emergency protest outside Downing Street that evening – a protest against Trump's retaliatory action, not against Assad's murder of civilians, including children; Corbyn did not attend). Watson, with his own members' mandate and his position as party deputy leader not depending on Corbyn's patronage, enjoyed the loud support of dozens of other MPs throughout the day.

That evening, appearing on Channel 4's *The Last Leg*, Ed Miliband was asked whether or not he regretted his position in 2013 that had effectively prevented the West from taking action against Assad in response to a previous poison gas attack (see Chapter Eight). He replied: 'I have thought a lot about it and whether it was the right thing to do, but I think in the end, in my heart of hearts, I do feel it was.'

Miliband's legacy to his party, however, in this and in other areas, was not universally embraced.

*   *   *

Vote Leave had triumphed. In the early hours of the morning after the night before, feelings were running high in Labour's ranks. Chris Bryant, the passionately pro-Remain Labour MP for the Rhondda and shadow Leader of the House, delivered to a live TV audience what many considered the most memorable quote of the night. In reference to his former leader, Ed Miliband, Bryant said: 'I might go and punch him because he's a tosspot and he left the party in the state it's in.'

Politics isn't all about party leaders, of course. But there is little doubt that the roles played by successive Labour leaders have shaped the party's course as well as its destination. In the internet age, just as in the television age that preceded it, leadership matters. A party's message at election time is, rightly or wrongly, indistinguishable from its leader. That does not mean that the only thing a struggling party requires to turn around its fortunes is a new, voter-friendly leader. But equally, without such a figure, even a previously successful election-winning organisation can sink to historic defeats.

The contention of this book is a simple one: that the definitive moment that sent Labour into its self-destructive spiral can be traced back ten years, to Saturday 6 October 2007, when Gordon Brown, having blatantly encouraged speculation that he would go to the country, beat a humiliating retreat and tried, implausibly, to make his U-turn look like firm leadership. Brown begat Miliband begat Corbyn. As Prime Minister, Gordon Brown created the circumstances which made it all the easier for his chosen candidate to seize the crown (in fact his preferred candidate was Ed Balls, but given a choice between the final two names in the 2010 leadership ballot, he chose Ed Miliband, not David). It was Brown who, with a staggering level of self-regard, chose to embark upon a decade-long feud with Tony Blair, his boss, his leader and his Prime Minister, whose authority Brown never accepted or respected. It was this needless rivalry that poisoned the New Labour well and forced others to choose between camps which essentially agreed on policy and strategy, camps whose only area of real disagreement was the identity of who should occupy 10 Downing Street.

There was an opportunity in 2007, after Blair had departed the field, for Brown to seek to heal the divisions caused by the long and tiring battle. Brown could have brought ministers, MPs and activists together to fight for a unified Labour Party against the threat of a resurgent Conservative Party. In those first few months of the summer of 2007, Blairites kept their views to themselves, were even willing to accept that perhaps they had been wrong about Brown, that maybe, just maybe, he was, after all, turning out to be the master statesman his supporters had always claimed he would be once the highest office had been reached. Perhaps this new Brownite dispensation could work after all, with the taciturn, dour but trustworthy Prime Minister glowering benignly upon a grateful nation.

But when the polls turned in the wake of the Election That Never Was, the opportunity to heal divisions was lost. In the space of a single weekend in early October, the ceasefire ended and the two Labour camps returned to a war footing. Every one of Brown's missteps and mistakes from that moment on – and there were many – became yet another building block in the case against his leadership that was being constructed by his enemies in the party. Offering loyalty to a man who had benefited from (if not actively contributed to) the coup that deposed Blair in 2006 had been difficult but doable; maintaining it in the face of a series of unforced errors and appalling opinion poll results came to be seen as electoral suicide.

The final episode of Aaron Sorkin's cult television drama *The West Wing* was broadcast more than a year before Brown became Prime Minister. Yet the fictional drama, centred on the staff of a fictional Democratic US President, still inspires political analysis, comparison and similes, in the UK as well as in America.

Richard Angell, the director of Progress, believes Martin Sheen's commander in chief provides a relevant comparison with Prime Minister Brown. 'Bartlett never achieved anything,' said Angell, a *West Wing* obsessive.

> We see him react as a Democrat to daily events and to crises, and he reacts well and with clear values. But by the end of the series, you thought, 'Well, what did he actually do while he was in the White House that he was elected to deliver?' Brown was like Bartlett. It's hard to think of a single thing he set out to achieve before becoming Prime Minister that he then delivered in No. 10. He did wonders dealing with the crises that crossed his desk – and he did so with Labour values on display. The international global crash was a case in point – no one could have coped with the fallout better.
>
> But what did he leave behind that was the result of a deliberate change in government policy? He lost sight of the big picture – and of the voters – jumping from initiative to initiative. He made more speeches about taxing plastic carrier bags than he did about crime – and he never actually delivered the tax on carrier bags.

If Brown was the hubristic protagonist in a Shakespearean tragedy, what of his successor, Ed Miliband? Hopi Sen, the respected Labour blogger, wrote, during the 2015 leadership election, about the danger of the 'one-steppers'.

'To be a one-stepper is to see someone saying something you largely agree with, but which others in your party do not, and to stand one step to their left and attack them for their heresy,' he wrote. 'It's an advantageous position to take, just one step to the left. You are not decrying everything the person to your right says, of course. They make many valuable points. Indeed, you would include much of their perspective in your own analysis. You'd appreciate their support. It's just that here, and here, and here too, they depart from what is right and purposeful, from the values of our movement.

'That's why one-steppers lose you elections. In the rush to tactical advantage, they forget there's always a place one step to the left, and someone will always see the advantage of occupying it. One place to the left of Tony. One place to the left of Gordon. One place to the left of Ed. One place to the left of Yvette. One place to the left of Andy. Or maybe the other way round.'

The analogy is useful because it pinpoints Ed Miliband's strategy neatly and explains why he became its prisoner while he was Labour's leader. On Syria, on railway nationalisation, on tax, on Iraq – having won the leadership against his brother, he couldn't renege on the stance that had delivered his victory. And the party paid the price at the ballot box.

But it is Miliband's reforms to the party for which he will not be easily forgiven or forgotten. A seemingly inconsequential argument about who should be the candidate in a Labour seat (see Chapter Six) was blown out of all proportion by Miliband's gross misjudgement and his decision to involve the police. Becoming the victim of a chain of events he himself initiated, Miliband found himself recommending structural and procedural changes to the relationship between Labour and the trade unions, reforms which the party could ill afford from a financial perspective and did not require from a political one. But Ed wanted his Clause IV moment, and he got it.

And to compound his errors, Miliband, when faced with defeat at the hands of the electorate, chose to follow the example of his predecessor, flouncing off huffily into the sunset rather than instituting a difficult post-mortem of the election defeat while remaining leader during the inevitable interregnum between his and his successor's tenures. Perhaps if he had shown leadership at the most difficult time – in the months after 7 May 2015 – he could have properly established the reasons for Labour's loss and what was needed to maximise the chances of victory next time. He might have taken the bulk of a sympathetic and admiring party with him in a new appeal for discipline and courage in the face of the Conservatives' overall majority.

But he didn't. Instead he bequeathed to Labour a set of election rules ripe for exploitation by entryists while at the same time giving the party no choice but to implement them in a leadership campaign at precisely the wrong time.

It is true that without the gross stupidity of those Labour MPs who 'lent' their vital nominations to Corbyn with no intention of supporting someone so ridiculously left wing, then Labour would have elected a moderate and undoubtedly competent leader. But the election would still have come at the wrong time, without a full explanation and appreciation of what exactly had gone wrong in the previous ten years.

It is Miliband, not Brown or even Corbyn, who must shoulder the largest share of the blame for what has happened to the Labour Party. And it is those MPs and trade union leaders who nominated Ed Miliband, who believed that electing a less capable leader with whom they agreed was preferable to having a more capable leader with whom they agreed slightly less, who should share that blame.

When Jeremy Corbyn, Brown's successor-but-one, was first elected as party leader, he was considered a symptom of Labour's decline rather than its cause. Does the result of the 2017 general election mean that Labour, far from being in its death throes, is actually on the brink of a new lease of political life, even of an extended period of government?

The theme of this book is not that Labour has died or even that it will necessarily die in the near or medium-term future; it is that it is in a constant state of dying that may or may not result in its final demise – the 'Walking Dead' of British politics, still moving, and dangerous. Labour's many and varied missteps under Corbyn seem to have been forgiven, for now, by a sizeable chunk of the electorate. But this does not mean that the fundamental fault line in the party has disappeared, merely that it has, for now, been camouflaged effectively. But it remains, like a festering sore that has been hastily bandaged without having been treated with antibiotics, in the hopeful expectation that so long as the bandage is not removed, life can go on as normal. Yet sooner or later the wound will have to be inspected.

The two wings of the Labour Party simply cannot coexist indefinitely, especially since the balance of power in the party and wider movement is a mirror image of the balance in the parliamentary party. A majority of Labour MPs are now being held hostage by a party, a trade union movement and a national executive committee that regards them with mistrust and suspicion. The feeling is mutual.

A number of different scenarios could play out in the next few years: either Labour will win a general election in the near future, or it won't. If it loses – most likely to whomever succeeds Theresa May in the next few years – it will once more fall victim to internal strife. The barricades on both left and right will be occupied, and each side will be angrily accused of betrayal. It was always thus.

The consequences of a Labour general election victory would be dramatic. It is surely unlikely, to say the least, that Prime Minister Corbyn would not wish to reverse many of the employment reforms made in the 1980s, whatever the party's manifesto had declared. But how many of his moderate MPs would support a return to the closed shop, mass picketing or the abolition of pre-strike ballots? And if such measures were not brought forward, how long could Corbyn hold on to his support among the angry Marxist left whose consistent criticism of the Blair-Brown era of government was its refusal to repeal those laws? Does he wish to go down in history as yet another class traitor?

Perhaps he might seek to save his reputation as a radical by removing Trident missiles from UK territory. Even during the 2017 general election, while conceding that the party's policy remained one of support for Trident, Corbyn promised a post-election review, in government, of the country's defences. That such a review would conclude that Trident should be dismantled is hardly in doubt, but how many Labour MPs would support the government on that policy? Enough to defeat it seems the most likely answer.

Corbyn and his closest supporters are aware of these risks, which is why deselection of moderates will remain on the agenda for the time being. Only by removing and replacing sitting moderate Labour MPs can Corbyn's agenda be progressed. Yet the political risks associated with mass deselections, the resultant coverage and the public analysis of the agenda that drove such ruthless treatment of MPs, could hole the party below the waterline, or even provoke a formal split, before the next general election.

Alternatively, it is quite possible, especially given the willingness of formerly hostile moderate MPs to capitulate and bite their tongues in the face of Corbyn's 'triumph' at the 2017 election, that they will hold their noses and vote for whatever the whips tell them, even if they are instinctively opposed to such measures. Such a scenario might be all the more likely once Prime Minister Corbyn has actual government patronage at his disposal. That uneasy alliance, ugly and detestable in its cynicism and dishonesty, remains the best hope for the long-term survival of the Labour Party.

Few in the Labour Party expected to win 40 per cent of the vote at the 2017 general election or to come within 2 per cent of the Conservatives. But it would be a mistake to credit Corbyn or his supporters with some form of hitherto unidentified political genius only available to them; had the normal rules of politics endured, had Labour gone down to the dismal defeat the opinion polls and almost everyone else had predicted, his supporters would have declared a moral victory anyway. Principle is always to be put before popularity – that the two coincided briefly in June 2017 was convenient but not necessary for the continued devotion of Corbyn's supporters.

Jeremy Corbyn and Donald Trump are what happens when a movement gets tired of making compromises, impatient with difficult decisions and opts instead for easy answers, whether that means renationalisation, nuclear disarmament or building a wall. Until the summer of 2017, Corbyn had achieved the remarkable goal of combining populism with unpopularity: the populism was deftly employed to attract sufficient numbers of politically committed individuals to his banner during the leadership election of 2015. He did what all populists, including Trump, do in pursuit of success: he told the crowds exactly what they wanted to hear. After thirteen years in government and five years in opposition, those members wanted to believe that radical socialism, so brutally rejected by the electorate in 1983, could be seen as the answer to the party's – and the country's – problems by the time the next election came around.

In fact, Corbyn was not the first UK politician successfully to surf a wave of populism with tales of the sunlit uplands that could be reached if only you had the faith to get there. Both Nicola Sturgeon and her predecessor as Scotland's First Minister, Alex Salmond, had – almost successfully – led the Yes campaign for Scottish independence a year before Corbyn's election as leader, during which the opinion polls revealed no small market for wish fulfilment in denial of the hard facts.

How much of Corbyn's advance in 2017 was down to his own efforts, and how much of it owed to Theresa May's appalling election campaign? In the US in 2016, commentators and experts dismissed Donald Trump and assumed that the most qualified candidate would win the presidency, despite Hillary Clinton's well-known negatives with the public, the lack of trust they had in her as a member of the political establishment, and her brittle personality. The major difference between America in 2016 and Britain in 2017 was that the populist candidate in the UK lost, but will be given another go: the Republican establishment would have quickly disowned Trump had the electoral college not awarded him the prize voters denied him (Clinton received almost 3 million more votes but Trump won the electoral college 304–227). The game of low expectations played into Corbyn's hands perfectly. Labour loves its losing leaders far more than it does its winning ones (which is just as well, since there are so many more in the former category).

* * *

Corbyn's critics in the Labour Party like to point out – privately, naturally – that the situation is nowhere near as bad as it was in the 1980s, when newspaper reports of the 'loony left' were constant and Militant-controlled councils used the party as camouflage in their attempts to bankrupt cities in order to put workers out of jobs as a political gimmick. For example, they say, none of the regional party executives in England or Wales have anywhere near a majority of Corbyn supporters as members (although at the time of writing, prospects for Scottish Labour's moderates look grim). Good organisation, the skills that kept the levers of power out of the hands of the hard left for many years, can still achieve victories at local and national level. Yet in the 1980s, the leadership itself never came close to being captured by the Bennite left. An almost-successful challenge by Benn for the deputy leader's post in 1981 came to represent the left's peak in the late twentieth-century era. Corbyn's leadership victory in 2015 presented moderates with an existential crisis; his decent, career-saving performance, against all expectations, at the general election of 2017 solidified his grip on the party, as did subsequent (and consequent) decisions made by party conference later that year. The review of party rules and procedures being carried out by Katy Clark is unlikely to result in any kind of advance for the forces of moderation in the Labour Party.

Perhaps a hard-left political analysis is what the British electorate will be convinced should be brought to bear in government at the next election. For a functional, united party of the left, such an event would be challenging enough; for a party still irreconcilably riven between right and left, such an event could prove calamitous – for the party but, more importantly, for the country.

The last decade has been a series of unforced errors by the Labour Party, its leaders, its MPs and its membership. None of the calamities which befell it in the ten years since 2007 needed to happen; they occurred because of conscious political decisions that were avoidable.

And if, in the next few years, Labour's death certificate needs to be issued, the cause of death will be a single word: suicide.

ABOUT THE AUTHOR

© Jack Donaghy

Tom Harris is a former Labour MP and served as a minister in Tony Blair's and Gordon Brown's governments. He is now a columnist for the *Daily Telegraph* and a political consultant.

INDEX